LITERACY,
ECONOMY,
AND POWER

LITERACY, ECONOMY, AND POWER

Writing and Research after
Literacy in American Lives

EDITED BY

John **Duffy**

Julie Nelson **Christoph**

Eli **Goldblatt**

Nelson **Graff**

Rebecca S. **Nowacek**

Bryan **Trabold**

Southern Illinois University Press / *Carbondale*

Portions of chapter 1 originally appeared in *The Cherokee
Syllabary: Writing the People's Perseverance* (Norman:
University of Oklahoma Press, 2011); chapter 11 copyright
© 2013 by Paul A. Prior; portions of chapter 12 originally
appeared in Patrick W. Berry, Gail E. Hawisher, and
Cynthia L. Selfe, *Transnational Literate Lives in Digital
Times* (Logan: Computers and Composition Digital Press
/ Utah State University Press, 2012), retrievable at http://
ccdigitalpress.org/transnational; epilogue copyright ©
2013 by Harvey J. Graff

22 21 20 19   5 4 3 2

Library of Congress Cataloging-in-Publication Data
Literacy, economy, and power : writing and research after
"Literacy in American lives" / edited by John Duffy, Julie
Nelson Christoph, Eli Goldblatt, Nelson Graff, Rebecca
S. Nowacek, Bryan Trabold.
    pages cm
Includes bibliographical references and index.
    ISBN-13: 978-0-8093-3302-8 (pbk. : alk. paper)
    ISBN-10: 0-8093-3302-3 (pbk. : alk. paper)
    ISBN-13: 978-0-8093-3303-5 (ebook)
    ISBN-10: 0-8093-3303-1 (ebook)
1. Literacy—Social aspects—United States. 2. Literacy
programs—United States. 3. Composition (Language
arts) I. Duffy, John, [date] II. Christoph, Julie Nelson.
III. Goldblatt, Eli. IV. Graff, Nelson. V. Nowacek, Rebecca
S. VI. Trabold, Bryan.
LC151.L48217 2014
302.2'244—dc23

Contents

LITERACY,
ECONOMY,
AND POWER

Introduction

A s we write this sentence, more than a decade has passed since the publication of Deborah Brandt's *Literacy in American Lives* (2001). At the time of publication, *Literacy in American Lives* was one of many voices in the boisterous, interdisciplinary, and ultimately transformative conversation about literacy that had become known, collectively, as "the New Literacy Studies," the theoretical conception that construed literacy, as Brian Street (1995) writes, "as an ideological practice, implicated in power relations and embedded in specific cultural meanings and practices" (p. 1). This conversation was in full swing when *Literacy in American Lives* appeared, and Brandt's book seemed yet another contribution to the series of carefully researched, thoughtfully argued works that were changing understandings of literacy from an individually acquired, ideologically autonomous skill to a social and cultural practice (see, among many published previous to Brandt's book, Scribner and Cole, 1981; Heath, 1983; Street, 1984, 1993, 1995; Farr, 1993; Barton, 1994; Moss, 1994; Collins, 1995; Besnier, 1995; Gere, 1997).

Yet, *Literacy in American Lives* would eventually emerge from this conversation to become a preeminent, if not the preeminent, voice in literacy studies. Consider that in the decade-plus since its publication, Brandt's book has garnered three major book awards, the MLA Mina Shaughnessy Prize, CCCC's Outstanding Book Award, and the Grawemeyer Award in Education from the University of Louisville. More, the book is routinely cited in literacy scholarship, appears almost de rigueur on graduate syllabuses on literacy, and has made Brandt a much sought after speaker at national conferences and at universities in the United States and abroad.

The influence of Brandt's work was not immediately apparent. The early reviews of *Literacy in American Lives* were enthusiastic, though not unequivocally so. D. K. Kaufmann in *Choice* calls the book "powerful" but writes, "[Brandt's] focus on economic influences sometimes obscures the other uses of literacy she defends" (2002, p. 1471). Joseph Zimmer (2002, p. 432) in *The Journal of Adolescent and Adult Literacy* takes a different view: "While economics are important, Brandt does not slight social and cultural factors that cannot be separated from the rich context of literacy in people's lives." Zimmer finds the book "fascinating" and "important," praising its methodology, highlighting the use of the life history interview, and terming the book a "great addition to the history of literacy." Diane Lemonnier Schallert and Suzanne E. Wade (2005) in the *Reading Research Quarterly* describe Brandt's book as a "beautifully argued and densely illustrated thesis about the economic value of the everyday literacy of people living in the 20th century" (p. 523). These reviewers praise, as does Zimmer, the book's methodology, writing that Brandt's interviews with eighty people, from ages ten to ninety-eight, living in south central Wisconsin was "so important, so unusual, and so ultimately compelling" as to deserve special notice. Schallert and Wade further note that Brandt's innovative concept of literacy "sponsors"—described in the book as "agents, local or distant, concrete or abstract, who enable, support, teach, and model, as well as recruit, regulate, suppress, or withhold, literacy—and gain advantage by it in some way" (2001, p. 19)—enabled Brandt to define literacy as a "commodity" and a "resource," at once "political, economic, intellectual, and spiritual" (Schallert and Wade, 2005, p. 523). Offering yet another lens, Beth Daniell's (2003) review in *College Composition and Communication* features the voices of Daniell's advanced writing students, who described their reactions to the book and how it invited them to understand literacy in contexts of their own lives. Among these reactions was the student Joanna's assessment that "Brandt does not simply bring the sociological background and history of literacy to our attention but also finds a way to make it moving . . . giving substance to the academic. It is not often that I find myself introspective after reading an educational study, yet Brandt created something that does just that" (p. 359).

Looking back at these reviews, we are struck by how prescient they were in identifying the moves and methods that have made *Literacy in American Lives* required reading for literacy researchers. Read collectively, the early reviews address in *Literacy in American Lives* the insistence on viewing literacy through a *historical* lens, which represents a departure from the "ethnographic present" that was the focus of much research in New Literacy Studies. They note, as well, the introduction of *sponsorship*, the conceptual innovation used to track the forces that encourage or constrain literacy. More, early reviewers single out Brandt's use of a *methodology*, life history interviews, that admit the voices and experiences of ordinary people into literacy research. Finally, some reviewers explore the possibility of adapting Brandt's work for *pedagogical* purposes, as a way of promoting literacy teaching and learning.

Few of these moves and methods, of course, are original to Brandt. The history of literacy has long been a preoccupation of historians (Graff, 1979; Soltow and Stevens, 1981; Kaestle, 1991) and the use of oral testimony, whether known as "oral history," "life story research," "biographical sociology," or other designations, has been a favored methodological tool of historians, anthropologists, sociologists, and other scholars (Bertaux, 1981; Thompson, 1978). Even Brandt's signature concept of "sponsorship," which may prove to be her most enduring contribution to literacy studies, has its roots, as Brandt acknowledges (2001, p. 214n), in older traditions of the patron and patronage. What makes Brandt's work unique, in our view, is the way in which these perspectives, concepts, and tools are brought together in a single volume, applied rigorously and perceptively to the study of literacy, and rendered in language that is clear, insightful, and humane.

This volume explores the influence, more than ten years after its publication, of *Literacy in American Lives* on current literacy research. In what ways, that is, have the perspectives, concepts, and methods of Brandt's volume shaped contemporary theory and research in literacy? What questions has the book raised for scholars? How, for example, has Brandt's insistence on the historicity of literacy influenced current work? How has the concept of sponsorship been appropriated and used in more recent studies of writing? To what extent has Brandt's use of oral testimonies been adapted for research in other contexts and used with other populations? And in what ways, if any, has *Literacy in American Lives* inspired teaching and learning? Has the book proven a useful tool for students as well as scholars of literacy?

To address these and related questions, we asked eighteen accomplished scholars of literacy to share examples of their work that reflect their readings of *Literacy in American Lives* and that exhibit, either explicitly or implicitly, the influence of Brandt's work upon their own. We made these requests because, first, we were interested, as scholars of literacy ourselves, in how *Literacy in American Lives* has shaped the ongoing development of literacy studies, whether historically, conceptually, methodologically, pedagogically, or in other ways. More, we hoped to collect in one volume some of the smartest, most creative, and most thought-provoking recent research in literacy studies. Finally, we wanted to acknowledge the passage of more than a decade since the publication of *Literacy in American Lives*, a book that has amplified understanding of how literacy is learned and used. *Literacy, Economy, and Power: Writing and Research after Literacy in American Lives*, then, is a collection of essays that takes as its beginning point a work published in 2001 to explore the current state of literacy research. We look to the recent past to better understand present and future questions in literacy studies.

The Organization of This Book

This volume is organized into three sections that treat, roughly speaking, literacy in the past, the present, and the future. The book concludes with a meditation on the role of interdisciplinarity in literacy studies and an afterword that speaks eloquently to the importance of Brandt's contribution.

The first section, "Looking Back at Literacy: What It Did to Us; What We Did with It," is a set of four essays that represents the historical perspective that is the foundation of *Literacy in American Lives*. The first of these essays, Ellen Cushman's "Elias Boudinot and the *Cherokee Phoenix*: The Sponsors of Literacy They Were and Were Not," examines the story of Elias Boudinot, the editor of the *Cherokee Phoenix*—the first Native American newspaper, published in the Cherokee and English languages. In telling this story, Cushman complicates Brandt's concept of sponsorship by showing how sponsors and the sponsored must in many cases negotiate the tensions inherent in differing interests, cultures, languages, and even writing systems. "At the perimeter marked by acts of sponsorship," Cushman writes, "one finds the workings of power—the economic and political forces that allow and circumscribe its circulation between individuals and groups for gain" (p. 15). Other essays in this volume return to this theme.

Rhea Estelle Lathan's history of speaking, writing, and teaching in South Carolina's Citizenship Schools of the 1950s, "Testimony as a Sponsor of Literacy: Bernice Robinson and the South Carolina Sea Island Citizenship Program's Literacy Activism," recalls the role of literacy in the civil rights struggle and demonstrates the inseparability of literacy and culture. In relating the story of Bernice Robinson, the first South Carolina Sea Island Citizenship Education Program teacher, Lathan illustrates the "symbiotic relationship between sacred and secular ways of knowing, being, learning, and living" in African American culture and how this relationship informed the uses and meanings of literacy (p. 43). Lathan, additionally, expands the existing vocabulary of African American literacy theory, and literacy theory more generally, through her discussion of testimony as a sponsor of literacy that crosses traditional boundaries between the sacred and the secular.

Carol Mattingly's contribution, "Beyond the Protestant Literacy Myth," is a work of historical repair. Mattingly questions what she calls the "Protestant Literacy Myth" and its "accepted assumptions about American literacy, including beliefs that Protestants valued literacy while Catholics did not and that women were always less literate than men" (p. 46). Through a careful consideration of multiple historical sources in Europe, Canada, and the United States, Mattingly shows how Catholic religious orders in the eighteenth and nineteenth centuries and, in particular, the women of those orders, such as the Ursuline Sisters, expanded through their evangelizing efforts the literacy opportunities of Native American, French, and African American students. Mattingly's work offers both an important corrective and an alternative narrative to the "Protestant Literacy Myth" while providing striking examples of literacy sponsorship in early American history.

Our historical section concludes with Morris Young's "Writing the Life of Henry Obookiah: The Sponsorship of Literacy and Identity." Young traces the literate and cultural voyage of Henry Obookiah, a native Hawaiian youth transported to Connecticut for schooling in the nineteenth century, who subsequently played a critical role in bringing literacy to the Hawaiian Islands. Obookiah's personal literacy narrative, as Young relates it, was, therefore, inextricably tied to literacy development in the Hawaiian Islands and the resulting "problems of development and colonial imposition: disease, rapid transformation of indigenous culture, and erosion of self-determination, among other consequences" (p. 62). In recounting Obookiah's paradoxical and in some ways poignant accomplishment, Young enlarges Brandt's concept of sponsorship by showing how written texts, which are typically considered a product of sponsorship, may actually function through their circulation and reception as sponsors of literacy.

The second section of *Literacy, Economy, and Power*, "Looking Now at Literacy: A Tool for Change?," shifts the discussion to contemporary settings, both domestic and international, to consider how literacy functions in community and institutional settings. The essays in this section also advance the discussion of theory and methodology in literacy studies with a nod to Brandt's work.

In "Sponsoring Education for All: Revisiting the Sacred/Secular Divide in Twenty-First-Century Zanzibar," Julie Nelson Christoph's research methodology both borrows and departs from Brandt's. Using evidence from oral interviews surveying literacy practices and attitudes toward literacy of seventy-five adults throughout Zanzibar, Tanzania, Christoph argues that centralized, secular literacy initiatives—such as UNESCO's Education for All—founder when they fail to acknowledge the decentralized, volatile nature of literacy networks of the twenty-first century. Christoph offers a provocative consideration of the role of Islam as "an important but largely unrecognized sponsor of literacy in Zanzibar," whose goals may not align well with those of officially recognized government literacy campaigns (p. 80).

Kim Donehower takes us in a different direction, revisiting one of Brandt's earlier works, *Literacy as Involvement* (1990), and its uses in the sustainability of rural communities. Donehower's essay, "Connecting Literacy to Sustainability: Revisiting *Literacy as Involvement*," demonstrates how Brandt's volume "offers a method for analyzing community reading and writing activities to better understand their role in community sustainability" and explores the "possible connections between Brandt's work and those of political theorists who work on issues of social capital and associational democracy" (pp. 98–99).

Bruce Horner and Min-Zhan Lu, in their essay "Toward a Labor Economy of Literacy: Academic Frictions," jump ahead, considering recent work by Brandt, "When People Write for Pay" (2009), to interrogate dominant—and flawed—models of academic literacy in composition studies. Horner and Lu call for a language and literacy model that can accommodate the increasingly global nature of English literacy, including translingual literacies, English as a lingua franca, and world Englishes, and that will highlight "the necessity and contribution of the labor of readers and writers for the production and transformation of meaning" (p. 111). They call this the "translation model" of literacy, a model that "recognize[s] the fact of semiodiversity, the multiplicity of meanings, the complexity of choosing from among them, and the inevitability of the necessity of the labor of doing so in reading and writing" (p. 119). Horner and Lu call for theoretical models that recognize the "frictions" of literacy or the role of language users in translating and reconstructing meanings in acts of reading and writing.

Eli Goldblatt and David A. Jolliffe in "The Unintended Consequences of Sponsorship" examine Brandt's notion of sponsorship as it applies to literacy teaching in two communities, one in the Arkansas Delta, the other in urban Philadelphia. Recounting their work in community literacy projects that require significant sponsorship investments from institutions in two communities, Goldblatt and Jolliffe argue that Brandt's conception of a sponsor as one who "gains advantage" from sponsorship does not "exhaust the story of sponsorship." Further complicating Brandt, the authors contend, "Sponsors take risks, too. Indeed, sponsors can be harmed, altered, or even transformed by the population and pedagogy they contract to teach" (p. 127).

Beverly J. Moss and Robyn Lyons-Robinson in "Making Literacy Work: A 'Phenomenal Woman' Negotiating Her Literacy Identity in and for an African American Women's Club" are also concerned with the question of sponsorship and how it functions in community settings. Their essay traces the experiences of a nominal sponsor of literacy, a college-educated member of a women's club, to explore the ambivalence a sponsor may feel about her role as sponsor and the implications of this. In doing so, they seek to extend Brandt's concept such that it accounts for refusals, or at least demurrals, of the role of sponsor. Moss and Lyons-Robinson's essay demonstrates how multiple ethnographic methods, including interviews and participant observation, can be used to trace sponsorship patterns.

Michael W. Smith, in "Seeking Sponsors, Accumulating Literacies: Deborah Brandt and English Education," takes us into the classroom, discussing how Brandt's work can be generative for both students and teachers. By asking students and teachers to consider how literacy has been sponsored, Smith suggests, both groups become more aware of how literacy works and how it shapes the experiences of reading and writing.

In the final essay in this section, "Combining Phenomenological and Sociohistoric Frameworks for Studying Literate Practices: Some Implications of Deborah Brandt's Methodological Trajectory," Paul Prior considers the place of theory, and specifically phenomenology, as this informs the concept of sponsorship and literacy studies more broadly. Arguing that phenomenology was once central to but has largely disappeared from Brandt's work, Prior explores the ways in which "combining phenomenological and sociohistoric frameworks can inform literacy research" (p. 166). To illustrate, Prior reviews three approaches to phenomenology and reviews a research project in which an art and design group created a web-based art object. A study of these creative processes, Prior writes, demonstrates that a phenomenological combined with a sociohistorical approach will lead to deeper, more robust understandings of literate activity.

The final section of this volume, "Looking Forward at Literacy: The Global and Multimodal Future," features the essay "Beyond *Literate Lives*: Collaboration, Literacy Narratives, Transnational Connections, and Digital Media," by Cynthia L. Selfe and Gail E. Hawisher. Selfe and Hawisher have pushed us into the twenty-first century in their ongoing study of globalized digital literacies. Their essay for this volume seeks to extend Brandt's "groundbreaking methodology" by including feminist and collaborative approaches to data gathering, by working in global and transnational contexts, and by using digital media, particularly video, "both as a method of data gathering and as a method of reporting on our research to others in and out of the profession" (p. 185). Thus, Selfe and Hawisher adopt and transform Brandt's methods in ways that point to new directions for research that examines literacy in the twenty-first century, in various media, and in global contexts.

Literacy, Economy, and Power concludes with reflections by Harvey J. Graff and Anne Ruggles Gere. In his epilogue, Graff reflects upon the development of literacy studies in terms of the history of interdisciplinarity. Drawing upon his own experiences in creating the literacy studies initiative at Ohio State University, Graff discusses the history of interdisciplinarity from the late nineteenth century to the present and delineates its critical, comparative, and historical foundations. His essay concludes with a consideration of Deborah Brandt's place in this history.

The final contribution comes from Gere, whose afterword, combining personal and professional observations, both celebrates Brandt's influence but also "resist[s] thinking of her research in the past tense" (p. 228). Reflecting on her original review of *Literacy in American Lives*, Gere contemplates what Brandt's work has meant both to her own research and the wider field but also looks to the future, calling upon Brandt to continue offering work that will, in Gere's words, "help me understand my world a little better, contribute to the richness of my graduate seminars, and inform my scholarship" (p. 229). We imagine Deborah Brandt would not have it any other way.

It would be a mistake to attribute too great an influence to any single text when considering the history of an idea or the development of an academic discipline. So, too, would it be erroneous to attribute present work in literacy studies to the publication of any single book, no matter how significant. And yet it does seem fair to say that *Literacy in American Lives* continues to offer perspectives, concepts, and methods for current literacy research. Even a cursory consideration of the essays collected in this book, all of which in one way or another may be read as a response to *Literacy in American Lives*, reveals an enormous range of purposes, theories, methods, and settings for literacy research: past and future, local and global, print and digital, and more.

The contribution of *Literacy in American Lives*, therefore, may be perhaps best understood on at least two levels. The first is the content of the book itself, in particular its insistence on literacy as historically grounded, its understanding of literacy as a resource, its conceptual contribution of sponsorship, and its use of a methodology that brings the voices and perspectives of ordinary people into the history of literacy. Taken together, these perspectives present a striking vision of how literacy was learned in the twentieth century, what forms it took, who promoted and received it, what values it had for those who practiced it, and how these values were diminished or enhanced in the rapid American shift from an industrial to an information economy.

A second measure of the significance of *Literacy in American Lives* is in the questions it raised and continues to raise for literacy researchers. What is the nature of the thing we investigate? Why does it matter? What are its purposes? How do we investigate these as they change over time? The dazzling variety of essays gathered in this collection indicates the generative nature of such questions, the ways in which they open rather than foreclose possibilities for studying written language. *Literacy in American Lives* speaks to us, then, through its specific arguments but also through the broader questions it raises about literacy and literacy research.

Perhaps this is the most important contribution, finally, that a scholarly book can make to its field. Even the most dominant theories are eventually overturned or discarded: Think of the prominence of positivism in philosophy, behaviorism in linguistics, or the rise and demise of New Criticism in literary studies. Methodologies, too, may wax, wane, and evolve in a given discipline: Consider the profound changes in attitudes toward the ethnographer that have characterized anthropological research over the last thirty years. The most enduring contribution of a scholarly work, then, may be found in the quality of its questions and in the ways in which they continue to resonate for scholars in the discipline.

This volume addresses some of the questions raised by Brandt's *Literacy in American Lives*. These questions continue to resonate for us and for the scholars who have contributed to *Literacy, Economy, and Power*, more than ten years after the publication of Brandt's book. We suspect comparable questions will continue to resonate ten years from now—and in ten years beyond that—even as new questions about literacy arise, challenge, stimulate, and provoke. We invite you to consider with us the questions that *Literacy in American Lives* has raised to date and the ways in which these questions have been explored and reinterpreted in the essays collected here.

References

Barton, David. 1994. *Literacy: An Introduction to the Ecology of Written Language.* Oxford, England: Blackwell.

Bertaux, Daniel. 1981. *Biography and Society: The Life History Approach to the Social Sciences.* Beverly Hills, CA: Sage.

Besnier, Niko. 1995. *Literacy, Emotion, and Authority: Reading and Writing on a Polynesian Atoll.* Cambridge: Cambridge University Press.

Brandt, Deborah. 1990. *Literacy as Involvement: The Acts of Writers, Readers, and Texts.* Carbondale: Southern Illinois University Press.

———. 2001. *Literacy in American Lives.* New York: Cambridge University Press.

———. 2009. "When People Write for Pay." *JAC, 29,* 166–98.

Collins, James. 1995. "Literacy and Literacies." *Annual Review of Anthropology, 24,* 75–93.

Daniell, Beth. 2003. Review of *Literacy in American Lives,* by Deborah Brandt. *College Composition and Communication, 55*(2), 356–59.

Farr, Marcia. 1993. "Essayist Literacy and Other Verbal Performances." *Written Communication, 10*(1), 4–38.

Gere, Anne Ruggles. 1997. *Intimate Practices: Literacy and Cultural Work in U.S. Women's Clubs, 1880–1920.* Urbana: University of Illinois Press.

Graff, Harvey. 1979. *The Literacy Myth: Literacy and Social Structure in the Nineteenth Century.* New York: Academic Press, 1979.

Heath, Shirley Brice. 1983. *Ways with Words: Language, Life, and Work in Communities and Classrooms*. Cambridge: Cambridge University Press.

Kaestle, Carl F. 1991. "Studying the History of Literacy." In *Literacy in the United States: Readers and Reading since 1880*, by Kaestle, Helen Damon-Moore, Lawrence C. Stedman, Katherine Tinsley, and William Vance Trollinger Jr., 3–32. New Haven: Yale University Press.

Kaufmann, D. K. 2002. Book review: *Literacy in American Lives*, by Deborah Brandt. *Choice*, 39(April 7–9), 1471.

Moss, Beverly J., ed. 1994. *Literacy across Communities*. Cresskill, NJ: Hampton.

Schallert, Diane Lemonnier, and Suzanne E. Wade. 2005. "The Literacies of the 20th Century: Stories of Power and the Power of Stories in a Hypertextual World." *Reading Research Quarterly*, 40(4), 520–29.

Scribner, Sylvia, and Michael Cole. 1981. *The Psychology of Literacy*. Cambridge: Harvard University Press.

Soltow, Lee, and Edward Stevens. 1981. *The Rise of Literacy and the Common School in the United States: A Socioeconomic Analysis to 1870*. Chicago: University of Chicago Press.

Street, Brian V. 1984. *Literacy in Theory and Practice*. Cambridge: Cambridge University Press.

———, ed. 1993. *Cross-Cultural Approaches to Literacy*. Cambridge: Cambridge University Press.

———. 1995. *Social Literacies: Critical Approaches to Literacy in Development, Ethnography and Education*. London: Longman.

Thompson, Paul Richard. 1978. *The Voice of the Past: Oral History*. Oxford: Oxford University Press.

Zimmer, Joseph E. 2002. Review of *Literacy in American Lives*, by Deborah Brandt. *Journal of Adolescent and Adult Literacy*, 45(5), 432.

PART ONE

Looking Back at Literacy:
What It Did to Us; What We Did with It

1. Elias Boudinot and the *Cherokee Phoenix*: The Sponsors of Literacy They Were and Were Not

Ellen Cushman

Fig. 1.1. Newspaper masthead of the second issue of the *Cherokee Phoenix*

The *Cherokee Phoenix* is the first newspaper published by an Indian tribe in the United States, and it included the Cherokee syllabary, the first indigenous writing system, in many issues (see fig. 1.1).[1] Invented by a Cherokee silversmith, treaty signer, and student of the language named Sequoyah over a ten-year process (Cushman, 2011c), the Cherokee syllabary was accepted by the Cherokee tribal council in 1821, though it was another five years before the Cherokee syllabary would appear in print. In between times, Cherokees learned, read, wrote, and communicated in script using Sequoyan in great numbers. Samuel Worcester, a Moravian pastor to the Cherokee, estimated that three-fourths of the people were fluent with the writing system before Sequoyan moved to print (Worcester, 1828b). Interestingly, "there had been no schools, and no considerable exertions of any kind, certainly none that were systematic, to effect this" high reading and writing rate in Sequoyan (Worcester, 1828b, p. 330). Worcester believed the rapid dissemination and uptake of this writing system were due in large part to the instrumentality of the writing system. First, it corresponds fairly well to the sounds of spoken Cherokee, and second, the small number of syllables were easily represented by the eighty-six original characters in the writing system (Worcester, 1828b).

Research on the Cherokee writing system confirms Worcester's thinking about its instrumentality. Margaret Bender's (2002) ethnography of

Cherokees in the Qualla boundary of North Carolina suggests that adult Cherokee language learners develop facility with the writing system because it represents fairly closely the sound units. She found that the reading and spelling practices of Cherokee readers and writers suggested to her that there might be semantic meanings encoded with each character (p. 122). Following these leads, I conducted a linguistic analysis of each character in the writing system to show the potential meaning resting latent within each character that becomes activated by its positioning in a word (Cushman, 2011a). The instrumentality of the Cherokee writing system might well be one reason why its use has persisted (Cushman, 2011b).

Sequoyah's writing system originally contained eighty-six characters with eighty-five being retained when it moved into print in the *Cherokee Phoenix*. Commissioned by the Cherokee Nation in 1826, the typeset used to publish the *Cherokee Phoenix* and the press itself were finally ready by 1827. Because the punches and matrices took some time to cast for the Cherokee typeset, the Cherokees set about building a log house for the press and hiring staff in the nation's capital, New Echota, in what is today Georgia. In January 1828, the press, types, and other materials necessary for printing the paper arrived in New Echota, with the first issue of the *Cherokee Phoenix* being published in February. Two years before the press had even arrived at the nation, Elias Boudinot had been charged by the Cherokee Nation to serve as the first editor of the *Phoenix*, to secure funding from outside sponsors for procuring the typesets in both English and Cherokee, and to establish an office in New Echota.

Through an exploration of Boudinot's role as editor as well as an analysis of the content of the *Phoenix*, this chapter provides an understanding of the ways in which the work of literacy sponsors requires the consent and support of those sponsored. Drawing upon data gathered over five years of ethnohistorical research, this chapter illustrates Boudinot's role as an editor of the *Cherokee Phoenix* to nuance the notion of literacy sponsorship and to further develop understanding of regional histories of literacy.

Deborah Brandt's notion of literacy sponsors offers detailed portrayals of individuals who come to develop reading and writing skill sets through their sponsors, who, in turn, gain some advantage from their forms of sponsorship. Brandt's notion allows scholars to view the influence of large-scale economic and political forces through individuals' choices to facilitate or limit particular reading and writing practices. Sponsors are "any agents, local or distant, concrete or abstract, who enable, support, teach, model, as well as recruit, regulate, suppress, or withhold literacy—and gain advantage by it in some way. . . . Sponsors are delivery systems for the economies of literacy, the means by which these forces present themselves to—and through—individual learners" (Brandt, 1998, p. 161). While sponsors are agents who enable and discourage particular kinds of literacy for their own gain, they're also often beholden to the very people who sponsored them in the first place.

Their individual talents for delivering and withholding access to particular forms of literacy reveal economic and political forces that shape and delimit the types of literacy available and to whom. Sponsors of literacy are "an especially tangible way to track connections between literacy as individual development and literacy as an economic development because of how closely literacy in the twentieth century grew integral to the interests of corporate capitalism" (Brandt, 2001, p. 26). At the perimeter marked by acts of sponsorship, one finds the workings of power—the economic and political forces that allow and circumscribe its circulation between individuals and groups for gain. This boundary also reveals the ways in which those who sponsor are ultimately impacted, for better or worse, by their sponsorship efforts.

With these findings, this chapter contributes to regional histories of American literate lives (Brandt, 2001; Rumsey, 2008, 2009; Powell, 2007; Royster, 2000). Regional histories provide unique vantage points on American lives at particular times and under a variety of circumstances.

> From a regional perspective, historians are able to demonstrate how unequal distributions of literacy related to unequal distributions of other things—wealth, roads, schools, trade, political privilege. . . . Regional histories also illuminate the value of literacy as a resource. In the early days of mass literacy, the worth of individual literacy would rise with the rates of literacy in a region. (Brandt, 2001, p. 28)

Defined along geographical boundaries, regional histories connect places and populations to economies of exchange and literacy. They reveal the unevenly distributed wealth, opportunities, and infrastructural resources of homesteads, farms, towns, and cities and, by doing so, certainly provide a useful place to begin mapping individual literacy achievement against a national backdrop of various economies of literacy.

The case of Boudinot and the *Cherokee Phoenix* lends dimension to regional histories of literacy because it shows how Cherokees' development of reading and writing proved, on the one hand, threatening to some and advantageous to other outsiders and, on the other, useful for sustaining the value and use of Sequoyan inside the tribe. Boudinot's role of sponsor shows his unique positioning as mediator between audiences of English and

Cherokee readers, providing both access to the inside world of Cherokees and outside world of political and legal battles. Boudinot found himself caught betwixt and between the contested boundaries of Georgia, the federal government, and the Cherokee Nation. His role as sponsor and mediator, complicated by this positioning, ended not well.

ᏍᏳᎦ (Galagina), the Buck

Known as Buck Watie to the Cherokee in Spring Place, where he attended the Moravian Mission school (near, what is today, Chatsworth, Georgia), Elias Boudinot was the eldest of nine children born to Oowatie and Susanna Reese. On route to attend the American Board School in Cornwall, Connecticut, Buck Watie met the American Bible Study president, Elias Boudinot. Impressed by the elder Boudinot, Buck Watie changed his name and enrolled in the American Board School as Elias Boudinot (Perdue and Green, 1995, pp. 5–8). While attending the American Board School, Elias Boudinot learned about the missionary purpose of the school to train students as "physicians, teachers, interpreters, and ministers so that they could 'communicate to the heathen nations, such knowledge in agriculture and the arts as may prove the means of promoting Christianity and civilization'" (Fries, quoted in Perdue and Green, 1995, p. 7). The American Board School recruited the most talented tribal peoples to their classrooms, which were designed to bring light to the "backward savage," who would then work to forward this civilizing mission. Though he lost fluency with the Cherokee language while attending it, the American Board School did enable his contact with powerful northeasterners, taught him privileged language conventions of English, and, upon graduation, ostensibly sanctioned his role as an agent for their civilizing efforts.

Boudinot's role in bringing home to the Cherokee a message of salvation and civilized ways in the pages of the *Phoenix* has been the subject of the writings of William McLoughlin (1986, 1984) and Theda Perdue (1977). Numerous histories have traced Cherokees' acquiescence and resistance to becoming civilized as played out in the pages of the *Phoenix* (Thornton, 1985, 1993; Young, 1981; McLoughlin, 1984). These historians have been inclined to see Boudinot not as a traditional Cherokee but instead as deeply immersed in white culture and imbued with negative attitudes toward his people. "Since Elias Boudinot had been educated in mission schools," Perdue (1977) comments:

> he no doubt had absorbed White attitudes toward aboriginal Cherokee culture. Like most well educated men of the early 19th century, he subscribed to a hierarchical view of human cultures and

> societies. . . . Thus, Boudinot was probably ashamed of his tribe's
> "savage" heritage and was interested in the "manners and customs"
> of the Cherokees only as a demonstration of how far they had pro-
> gressed up the ladder of social development. (pp. 215–16)

Several problems rest in this reading of Boudinot and his efforts with the
Phoenix. First, she speculates that Boudinot was "probably ashamed of his
tribe's 'savage' heritage" (p. 216), as though she can infer his emotional and
psychological stance toward his people. Second, Perdue presumes that given
Boudinot's education, he would automatically subscribe to "a hierarchical
view of human cultures and societies." She views Boudinot as using the
Cherokee Phoenix as a mechanism for Cherokees' assimilation and as a mile-
stone marking an important phase in the loss of Cherokee culture.

Arguments about Boudinot's assimilation rest on a modernist notion of
tradition challenged by Mignolo (2007).

> "Tradition" is not outside modernity but in its *exteriority*: It is *an
> outside* invented by the rhetoric of modernity in the process of
> creating *the inside*. The outside of "tradition" is invented in or-
> der to insure the inside as the locus of enunciation of knowledge.
> "Tradition" is not a way of life that predated "modernity" but an
> invention of the rhetoric of modernity. (p. 472; original emphasis)

Historians who have focused on Boudinot's assimilation and who have presumed his "shame" of his Cherokee heritage have worked from the troubled and troubling modernist binaries of traditional/assimilated, authentic/
sellout, inside/outside, and the like. The modernist perspective invents the
exteriority of "traditional Cherokee culture" as the necessary other to the
interiority of "white, civilized society." Presenting Boudinot as assimilated
and ashamed of his people, Perdue maintains the imperialist interiority as
the locus of knowledge. When read from a modernist perspective, Boudinot
can only be understood as a sellout of his people. His story and the story
of the *Phoenix* tell more about the fluidity and contingency of his position
than the American Indian scholarship to date on Boudinot has revealed.[2]

Scholars can begin to understand better Boudinot's role as editor of the
Cherokee Phoenix when viewed from the lens of literacy sponsorship. As a
literacy sponsor seeking to publish Cherokee knowledge, laws, traditions,
and language, he could not do so without the endorsement of the General
Council and Cherokee people, on the one hand, and, on the other hand, he
needed to maintain his white readers' continued good faith in the authority
and validity of the paper's content as being from and by Cherokee people.
Boudinot's efforts reveal the complex role of literacy sponsor as mediator

that he and the *Cherokee Phoenix* played at this time. He needed to represent the tribe's language and values, especially through printing Sequoyan, as he needed to present the civilized face of the nation to generate and maintain the sympathies of northerners. As a Cherokee who came from the politically powerful Watie family who had also become fluent and versed in white ways, he was uniquely positioned to serve as a sponsor who mediated in these ways. Such a balancing act reveals the sociopolitical exigencies of the time in one individual, whose acts of sponsorship, while surely beneficial to him personally, ultimately came at a high cost. To illustrate this, the next sections explore how important it was for the Cherokee Nation to procure a press in order to communicate with outsiders on and in Cherokee terms.

Establishing the Press in Cherokee and English

The establishment of the Cherokee press occurred at a time of high reading and writing rates among Cherokees, who had been using the manuscript form of the writing system for a variety of purposes.[3] Worcester (1828a, p. 162) marveled at the representational economy of the Cherokee syllabary as a writing system and suggested that its ease of use was a "source of wonder."

Because the Cherokee language has fewer consonants, and each syllable ends in a vowel, the language ends up, according to Worcester's (1828a, p. 162) calculation, to have only ninety-six possible consonant-vowel combinations into syllables, compared to "1536 possible syllables in the letter." With its eighty-five characters, the economy and precision by which this writing system worked may have eased the tribe's quick progress in learning this new technology. Of the tribe's willingness to learn the syllabary in longhand before the invention of the printing press, James Mooney (1900, p. 110) finds that "no schoolhouses were built and no teachers hired, but the whole nation became an academy for the study of the system." Worcester describes this national reading and writing movement sans schools in somewhat more detail in a letter to Jeremiah Evarts, the corresponding secretary of the American Board of Commissioners for Foreign Missions (ABCFM). Evarts excerpted Worcester's letter in the ABCFM's magazine, the *Missionary Herald*, in 1826:

> I suppose there has been no such thing as a school in which it has been taught, and it is not more than two or three years since it was invented. A few hours of instruction are sufficient for a Cherokee to learn to read his own language intelligibly. . . . [T]here is no part of the nation, where the new alphabet is not understood. (American Board, 1826)

Perhaps because the writing system was so easy to learn, its widespread use in a variety of genres was made possible. Cherokees taught each other to read and write in Sequoyan, with some traveling days to sit by the side of another Cherokee fluent in Sequoyan to learn the syllabary, return home, and teach it to kin there (American Board, 1826). The Cherokees' use of the writing system, once learned, in manuscript form proliferated: "[G]reat numbers have learned to read: they are circulating hymns and portions of Scripture, and writing letters everyday: they have given a medal to the inventor of a wonderful method of writing their own language" (see fig. 1.2) (Worcester, 1827, p. 212). In part to remain in touch with loved ones who stayed in Georgia after the first voluntary removal to Arkansas, Cherokees became agents of their own mass literacy movement.

Fig. 1.2. Two verses of the Book of Genesis, the first to appear in Cherokee print in the *Missionary Herald*

This established value of the syllabary, then, both in terms of its ease to learn and in terms of its enabling long-distance communication, continued as the Cherokee writing system evolved into print. In fact, because the Cherokee writing system was already in such widespread use, the ABCFM hesitated to offer its endorsement of the Cherokees' establishment of their own press. They feared that Cherokees

> will cut themselves off from that respect and sympathy from the intelligent of other nations . . . should they make advances in literacy acquisitions [in Sequoyan]. . . . [F]or there are few *out of* their nation, who will be at pains to become familiar with the characters and sounds of this alphabet. (American Board, 1826, p. 47)

The ABCFM's lack of support mattered little to Cherokees. The point for Cherokees in seeing Sequoyan in print was to communicate with and in Cherokee communities. A number of Cherokees had already developed fluency with English and had been able to communicate in the language of those *out of* their nation. For Cherokees, the ease of learning Sequoyan, its close match to the language, and its widespread use made it imperative for the Cherokee Nation to develop a printing press capable of printing in Cherokee and English for the nation's newspaper.[4] Sequoyan would be printed by and for Cherokee people, with letters chosen for white readers.

When the writing system moved into print, the values attached to it both inside and outside of the Cherokee tribe multiplied. Indeed, the Cherokee writing system as an instrument for encoding speech worked so well for the tribe that they were eager, as a matter of convenience, continuity, and pride, to see the language in print. Within the context of the tribe, then, significant demand for print prompted the tribal leaders to request a typeset be cast for them.

While the value for Sequoyah's orthography was high among Cherokee, it was also an invention that sparked the imagination of white northeasterners and Europeans who both marveled at and were perplexed by its workings. John Pickering, a philologist who had developed an alphabetic orthography of the Cherokee language that was rejected by the tribal council, received a copy of the prospectus for the *Phoenix* with a letter from Boudinot sent from Echota, Cherokee Nation, dated December 17, 1827: "In this undertaking of the Cherokees I would not wish to promise much. I hope, however, that our Northern friends will not turn off with disdain. I will try to make the paper as respectable as my limited means will allow" (Pickering, 1887, p. 357). Pickering forwarded Boudinot's letter and prospectus to Baron Humboldt, another avid researcher of languages.

Pickering also took the liberty to subscribe Baron Humboldt to the *Phoenix* and notes that Boudinot's "English style is perfectly correct" (1887, p. 357). At the same time, Pickering framed these artifacts as surely a "great curiosity in Europe" (1887, p. 357), suggesting that their exotic nature would serve to generate interest if not support for the paper. The addition of a baron to the list of subscribers and the suggestion that the discourse of Boudinot is stylistically correct directly connected to the paper's introduction to the national and international scene and lent respectability to the Cherokee efforts. Boudinot was recruiting readers whose subscriptions would lend prestige and financial support to the paper. He pandered to their privileged sensibilities to ensure they not expect too much from the humble newspaper that was only as good as Boudinot's limited resources could muster. The newspaper would be a topic of discussion for Pickering and Baron Humboldt, both for its linguistic and political information.

Boudinot's efforts to secure a network of readers suggest the ways in which his sponsorship of the *Phoenix* would be indicated and sustained by the sponsorship of subscribers, especially as these readers would later turn into potential allies of the Cherokee Nation as it attempted to retain its land rights. Boudinot had to include Sequoyan in the newspaper because it satisfied the deeply held value and demand for it among the tribe. For curious outsiders, the *Phoenix* provided an imagined glimpse into Cherokee life and language and evidence of the brilliance of this civilized tribe. So long as Boudinot satisfied the competing yet overlapping demands of his readers, his role of sponsor was secure, as the next section makes clear.

The Scope of the *Cherokee Phoenix*

Though the Cherokee Nation outlined the goal and scope of the *Phoenix*, which were published in the prospectus in the second issue of the paper, Boudinot (1828b, February 28) frames this goal and scope within exigencies existing outside of the tribe:

> It has long been the opinion of judicious friends to the civilization of Aborigines of America, that a paper published exclusively for their benefit and under their direction, would add great force to the charitable means employed by the public for their melioration. . . . There are many true friends to the Indians in different parts of the Union. . . . On such friends must principally depend the support of our paper.

Boudinot situates the publication of this paper as though it were motivated by an effort to appease the Cherokees' "judicious friends" who seek "the melioration" of Cherokees. In the same breath, Boudinot also acknowledges that these friends would have this paper be by and for the Cherokees. Boudinot sponsors these friends, who provided the bulk of the readership for the Phoenix, by making available to them information in the *Phoenix*. Sympathizers were enabled to learn about the nation and its situation in the larger sociocultural milieu. Boudinot was enabled to continue publication of the paper because of their readership. The development of the paper coincided with two historical exigencies then: On the one hand, white readers wanted to know more of the Cherokee language, culture, traditions, and politics; on the other hand, Cherokees wanted a paper that would deliver their intelligence in their own prized writing system. Boudinot mediates these competing demands by sponsoring content in both English and Cherokee, to the extent possible.

Boudinot's prospectus for the newspaper promised to serve Cherokees' interests by sanctioning a space for the printed version of the language, laws, stories, letters, and Bible translations (many of which were gathered by Worcester):

> For it must be known that the great and sole motive in establishing this paper is the benefit of the Cherokees. This will be the great aim of the Editor, which he intends to pursue. . . . The alphabet lately invented by a native Cherokee . . . forms an interesting medium of information to those Cherokees who are unacquainted with the English language. For their benefit Cherokee types have been procured. The columns . . . will be filled, partly with English, and partly with Cherokee print; and all matter which is of common interest will be given in both languages in parallel columns. (Boudinot, 1828b, February 28)

Printing the first Native American newspaper with the first Native American writing system developed with the first ever set of types created for a Native writing system set a boundary for the Cherokees. The language and writing system were not intended for outsiders to understand. In other words, as a literacy sponsor, Boudinot provided different and differential access to the paper's content and intentionally so.

The prospectus continues to outline four ways in which the paper's content would tailor itself to its goal of benefiting Cherokees by including:

1. The laws and public documents of the nation.
2. Account of the manners and customs of the Cherokees, and their progress in Education, Religion, and the arts of civilized life . . .
3. The principal interesting news of the day.
4. Miscellaneous articles, calculated to promote Literature, Civilization, and Religion among the Cherokees. (Boudinot, 1828b, February 28)

The issues of every paper were organized into these four categorizes of content fairly consistently, with greater or lesser portions of the paper devoted to the first two as the need presented. The first issue, printed in February 21, 1828, includes the Cherokee Nation's constitution printed in both languages in columns next to each other (see fig. 1.3) (Boudinot, 1828, February 21). Because the Cherokee language needs far fewer characters to express meaning, large white spaces appear after each section of the Cherokee language.

| CONSTITUTION OF THE CHE- ROKEE NATION; *Formed by a Convention of Delegates from the several Districts, at New E- chota, July 1827.* WE, THE REPRESENTATIVES of the people of the CHEROKEE NATION in | .JᏙᎾᏆ.ᏒᎯᎫ ᏋᏫᎩ Ꮕ·ᎾᏐᎬᏏ. — J.ᏓᏔ ᎢᏑᏍᎩ Ꮟ-ᏂᎯᎢᏎᎦᎩ ᏉᏃᏃᎡᏬ-Ꮜ, ᎫᏖᏤᎷ ᏋᏎᎢ Ꮼ-ᎻᎦᎡᏎᎦ. ᎮᏋ ᏍᎯᏪᎲ ᎠᏋᎯᎦᎢᏈ ᎠᏍᎪᎥ ᎠᎦᏉᏬ, ᏋᏫᎩ ᎬᎾ-ᏃᏈ ᎠᏴᎦᎢᎦᎭ, ᏍᏪᎦᎲ ᎦᏴᏒᎢᎧᎦᎭ, ᎠᏓ ᎦᎦ ᏗᏴᏎᏆᏃᎧᏎᎦᎭ, ᎠᏓ ᎫᎡ ᎢᏏᎦᏉᎦᎢᏬ ᎥᎡ ᏃᏆ ᏋᏫᎩ ᎠᏍᎦᎢ ᏦᏤᎦᏬᎦᎭᎦᎭ, ᎾᎦᎤᏍ ᎦᏴᎯ |

Fig. 1.3. Preamble to the constitution of the Cherokee Nation, published in the first issue of the *Cherokee Phoenix*, 1828, p. 1

Cherokee in script does not have punctuation because word borders are indicated by space. Since one word in Cherokee can be equivalent to an entire compound, complex sentence in English, spacing between words alone suffices in showing sentence boundaries. Punctuation, however, was added to the Cherokee published in the *Phoenix* and to the verses of the Psalms. These conventions of punctuation would have indicated more to English-speaking audiences than to Cherokee readers, allowing readers to roughly match the Cherokee to the English. This side-by-side layout of columns does more than simply present information in a systematic way for the two audiences; white readers might have perceived themselves as privy to insider access to the Cherokee language through this design. This was the first time that the Cherokee syllabary in print was produced in a newspaper; its novelty would have served as a curiosity to outsiders simply on the face of it. Including punctuation with Sequoyan, Boudinot guides white outsiders to the boundaries of idea units in ways that Cherokees wouldn't have needed.

But this layout also served as one way to visually reinforce the parallel structure of the Cherokees' government to the US federal government. "By publishing official correspondence and documents, legislation passed by the National Council, and notices . . . Boudinot not only informed Cherokee readers of events in the Nation but also demonstrated to white readers the remarkable accomplishments of his people" (Perdue, 1983, p. 16). Boudinot's choice to include the Cherokee constitution in these two languages, side-by-side, despite having large portions of white space, presented these as visually equal systems of government.

The equality of the governments was also demonstrated in the content of the pieces. Note that the Cherokee constitution's preamble models its language closely to that found in the preamble of the US Constitution:

We the people of the United States, in order to form a more perfect union, establish justice, ensure domestic tranquility, provide for the common defense, promote the general welfare, and secure the blessings of liberty to ourselves and our posterity, do ordain and establish this constitution for the United States of America.

The ways in which this first publication of the *Phoenix* draws upon conventions and models of language, content, and design presented in the mainstream cater to white audience's desire to see Cherokees becoming civilized. At the same time, this arrangement allows Cherokees their own means to maintain exclusivity to their language. Boudinot's layout of the two languages side-by-side suggests the complexity of his role as literacy sponsor who had to provide differential access to language resources and information for his readers. He used white space and proximity in ways that reinforce the message of equality and of mediation between these two systems of government and language.

The establishment of the press secured a mutually sustaining and complex sponsor/sponsored relationship that was more than economically motivated. The advantages of having this readership were initially economic for the paper and for Boudinot. Boudinot wrangled with the Cherokee Nation over his pay that was $100 less than Isaac Harris, the white printer, until Boudinot eventually received $400 a year as an editor of the paper. Boudinot certainly gained personal status, a paycheck, and some measure of public acclaim as the editor of the *Phoenix*; at the same time, he was working on the behalf of Cherokees, presenting laws and public documents in the language. The sponsored audiences were both white and Cherokee, and the press in New Echota acted as a delivery agent that provided an avenue to reading and writing in Sequoyan and English literacy to the different audiences.

The Sponsor That Elias Boudinot Was and Wasn't

Through the *Cherokee Phoenix*, Elias Boudinot informed white sympathizers and Cherokees, published language lessons, and crafted a "civilized" face for the Cherokee. By publishing information regarding legal battles and unlawful acts of white people in both Cherokee and English, Boudinot acted as a sponsoring agent of the Cherokee Nation and tribe. He elicited sympathy from white reformers in the north and provoked hostility from the Georgia militia during the years leading up to the removal of the Cherokees.

In the July 1, 1829, issue of the *Phoenix*, George Lowrey, Sequoyah's cousin, translated a letter from Chief John Ross into Cherokee asking them to have faith in the law of the US federal government and not to be afraid of the words of President Andrew Jackson:

The Treatys entered into between us and the General Govt.' are very strong and will protect our right of soil. The Govt.' have agreed to keep our lines clear [referring to the borders with the Creeks] and keep all intruders off our lands. If Georgia was to extend her laws over us it would be a violation of our treaties with the Genrl. Govt. and the laws of the United States. We don't believe they will extend their laws over us. (Ross, 1985, p. 166)

Chief Ross was using the paper to ask Cherokees to trust in the treaties made with the US federal government, to understand that the state of Georgia had no legal right to extend their laws over the tribe, and to not be frightened of Jackson's posturing.

Boudinot, of course, had to sponsor this information and include it in the *Cherokee Phoenix*, though he did not agree with Ross's position; Ross and the Cherokee Nation hired Boudinot to publish this information and use the paper as a resource for providing correct legal information. This letter in Cherokee, printed in the same issue where the very topic of land rights was being discussed in English, was meant to calm growing uncertainty among the tribe's people about their impending removal. The press acted as an agent of information and reassurance for Chief Ross even as it worked to rally white sympathizers to the Cherokee cause. This same issue of the *Phoenix* explained for English-speaking audiences the causes and troubles behind the increasing strife among Cherokees, Creeks, and the state of Georgia.

As the state of Georgia increasingly attempted to extend its legal authority over the nation, the nation continued to argue its case for sovereignty using Boudinot and the press as an important resource manager for reading and writing in Cherokee and English to express and build alliances for their positions. The problem of Georgia's encroachment on Cherokee lands was exacerbated by the 1830 passage of the Indian Removal Act, which authorized Jackson to send agents into Cherokee country to recruit emigrants west. Jackson directed the Indian agent Colonel Hugh Montgomery to withhold the annual annuity owed to the tribe by the federal government for lands ceded in the 1819 treaty.

Strangulating their national treasury, the funding for the press was jeopardized, requiring Boudinot to travel the country to seek financial assistance from allies who subscribed to the paper and other white sympathizers. He returned to the nation after a year of fund-raising and after the US Supreme Court had ruled that the state of Georgia's laws did not extend over Cherokee land. But when Jackson and the Georgia militia refused to support the ruling, Boudinot saw little hope for the Cherokees' continued presence on their ancestral lands, and he supported removal. When the Cherokee Nation learned of his support for removal, they asked him as editor of the *Phoenix* not to publish his views. In protest of what he perceived to be censorship and with disregard for the Cherokee Nation's fight to remain on ancestral lands, he stepped down as editor.

Ultimately, the ways in which the press worked as a voice and face for the nation spelled the demise of Boudinot as its editor. His role as sponsor of literacy came to an end because he was understood as working against the tribe and nation with his support for removal. When he signed the Treaty of New Echota as one of a handful of Cherokees who advocated for the removal of the tribe, his fate was sealed, and he was assassinated in 1839.

The nation appointed another editor. The press and typecasts themselves, so valued among the Cherokee, continued to produce printed materials for the Cherokee concerning their removal, legal battles, and especially their ill treatment at the hands of the Georgia Guard. Ultimately, the fortunes of the new editor and sponsor of literacy also went the way of the nation. In a letter to Lewis Cass from Washington, D.C., on April 1836, Ross tells the story of the press's demise:

> The Cherokee Council, held in the spring of 1835 resolved to remove the nation's Printing Press to Red Clay, and to issue a paper at that place, in as much as the Cherokees were prohibited from holding their councils at New Echota within the limits of Georgia. . . . The Press, and materials were at New Echota and [the new editor, Richard Fields] sent a wagon for them. The messenger returned with information, that before he arrived at that place, the whole had been seized by the Georgia Guard. . . . Thus the public Pres[s] of the Cherokee Nation has been lawlessly taken, is yet retained, and has been recently used by the agents of the United States, in the publication of slanderous communications against the constituted authorities of the nation. (1985, p. 418)

The very gesture of the Georgia Guard stealing the press suggests the value, threat, and import the press had in developing a face for the Cherokee Nation. As a sponsor of literacy, the editor of the *Phoenix* used the press to provide differential access to language resources, conveying at once the Cherokee language, its tradition, and some tribal ways but, equally important, securing the sympathies and support of white northeasterners.

The printing press's arrival and production of the *Cherokee Phoenix* furthered a mass reading and writing movement that had been underway with the Cherokee script. The newspaper and press had significant political implications for the ways in which the Cherokee presented themselves as a sovereign nation to the US government and to the state of Georgia; it allowed tribal members to hear of news from Europe and other Indian tribes around the nation in Cherokee and English; it also provided a platform for white audiences to see inside the Cherokee language and US politics from an indigenous standpoint. The agents of the press used the rhetoric of "becoming civilized" in a way that provided support for claims to the rights and privileges that a nation of Cherokees might enjoy. Boudinot's role in all of this was one of stewardship, advocacy, mediation, and proxy and was always contingent upon the continued endorsement of the people and the officers of the nation he served.

For every way that the *Cherokee Phoenix* might disappoint historians as an ethnohistorical source (Perdue, 1977), when seen as the sponsor of information and meaning that it is, the paper and Boudinot's work might be rescued from critiques of what they did not do and instead be seen in light of what they did. Though results were surely mixed, the ways in which Boudinot sponsored literacy through the publication of the *Phoenix* in both Cherokee and English suggests another nuance to the notion of sponsorship itself: Sponsors work within mutually sustaining relationships with both those they sponsor and those who sponsor them. Sponsors (like Boudinot) are beholden to those sponsored by their efforts (the Cherokee people) and to those who put them in the position to sponsor in the first place (the Cherokee Nation). They are also impacted by the sponsorship efforts. Boudinot's case demonstrates in broad relief the remarkable stakes, efforts, and outcomes of sustaining such sponsorship positions and what happens when the sponsor makes choices that run contrary to the wishes and beliefs of his or her own sponsors and those he or she sponsors. Literacy sponsors serve at the behest of others.

Notes

1. All issues of the *Cherokee Phoenix* are now available in electronic reproduction from printed papers from the Georgia Newspaper Project, University of Georgia Libraries, Farmington Hills, Michigan, Thomson Gale, 2006, http://neptune3.galib.uga.edu/ssp/cgi-bin/tei-news-idx.pl?sessionid=7f000001&type=issues&id=chrkphnx (access limited by licensing agreements).

2. I am grateful to the reviewers of this chapter, whose thoughtful responses have helped me develop several key points. One reviewer writes of my need to develop more of my reasoning behind my critique of American Indian Studies scholars who have considered Boudinot and the *Phoenix*: "One is left with the dual impression that Cushman disagrees with Perdue and colleagues, but that her analysis depends heavily upon the primary sources unearthed and published by them." I do disagree with Perdue and

colleagues for reasons I've developed more here. I do not agree that my work relies heavily on the primary sources they "unearthed" and "published." My sister and mother subscribed to the *Cherokee Phoenix* and pointed out proudly to anyone who asked that it was the first Indian newspaper. This source was hardly hidden, "published by," or "unearthed by" these or any other scholars.

3. When referring to the Cherokee writing system, the term *literacy* does not apply. This writing system has morphographic features, meaning that each character potentially carries with it semantic, syntactic, morphological, and phonological information. It does not rely on the letter as literacy does but was, rather, created from an entirely different instrumental and cultural logic. For more on this, see Cushman, 2011a, 2011c.

4. Elsewhere, I have discussed the ways in which Cherokees' value for Sequoyan in print lent to the stabilization of the tribe as it created a national identity for itself, primarily in English. See Cushman, 2010.

References

American Board of Commissioners for Foreign Missionaries. 1826, February 22. "Cherokees." *Missionary Herald, 22,* 47.

Bender, Margaret. 2002. *Signs of Cherokee Culture: Sequoyah's Syllabary in Eastern Cherokee Life*. Chapel Hill: University of North Carolina Press.

Boudinot, Elias. 1828a, February 21. "Cherokee Constitution." *The Cherokee Phoenix*, col. B:1(1). 19th Century Newspapers. Gale, 2009. Accessed July 22, 2009.

———. 1828b, February 28. "Prospectus." *The Cherokee Phoenix*, col. B:1(2). 19th Century Newspapers. Gale, 2009.

Brandt, Deborah. 1998. "Sponsors of Literacy." *College Composition and Communication, 49*(2), 166–85.

———. 2001. *Literacy in American Lives*. Cambridge, England: Cambridge University Press.

Cushman, Ellen. 2010. "The Cherokee Syllabary from Script to Print." *Ethnohistory, 57*(2), 225–47.

———. 2011a. "The Cherokee Syllabary: A Writing System in Its Own Right." *Written Communication, 28*(3), 255–81.

———. 2011b. *The Cherokee Syllabary: Writing Peoplehood and Perseverance*. Norman: University of Oklahoma Press.

———. 2011c. "'We're Taking the Genius of Sequoyah into This Century': The Cherokee Syllabary, Peoplehood, and Perseverance." *Wicazo Sa Review Journal, 26*(2), 67–83.

McLoughlin, William G. 1984. *Cherokees and Missionaries, 1789–1839*. New Haven, CT: Yale University Press.

———. 1986. *Cherokee Renascence in the New Republic*. Princeton, NJ: Princeton University Press.

Mignolo, Walter. 2007. "Delinking." *Cultural Studies, 21*(2–3), 449–514.

Mooney, James. 1900. *Myths of the Cherokees*. Washington, DC: Bureau of American Ethnology.

Perdue, Theda. 1977. "Rising from the Ashes: The Cherokee Phoenix as Ethnohistorical Source." *Ethnohistory, 24*(3), 207–18.

———, ed. 1983. *Cherokee Editor: The Writings of Elias Boudinot*. Knoxville: University of Tennessee Press.

Perdue, Theda, and Michael D. Green, eds. 1995. *The Cherokee Removal: A Brief History with Documents*. Bedford Series in History and Culture. Boston: Bedford/ St. Martin's.

Pickering, Mary Orne. 1887. *Life of John Pickering*. Boston. Retrieved from http://books. google.com/books/about/Life_of_John_Pickering.html?id=cHyAiwyYksEC

Powell, Katrina. 2007. *The Anguish of Displacement: The Politics of Literacy in the Letters of Mountain Families in Shenandoah National Park*. Charlottesville: University of Virginia Press.

Ross, John. 1985. *The Papers of Chief John Ross*. Edited by Gary Moulton. Vol. 1, *1807–1839*. Norman: University of Oklahoma Press.

Royster, Jacqueline Jones. 2000. *Traces of a Stream: Literacy and Social Change among African American Women*. Pittsburgh, PA: University of Pittsburgh Press.

Rumsey, Suzanne. 2008. "Cooking, Recipes, and Work Ethic: Passage of a Heritage Literacy Practice." *Journal of Literacy and Technology: An International Online Academic Journal, 10*(1), 70–95.

———. 2009. "Heritage Literacy: Adoption, Adaptation, and Alienation of Multimodal Literacy Tools." *College Composition and Communication, 60*(3), 573–86.

Thornton, Russell. 1985. "Nineteenth-Century Cherokee History." *American Sociological Review, 50*(1), 124–27.

———. 1993. "Boundary Dissolution and Revitalization Movements: The Case of the Nineteenth-Century Cherokees." *Ethnohistory, 40*(3), 359–83.

Worcester, Samuel ["W."]. 1827. "Letter to Jeremiah Evarts, 2 September." *Papers of the American Board of Foreign Missions* 18.3.1, vol.5, part 2, no. 232. Microfilm reel 739, frames 609–10. Woodbridge, CT: Research.

———. 1828a. "Cherokee Alphabet." *Missionary Herald, 24*(5), 162.

———. 1828b. "The Invention of the Cherokee Alphabet." *Missionary Herald, 24*(10), 330.

Young, Mary. 1981. "The Cherokee Nation: Mirror of the Republic." *American Quarterly, 33*(5), 502–24.

2. Testimony as a Sponsor of Literacy: Bernice Robinson and the South Carolina Sea Island Citizenship Program's Literacy Activism

Rhea Estelle Lathan

> For the master's tools will never dismantle the master's house. They may allow us temporarily to beat him at his own game, but they will never enable us to bring about genuine change.
>
> —Audre Lorde, *Sister Outsider*

> As African American women intellectuals doing this work, we are obligated, as are our counterparts within the community, to be holistic, to remember our connectedness in both places. We are free to do our own intellectual business, and at the same time we are also obligated to have that work respond to sociopolitical imperatives that encumber the community itself. We, like our sisters (the African American women whom we study), are accountable ultimately to the merging of the interest of mind, body, and soul as part and parcel of the wholeness of the knowledge making enterprise, which includes accounting for our own social obligations as members of the group. We speak and interpret with the community, not just for the community, or about the community.
>
> —Jacqueline Jones Royster, *Traces of a Stream*

I begin with Audre Lorde and Jacqueline Jones Royster because they both superbly embody the objectives of this essay: to make a case for expanding definitions of literacy to include arenas where writing is in a symbiotic relationship with social and political obligations. Both Lorde and Royster are pushing for the transcendence of current intellectual frameworks, arguing that the problem is that the "master's house" is cognitive, not spiritual; these frameworks are too rigid, allowing little space for a testament to the survival of marginalized, underrepresented people, particularly African American women. Royster and Lorde are talking about transcendence; an understanding of both sacred and secular consciousness would improve our understanding of that transcendence. Admittedly, research in critical theory, musicology, African American studies, and composition studies has successfully argued that testifying is not simple commentary but dramatic narration requiring a communal reenactment of one's feelings and experiences. In the end, conventional academic uses of testifying hold fast to master frameworks, rarely moving testifying beyond religious contexts toward an intellectual practice.

I concede that several contemporary literacy scholars have begun the task of broadening the domain in which literacy is situated.[1] These studies suggest there is a great deal of complex literacy activity occurring outside standard academic contexts as well as what constitutes "community literacy" within local communities. However, standard frameworks traditionally follow a "master framework," marginalizing or ignoring "other" ways of knowing. By interrogating the intersections between sacred and secular literacy activities, I move toward a theory developed in an arena where grassroots people are aggressively fighting *for* and *with* literacy acquisition, revealing that the acquisition of knowledge requires *all* participants to take an active stand on the means and methods of writing instruction. Such an analysis leads to an awareness about the practices, meanings, and values of literacy activism within the context of a major literacy campaign: the South Carolina Sea Island Citizenship Education Program.

Ultimately, I follow Deborah Brandt by illuminating how individual ways of knowing, interpreting, and being are connected to larger social systems. However, through an extension of Brandt's theory of literacy sponsorship, I treat an African American cultural concept of testimony as a new and inclusive literacy tool. I explore these continuities and changes by looking specifically at the literacy activism of the late civil rights activist Bernice Robinson in an effort to expand representations of African American literacy activism.

Robinson's literacy activities provide a means of exploring one of the most significant eras in African American history: the Civil Rights Movement. Bernice Robinson is to Septima Clark what Ralph Abernathy is to Martin Luther King Jr.—essential. Therefore, my goal here is also a corrective effort to illuminate Robinson as a crucial thinker within the success of the Citizenship Education Program from its inception on Johns Island through its spread across the South and currently in Freedom School models across the United States. Like Clark, this program could not have succeeded without Robinson's intellectual activities. If we are going to call for a well-documented effect of African American literacy activism, Bernice Robinson must be included as a central actor and thinker.

Robinson was the first teacher within the Citizenship Schools, which operated first under the sponsorship of Highlander Folk School and later under the auspices of the Southern Christian Leadership Conference. The Citizenship Schools were described by activist Andrew Young as the base upon which the whole Civil Rights Movement was built. Robinson is one of the unsung heroes of the Civil Rights Movement. Through her involvement in the Civil Rights Movement, the Citizenship Education Program, and subsequent Freedom Schools, she both directly and indirectly had a hand in training more than twenty-five thousand people. It is for this reason that I begin the essay with a brief biographical background. Next, I unpack a detailed new literacy treatment of testimony, drawing on its linguistic, rhetorical, and cultural theory intersections. Finally, I redefine testimony to include African American sacred/secular ways of knowing and Brandt's concept of literacy sponsors. Within these treatments, I weave Robinson's radical literacy activism, demonstrating how testimony operates within the context of grassroots Civil Rights Movement literacy activism.

Bernice Robinson: A Brief Background

Bernice Robinson was born on February 7, 1914, in Charleston, South Carolina. Robinson proudly recalls that on that day it snowed in Charleston for the first time in over one hundred years. For her, snow in South Carolina on her birthday meant that she was destined to spend her life "disturbing the elements." Born to Haitian immigrants, Bernice was the youngest of nine children. Her father was a bricklayer and her mother a self-employed seamstress. They were not wealthy by any means, but Bernice recalls that her childhood was happy. There was rarely a meal that did not include a visiting child from the neighborhood. The Robinson children were raised to never complain about what they did not have, to be grateful and proud, and, most of all, to acknowledge that they never had so little that they did not have enough to share. Robinson's lessons began with her parents refusing to allow them to say they were poor. She explains, "My daddy would refuse to let us say that we were poor even though they didn't have much money" (1980).

The roots of this pride stemmed from the Robinsons' religious foundations. Her parents, Martha and Fletcher, were devout Christians raising their children in the African Methodist Episcopal Church (AME). The church's doctrine infused Bernice with its powerful and distinctive Afro-Christian ideology. This liberatory form of Christianity advocates for a means of weighing what African American people have been led to believe about Christianity against the reality of racist philosophies engrained in the consciousness of some practitioners of that faith. This way of knowing illuminates how a large part of the success of the Civil Rights Movement derives from the traditional intersection, within African American communities, between religious and secular organizations that formed around shared goals.[2]

Bernice Robinson attended Burke High School in Charleston through the eighth grade—the highest grade public schools in South Carolina would allow African American children at the time—but she received her high school diploma after attending night school in New York. She moved to New York City primarily because there were few employment opportunities for African American women in Charleston, other than domestic work, which her parents deemed too dangerous. While living in New York City, Robinson experienced academic, intellectual, and civic autonomy, studying real estate and cosmetology at the Pace Institute. Holding a variety of jobs gave her valuable experience and an opportunity to exercise an intellectual autonomy that she would draw on later while working with the Citizenship Schools. Robinson was also employed as a computer operator for the Internal Revenue Service, a beautician, a statistical clerk for the Veterans Administration, and a campaign worker for a state legislator while she sold real estate.

In 1947, her parents became ill, requiring live-in assistance, so she returned to Charleston to help with their care. Unfortunately, due to intense race and gender discrimination, employment opportunities in Charleston limited Robinson to independent tailoring and operating a beauty salon from home. However, the semi-liberatory experience in New York (including civic freedom) empowered Robinson, making her far less tolerant of overtly restrictive Southern covenants. While living in New York City, not only was she a registered voter, she could actually exercise full citizenship rights and vote. Charleston's "white only" primary denied her this privilege for no other reason than she was African American. Unwilling to accept the status of third-class citizen, Robinson took charge, working against racist oppression with full vigor by initiating activist efforts through Young Men's Christian Association (YMCA) and National Association for the Advancement of Colored People (NAACP) memberships. As an executive officer in both organizations, her focus was on eradicating racial discrimination and disenfranchisement. It was her work in these organizations along with her determination to achieve social equality that prompted her cousin, civil rights activist Septima Clark, to invite Bernice to a Highlander-sponsored United Nations Human Rights workshop held in August 1954.[3]

Test as Testimony: A Working Definition

A conventional understanding of testimony is to give an account of something: reporting on or explaining a situation or event that the speaker has personal knowledge of. In African American sacred or religious contexts, testimony is the retelling of an occurrence that includes visual accounts, prophetic experiences, and narratives. The storyline is usually delivered in dramatic fashion, re-creating a spiritual reality for the listener, who at the moment shares, vicariously, the experience that the person has gone through. Above all, the *purpose* of a testimony is to empower by communicating valuable, life-giving, life-changing solutions.

Testifying becomes an ideological framework and theoretical concept because of its unique manifestation within African American culture. It is determined by specific principles and predispositions attached to larger social systems bounded by time and space. Similar to literacy, testifying illuminates visions—ways of knowing—that include a continual interchange. Ultimately, testimony is a process through which individual acts of evaluation inform larger social systems—such as the Civil Rights Movement. With this in mind, as an African American cultural expression, testimony intersects both secular and sacred ideologies. Coupled with literacy activism during the Civil Rights Movement, a testifying ethos evolves along with the surrounding culture, developing—through intellectual engagement—innovative learning strategies and styles, testing new language in response to new perspectives on intellectually oppressive ideologies. Testimony, then, becomes an African American intellectual means of embracing critical intellectualism as an empowering activity—thinking, reasoning, and expressing—that begins by engaging oppressive ideologies while sharing about literacy customs that consciously choose an empowering response.

In 1955, during the peak of civil unrest in the United States, Bernice Robinson helped initiate and sustain a vital African American literacy campaign called the Citizenship Education Program (CEP) on the South Carolina Sea Islands. Robinson, the first CEP teacher, explains that the curriculum she developed for the program came from the expressed needs of participants. Robinson combined lessons of civic accountability with African American sacred/secular ways of knowing, including music and religious meditation. These are the very literacy activities that are fundamental to transcendence of self and society, which are also circulated through ritual symbolic practices, such as testimony.

In August 1955, Robinson accompanied Clark and Johns Island community activist Esau Jenkins to a Highlander residential workshop. This was an interracial workshop that included about forty college students, community leaders, union workers, teachers, and farmers. The topic was "World Problems, the United Nations and You"—a theme reflecting Highlander's mission to link the American struggle for justice with international solidarity. The workshop was not particularly successful in formulating plans central to a United Nations' effort, especially in the midst of 1950s domestic racial unrest. Toward the end of the weeklong session, Jenkins caused a stir by requesting Highlander's assistance in teaching Johns Island residents basic literacy—reading and writing—in order to pass the South Carolina Voter Registration Test. He delivered this request in the form of a sermon. Drawing on deeply felt experiences coupled with logical reasoning, Jenkins, evoking a testimony ethos, described the psychological consequences of the fact that the Sea Island School for African American children was painted black. Jenkins drew on the three primary characteristics central to a testifying ideology: a specific narrative, an intellectual exercise between a speaker and audience, and a group interaction affirming individual humanity. He infused, within his testimony, intense emotion and political vigor explaining how painting the schoolhouse black was done so "that we could be identified as who go to the school. It discouraged me when I got some pride. I quit [school]" (quoted in Carawan et al., 1967, p. 142).

Robinson's account of this scene illuminates the communal reenactment of Jenkins's feelings:

> And then he talked about the literacy on the islands. Well, you know, [it's] like you say, we accepted the black school, we accepted the whites and the colored fountain as a way of life. I knew that there was a lot of illiteracy all around me, but I accepted that as a fact, that there was nothing you could do about it. That was gonna be there you know, and there was nothing anybody could do about it. When Esau started talking about it, then, you know, it started to really coming through and something to think about. People can't read, you know. So he turned a whole workshop around (*laughs*) everybody became interested in this you know. (1980)

Crucial to the testifying ideology, this is an intellectual exercise between the speaker and audience. Once Jenkins "started thinking about it . . . it started to really coming through" to Robinson and others, giving them "something to think about": by thinking, reasoning, and expressing knowledge about a larger context. All this does more than require active engagement; it insists on the critical reexamination of old ideas. This is evident in the action taken by Highlander and those attending the workshop. Moreover, by drawing on a testifying ideology, Jenkins redirected the remaining days of the United Nations' workshop toward literacy activism through passing the voter-registration test. This testimony not only served as the catalyst for Robinson's participation in the Citizenship Education Program; it also became a channel for this crucial twentieth-century literacy crusade: the Freedom Schools.

Central to a testifying ideology is the group's interaction, which reaffirms individual humanity, helping dismiss any sense of isolation. As explained

above, testimony is most often a very specific narrative that explains a trag-
edy or bad time(s) a person has experienced. However, literacy narratives
often follow a master framework that elucidates—within a testimony—how
a greater power has safely carried that person through the difficult experience. I add that testimonies are intellectually sophisticated symbolic practices defined through an experience (individual or shared). Again, I return
to Robinson's response to Jenkins's testimony. As she moves through the
consequences of learning in a building painted black, she transcends with
Jenkins's testimony to break free of segregation's intellectual incarceration.

I primarily draw my use of testifying as an intellectual construct and
literacy tool from Geneva Smitherman (1977), who in *Talkin and Testifyin*
explains that testifying characteristics come out of the Black Church and are
part of African American traditions that form Black Semantics. Smitherman
defines testifying as follows:

> Testifyin, concepts referring to a ritualized form of black commu-
> nication in which the speaker gives verbal witness to the efficacy,
> truth and power of some experience in which all blacks have shared.
> In the church, testifyin is engaged in on numerous symbolic oc-
> casions; newly converted ex-"sinners" testify to the church con-
> gregation the experience of being saved, for instance, or on Watch
> Meeting Night, New Year's Eve, when church folk gather to "watch"
> the old year go out and the new one come in—they testify to the
> goodness of the Lord during the past year. A spontaneous expres-
> sion to the church community, testifyin can be done whenever
> anybody feels the spirit—it don't have to be no special occasion.
> Like Rev. C. L. Franklin, father of Aretha Franklin, might just get
> up in the pulpit any Sunday morning and testify to the goodness
> of God. Aretha talks about the greatness for her man and how he
> makes her feel in her well-known blues recording, Dr. FEELGOOD,
> and that's testifyin too. (p. 58)

Smitherman's definition of testifyin includes rhetorical principles, such
as *persuasive empowerment*, that are acquired by reporting on, or about,
a triumph, success, or good thing (e.g., Dr. Feelgood) in order to persuade the community/group to believe in a higher power or greater force
(e.g., God).

Literacy histories, which often follow a master framework, have missed
the use of testimony as a tool permeating literacy acquisition and use. However, if taken as a sponsor of literacy, testimony could be seen to share core
literacy principles. For example, within the sacred consciousness the practice

of testifying complicates a literacy narrative by including either an account of or response to a burden or problem. Robinson chose such a response as she initiated her literacy activism. The story goes that on January 7, 1957, Robinson walked into a room filled with fourteen adults ready and eager to participate in the South Carolina Sea Island Citizenship Education Program. Anxiously surveying fourteen expectant pairs of eyes, she contemplated how to begin:

> I guess I was nervous, I was more nervous than the people, because they didn't know what they were just coming to learn or to see what they could learn, that sort of thing. And, they came in that night and I told them that they ask me to teach this class. But, I'm not going to be the teacher, we gonna learn together. You gonna teach me some things and maybe there are a few things I might be able to teach you, but I don't consider myself a teacher. I just feel that I'm here to learn with you, you know, learn things together. I think that sort of settled the folks down. (1980)

Immersed deep in this intellectual practice is a shared knowledge about the acquisition of knowledge of a higher power (i.e., the community, God, etc.). Robinson's success in gaining control over past oppressive learning experiences as well as her efforts *not* to bring that ideology into the classroom is an example of testimony as literacy sponsor. Robinson enters the classroom and immediately dissolves the role of teacher in an effort to ease nervousness and preconceived perceptions of the teacher's role. This statement combined with her acknowledgment of an empowering force that helped her get through building the initial curriculum illuminates a testifying ideology. Ultimately, testimony includes specific communicative and epistemological principles and characteristics that intersect with literacy and larger social systems. In the case of the CEP, these social systems are not limited to the larger Civil Rights Movement but rather include a shared belief in a definitive transformative power.

A testifying ideology is derived from African American gospel culture and is fueled through traditional elements of African American intellectual design. For example, when Robinson shares her literacy activism experience, she is not simply retelling how she learned to teach. She is operating within a literacy ideology where testimony becomes an outward expression of an inward process: It involves engaging complex problems through a critical intellectual process. As an empowering concept, testimony extends beyond defeat to the power of sharing with the collective by touching what others have dealt with individually.

In the case of grassroots literacy activism, we see testimony as a means of rejecting limitations of past systems of literacy learning through a reexamination of those systems. The very organization of the classes demonstrates this intersection. Within these gatherings there was a continual exchange between spiritual and sociopolitical ideologies, methodologies, and pedagogies. Robinson clearly describes this phenomenon as follows:

> A typical [Citizenship School] class would begin with devotions. Someone would be assigned to carry on devotions for each class night. This relaxed and warmed up the group. Then homework was checked. Then we would have about thirty minutes of reading. I wrote down each word they had difficulty in pronouncing and used these words during our spelling period, which followed. The definitions of these words were also taught so the students would understand what they were reading. Then we would have a session in arithmetic, using the prices from grocery lists, catalogue orders, etc. Then we would go thru the process of applying for a [voter] registration certificate. [. . .] The goal of the classes was to create an awareness of the political structure in the local community, across the state, as well as nation who controlled funds for education, housing, employment etc. Blacks could not only be knowledgeable as to whom they should contact to eliminate what problems, but they could become candidates for these offices as well. (1980)

Ultimately, everyone gains strength—individually and collectively—from deeply felt experiences grounded in logical reasoning, coherent thought, and lucid expression. This gets paired with an embodied knowledge that freedom from intellectual incarceration is not only possible but imminent.

Engaging a revisionist literacy perspective illuminates the way in which access to literacy learning is experienced differently within racial, class, gendered, historical, religious, and geographical contexts. Particularly, an exploration of continuities and changes of the teaching and writing activism of the late Bernice Robinson expands representations of African American literacies. Most important, there exists an emerging theme rooted in African American cultural consciousness that weaves secular literacy activism and expression together with spiritual and material ways of being, knowing, acting, and living. This is a testifying ideology.

Testimony: A Multirhythmic Way of Knowing

Testimony, here, evolves from explorations into how literacy activities of the Civil Rights Movement and sacred expressions develop along with the surrounding culture, initiating innovative styles while testing inventive language in response to new expressions of traditional problems. Testimony thus gets situated as a critical literacy concept with a multirhythmic framework that accounts for formal, cultural, spiritual, and material ways of knowing, thinking, and being. A testifying consciousness is especially visible within the literacy activities of the Civil Rights Movement, where participants frequently interchange literacy activism with sacred ways of knowing and social change, illuminated by the fact that most literacy and political activities took place in private, protected worship spaces—mosques, private clubs, churches, and homes.

In testimony, literacy and rhetoric—the written and the oral—frequently work together. Historically, African Americans have had to make "the Word" their own in order to *do* language. For example, as Janet Duitsman Cornelius's (1992) work illustrates, for many enslaved people, the Bible provides the community with an identity. Admittedly, this acquisition of knowledge informed the legacy of colonial missionary literacy. Rejecting this legacy of oppression, enslaved people spoke the Word through reading and writing as an act of resistance as well as an assertion of identity. In African American rhetorical studies, this practice has been identified as Nommo. According to composition scholar Keith Gilyard, Nommo "is the belief in the pervasive, mystical, transformative, even life-giving power of the Word" (2003, p. 12). Geneva Smitherman adds that African Americans reinterpret this linguistic orientation and that Nommo actualizes the "fundamental unity between the spiritual and material aspects of existence" (p. 75). Smitherman concludes, "[T]he oral tradition, then, is part of the cultural baggage the African brought to America. Preslavery background was one in which the concept of Nommo, the magic power of the Word, was believed necessary to actualize life and give man mastery over things" (1977, p. 78). The African belief in the power and necessity of Nommo was so strong that a verbal battle was required to precede or accompany warfare. This performance was central within CEP teaching and learning activities. For example, participants—through the acquisition of knowledge—gained power over the list of "offenses" or the words on the South Carolina voter-registration form by gaining mastery over the words—learning the actual meanings and how to pronounce them. In Robinson's recollection of a lesson based on voter-registration forms, we see the principle of Nommo in action:

> As they would read and I taught them to read, every word they stumbled over we came to a spelling lesson and I'd pull the words out, put them on the board, break them into syllables and give the explanation, what the word means. I told Myles one night (Myles

was down here in class) and I was having this lesson. I was just
going down this list, giving them the meaning of this word just
from the top of my head. I was looking at the board and there were
a couple of words I didn't know the meaning of, and I said, "Mmm,
this word here means something." And Myles and I just laughed
at that. If I hadn't realized, you know we use words that we don't
know the meaning of, and rather than have them read this section
of the Constitution and just call words and not know what it was,
that they were being required to read. This is how we got started
in our program. (1980)

Paramount to testimony as a literacy sponsor, CEP participants moved com-
pleting a voter-registration application beyond a *simple* lesson in filling
out an application or learning vocabulary words. A deeper lesson was in
place. Participants were empowered through the infusion of a testimony
and vocabulary exercises.

Most crucial within this analysis is *how* the sacred vision underlies a
testimony ideology. For example, in the musical expression, a gospel singer
responds to the audience by testifying about a problem, dilemma, or the
trouble he or she has experienced—sharing the most sincere emotional
truths he or she knows. However, the testimony does not stop at just acknowledging a burden or waging a complaint. It also recognizes the presence
of a power or spirit greater than the force behind the incident. In a sacred
context, this is usually recognized through a nonverbal expression, such
as moans or shouts.[4] The spiritual, not religious, understanding is crucial
here. Craig Hansen Werner (1998) best explains the multiple identities and
interpretations of a higher power within African American culture:

> [I]t takes an energy bigger than yourself, the wellspring of healing
> that South African pianist Abdullah Ibrahim called "water from
> an ancient well." For the classic gospel singers, the source is God;
> for soul singers, it's love. Bob Marley calls it Jah. George Clinton
> envisions Atlantis, the Mothership. Arrested Development imag-
> ines a tree in Tennessee. (pp. 30–31)

It is important to add that this power also includes an expectation of being
saved, delivered, or rescued *from* the oppressive force *by* a superior, higher,
and more powerful being. However, no matter how the power is identified,
personal power and autonomy must include communal liberation. Survival
depends on testifying about a connection with a higher power.

Basically, as the opening epigraph explains, a testimony usually expresses
what we share on our own (individually) when the coincidences and miracles

happen, providing evidence of a dominant energy or power—God—that could not be explained through material means. Testimony yields personal knowledge about a time or space when individuals are confronted with evidence of a higher power they could not deny. This force is spiritual, real, and central to testimonies within gospel literacy. For example, Robinson explains that she does not know where or how she acquired her instructional tools and methods, declaring, "I don't know yet how I did it. It was something that hit me when talking. [. . .] I don't know yet how I did it."

Within African American intellectual traditions, a testimony has sacred and secular implications. It is a communicative, literate practice with non-material dimensions including faith, hope, courage, willingness, humility, unconditional love, perseverance, open-mindedness, awareness, vigilance, self-discipline, sharing, caring, and service. Within African American consciousness, testimony is a way of verbally acknowledging and affirming the power of a greater being, by speaking of, recognizing, or affirming a significant experience outside the sacred context. A conventional definition is giving an account of something: reporting on or explaining a situation or event that the speaker has personal knowledge of. In sacred contexts, testimony includes visual accounts or prophetic experiences. On the surface, it is the retelling of an occurrence, story, or stories. However, the purpose of testimony is to persuade or communicate valuable life giving/changing knowledge.

Earlier I defined literacy as a way of knowing, a process by which decoding and making meaning are used in their social contexts, in other words, the way in which individual acts of composition (reading and writing) are attached to larger social systems. Here I reinvoke that definition, illustrating how literacy acquisition and use intersect with testimony (a practice of communicating knowledge as well as life experiences while relating them to a larger social system, in this case, the Civil Rights Movement). Testimony, then, is a literacy tool that includes ways of knowing that not only sponsor the practices, meanings, and values of literacy but become central to CEP participants' literacy acquisition and use.

Testimony: A Literacy Sponsor

Testimony serves as a viable sponsor of literacy. Deborah Brandt, who introduced the concept of literacy sponsors, describes the sponsor as "agents, local or distant, concrete or abstract, who enable, support, teach, and model, as well as recruit, regulate, suppress, or withhold literacy" (2001, p. 19). These sponsors most often refer to people—"older relatives, teachers, religious leaders, supervisors, military officers, librarians, friends, editors, influential authors." I add, however, that connected to African American ways of knowing are sacred/secular practices motivating the sponsored to identify with the cultural meanings and cultural activities associated with an institutional site. For example, testimony as a way of knowing can often inform both sacred and secular sites. As Robinson describes a typical class, a testifying ideology is present. Devotions in sacred context include prayer and an account of an experience where an often negative outcome resulted in a positive experience.

Testimony as a sponsor of literacy happens when Bernice Robinson gives an account that includes both her personal knowledge about literacy acquisition and use as well as her lived experience and testimony. Robinson's account embodies logical reasoning and shared understanding. Specifically, she explains how oppressive literacy learning (intolerance and close-mindedness) informs her teaching and teacher perspective:

> So that's the control that the teachers had in those days. We had to learn how to do laundry, we had to learn how to wash, we had to learn how to iron. All that was when, you started in the seventh grade and went from the seventh through the ninth grade. Cooking, sewing, and laundry. You didn't ask whether you had to take it, you took it. You had to take it. The girls had to take that. And, uh, I remember that the teacher had me to iron a white shirt over and over again.
>
> And I had to wash that shirt every time I had to iron it. I had to wash it out first and then I had to iron it again. Starch it and iron it. And the reason why is because on the collar, I would get what they called "cat faces"—creases, and I couldn't get it straight and of course, we didn't have any electric iron, you know. We had the flat irons, see? It was heated, you know, on the charcoal thing and you had to wipe it off and I would smear it, and I would get it—oohh, I said I never wanted to see a white shirt again in my life. (1980)

Robinson's learning was limited to domestic employment, a vocation that clearly went against her family philosophies. She was denied any formal instruction promoting critical thinking. Her desire was to study classical music. The absence of empowering learning tools takes up the testifying ideology of engaging personal knowledge. Throughout her life, Robinson had been "forced" to accept learning tools that sought to keep her under control, whether it was an iron or a black-painted school.

Robinson's account is useful here for two reasons. First, it provides a means of shifting literacy acquisition from its comfortable cognitive position to a place where literacy is felt; Robinson "feels" teaching and learning are reciprocal, making allowances for the emotion and souls of people who are doing/experiencing literacy. Second, Robinson initiates a perspective for exploring literacy learning that demonstrates a symbiotic relationship between sacred and secular ways of knowing, being, learning, and living. Literacy, here, is felt; it is embodied.

To the extent that any African American literacy theory embraces a broad spectrum of the African American community, it must also consider the institutions, spiritual ideologies, and consciousness—thinking and souls—that connect the community individually to larger social systems. This especially includes the spiritual and religious spaces as well as the various forms of expression—music, dance, poetry, preaching—both sacred and secular, that articulate shared perceptions developed in those spaces. Testimony's communicative and epistemological principles intersect with literacy learning. In the case of Bernice Robinson, testimony includes individual accounts that permeate the practices, meanings, and values of literacy acquisition and use.

Notes

1. See Farr, Seloni, and Song's (2010) study of the social networks of Mexican American families in a Chicago Mexican American community; Duffy's (2007) study of the literate and rhetorical history of a Hmong American community in Wisconsin; Heath's (1983) ethnography of literacy in Trackton and Roadville, working-class African American and white communities in the Piedmont Carolinas; Scribner and Cole's (1981) ethnography of literacy among the Vai in Africa; and Moss's (2003) study of literacy in African American churches.

2. The most notable of these organizations is the Southern Christian Leadership Conference (SCLC), whose primary mission was and is social activism in favor of racial equality.

3. The Highlander Folk School, established in 1932 and now called the Highlander Research and Education Center, was located in Monteagle, Tennessee. Through the request of Sea Island civil rights activist Esau Jenkins, Highlander sponsored an adult literacy program called the Citizenship Education Program (CEP). With some hesitation, Robinson accepted the responsibility as the first teacher for the Highlander-sponsored program, developing and applying a powerful intellectual learning model that connected personal liberation with collective empowerment with literacy activism.

4. Kimmika L. H. Williams argues that "the ontology of African-influenced spirituality includes (1) God (2) spirits (3) men and women, (4) plants and animals, and (5) inanimate objects or 'things.'" 2003, p. 93.

References

Brandt, Deborah. 2001. *Literacy in American Lives.* New York: Cambridge University Press.

Carawan, Guy, Candie Carawan, Bob Yellin, and Ethel Raim. 1967. *Ain't You Got a Right to the Tree of Life? The People of Johns Island, South Carolina, Their Faces, Their Words, and Their Songs.* New York: Simon and Schuster.

Cornelius, Janet Duitsman. 1992. *When I Can Read My Title Clear: Literacy, Slavery, and Religion in the Antebellum South.* Columbus: University of South Carolina Press.

Duffy, John. 2007. *Writing from These Roots: Literacy in a Hmong-American Community.* Honolulu: University of Hawaii Press.

Farr, Marcia, Lisya Seloni, and Juyoung Song. 2010. *Ethnolinguistic Diversity and Education: Language, Literacy, and Culture.* New York: Routledge.

Gilyard, Keith. 2003. "Introduction: Aspects of African American Rhetoric as a Field." In *Understanding African American Rhetoric: Classical Origins to Contemporary Innovations,* edited by Ronald Jackson III and Elaine B. Richardson, i–xviii. New York: Routledge.

Heath, Shirley Brice. 1983. *Ways with Words: Language, Life, and Work in Communities and Classrooms.* Cambridge: Cambridge University Press.

Lorde, Audre. 1984. *Sister Outsider: Essays and Speeches.* Trumansburg, NY: Crossing.

Moss, Beverly J. 2003. *A Community Text Arises: A Literate Text and a Literacy Tradition in African-American Churches.* Cresskill, NJ: Hampton.

Robinson, Bernice. 1980, November 9. Unpublished Interview by Sue Thrasher and Eliot Wigginton. Highlander Education and Research Center Archives New Market, TN.

Royster, Jacqueline Jones. 2000. *Traces of a Stream: Literacy and Social Change among African American Women.* Pittsburgh: University of Pittsburgh Press.

Scribner, Sylvia, and Michael Cole. 1981. *The Psychology of Literacy.* Cambridge, MA: Harvard University Press.

Smitherman, Geneva. 1977. *Talkin and Testifyin: The Language of Black America.* Boston: Houghton Mifflin.

Werner, Craig Hansen. 1998. *A Change Is Gonna Come: Music, Race & the Soul of America.* New York: Plume.

Williams, Kimmika L. H. 2004. "The Ties That Bind: A Comparative Analysis of Zora Neale Hurston and Geneva Smitherman." In *African American Rhetoric: Interdisciplinary Perspectives,* edited by Ronald Jackson III and Elaine B. Richardson, 86–107. Carbondale: Southern Illinois University Press.

3. Beyond the Protestant Literacy Myth

Carol Mattingly

Literacy historians have long credited the Protestant mandate to read Scripture for advances in literacy, with historians of American literacy pointing to New England Puritans as the model for the Protestant impetus to literacy.[1] This belief is commonplace in our best histories. For example, Lawrence Stone identifies the "critical element" of mass literacy "not so much as Christianity as Protestantism" (1969, p. 77) and declares, "At the deepest psychological level, Tridentine Catholicism remained a culture of the image. It intensified the worship of saints, and indulged in ever more lavish embellishment of churches with paintings, glass and sculpture. Protestantism, by contrast, was a culture of the book, of a literate society" (1969, p. 78). Kenneth Lockridge similarly claims that "it is possible to hold great respect for the Protestant impulse as the sole force powerful enough to work a transformation in the level of literacy" (1974, p. 45). Harvey J. Graff finds that Irish Catholics in nineteenth-century Canada had a lower literacy rate than Protestants because Irish Catholics' religion "importantly influenced their disadvantaged status" as "Protestantism provided a greater impetus to literacy than Catholicism—a link that historians should well expect" (1979, p. 58); and E. Jennifer Monoghan, in noting the complex "religious, social, political and economic base" influencing literacy, nonetheless assumes, "The [Protestant] religious motive was paramount" (2005, p. 32). The claim surfaces in numerous other texts related to literacy studies. In the most used history of rhetoric text in English Departments, for example, Patricia Bizzell and Bruce Herzberg claim, "The spread of Protestant Christianity in the eighteenth and nineteenth century aided women's efforts to become better educated. . . . Protestantism encouraged women to be literate so that they could read the Bible" (2001, p. 987).[2] This overarching, seemingly self-evident belief in Protestantism and firsthand experience with biblical texts as the primary promoter of literacy in America has overshadowed other important efforts, leading to an incomplete understanding of American literacy history.

The Protestant narrative was created amidst patriarchal and religious attitudes that have shaped how we see ourselves and the stories we continue to tell, obscuring other valid narratives and promoting prejudicial inaccuracies. In this chapter, I use Catholic literacy efforts as a test case to question some accepted assumptions about American literacy, including beliefs that Protestants valued literacy while Catholics did not and that women were always less literate than men. I suggest that competition among religions to attract and maintain members may have been more important in the sponsorship of literacy than religious beliefs per se.

The American Protestant grand narrative arises partly because historians have synecdochically focused on early English colonies, primarily the New England colonies, to craft a narrative of literacy for all of America; however, prior to English settlement, French, Spanish, and Portuguese conquerors and missionaries introduced themselves to the New World as sponsors of literacies from a European Catholic tradition. As Jamie Candelaria Greene (1994) has noted, the presentation of American literacy as an English (Protestant) enterprise demonstrates an ethnocentric bias. For example, members of the religious Franciscan order both accompanied the first Spanish conquistadors to the Americas and continued to emigrate with the purpose of educating and "civilizing" native inhabitants. Franciscans and other religious orders created schools for natives and for children of the invading armies and settlers, teaching in both Spanish and Latin languages throughout Spanish-conquered Americas, including areas that would become part of the United States (Barth, 1945, p. 50; Gallegos, 1992, pp. 26, 34). The primary purpose, of course, was to extend the Christian religion and Spanish/European culture, to "impose a foreign world view on the native population" (Gallegos, 1992, p. 67).

Similarly, members of Catholic religious communities followed French explorers and settlers to the New World to spread French and Catholic culture. Jesuits had arrived in Quebec as early as 1610, and Ursuline sisters joined them in 1639, establishing the first schools for girls and young women in the Americas. The Ursulines also settled a community of religious women in New Orleans in 1727, shortly after their arrival founding a school for girls. Like Protestant groups, Catholics saw the Americas as a place to extend their religious and cultural vision. During the colonial period, Catholics established early schools in what would become Arizona, California, Florida, Illinois, Louisiana, Maine, New Mexico, New York, Maryland, Michigan, Pennsylvania, and Wisconsin, some as early as the sixteenth century (Buetow, 1970, pp. 1–37).

An important aspect of the Protestant narrative hinges on the importance of literacy in conducting oneself as a Protestant. Protestants often differentiated themselves from "papists" by pointing to their personal involvement with Scripture. Protestants, according to the narratives of most literacy historians, did not rely upon clergy as intermediaries but could interpret God's word themselves, especially through the reading of the vernacular Bible (as opposed to the Catholic emphasis on Latin, for example, or Catholic distrust in anyone but the clergy for interpreting the Word). Because of this belief in the individual's ability, right, and duty to read Scripture, reading was promoted by Protestant leaders beginning with Martin Luther, a theory that has become commonplace in literacy studies.[3]

However, Richard Gawthrop and Gerald Strauss (1984) have argued that while Luther called for general, basic reading and writing for both boys and girls, he "favoured the school as a specialized facility for preparing a professional cadre capable of assuming positions of leadership in church and state: pastors and preachers, theologians and church administrators, lawyers and bureaucrats, teachers, physicians" (p. 32). And, "by the second half of the 1520s he no longer thought that this internal change [within the individual conscience] could be effected by means of private Bible study" (p. 35). Instead, the common schools thus established rarely provided or taught the Bible, instead using catechisms "suitable for memorizing" (p. 37) to promote respect, loyalty, and acceptable social conventions (p. 38). According to Gawthrop and Strauss, education in reading and writing increased as citizens, "more alert to the importance of literacy as a precondition of keeping or raising one's place in society," demanded it (p. 38). Gawthrop and Strauss conclude that "the facts as we can establish them do not substantiate the generally accepted notion—which no one has ever felt obliged to prove—of a causal link between the Lutheran Reformation of the sixteenth century and popular Bible reading" (p. 41).

The New England colonies may indicate a trend similar to that suggested by Gawthrop and Strauss for earlier European literacy efforts; the complexity suggested by other-than-religious literacy sponsors, such as commercial interests, supports the exploration of alternatives to the dominant American literacy narrative. New England saw little growth in literacy levels during the first generations of settlers, when one might expect the Protestant fervor to be especially intense; leaders placed greatest emphasis on readying a future generation of professionals, especially a ministry to lead the people. Early schooling laws in New England, often cited as evidence of Protestant interest in literacy, established Latin grammar schools, where children were expected to learn Latin, perhaps Greek, writing, and numbers, not reading, as the presumption was that children would learn reading at home, an expectation that went largely unmet (Monaghan, 2005, pp. 31–43). Leaders' early schooling emphasis focused on preparation for scholarly and commercial careers suitable for a chosen people, not on Scripture reading. When the schools began to teach reading because children entered schools unable to read, those schools relied largely on moral primers and catechisms, often primarily oral, not on reading Scripture.

An Alternative Narrative

The reification of Protestantism as the source and guardian of literacy in America originated within an exclusionary structure of power and prejudice, and the remnants of the stories thus created continue to eclipse alternative narratives. One such example includes narratives about Catholics' disinterest in or hostility to literacy. Graff (1967, p. 135) suggests in *Legacies* that "Catholicism has suffered a too negative, too unilaterally condemnatory press" on the subject of literacy promotion. He is accurate here. The accepted premise that morality and literacy were linked, along with bitter prejudice toward Catholics, helped establish the notion of Catholics' antagonism toward literacy, ignoring the socioeconomic context that assured a less literate Catholic population. The illiterate nineteenth-century Irish Catholics Graff (1979) focuses on in his *Literacy Myth* derived from a long history of the types of oppression scholars have recently recognized as impeding literacy acquisition, including laws and social circumstances that precluded advancement in literacy. Before coming to North America, Graff's Irish had suffered from centuries of conquest in which they were divested of property and civil rights. Already forced into the darkest poverty by centuries of domination and oppression, Irish Catholics were further disadvantaged by British penal laws beginning in the late seventeenth century. Commonly called "popery" laws, these codes assured continued economic, social, and literacy deprivation for Irish Catholics. The laws banished most Catholic clergy, who were often educators, and greatly limited the activities and influence of others. After centuries in which their lands were confiscated, Catholics were further barred from buying and restricted from inheriting land. They were prevented from practicing law, from holding office, or from participating in other civil activities. The laws restricted meaningful attendance at established schools and forbade Catholics from creating their own schools or sending their children abroad to be educated.[4]

Literacy historians have largely dismissed or omitted Catholic efforts at literacy in the New World, accepting the stories of Catholics' disinterest and ignoring the persecution that continued throughout British American colonies. Once the British gained control of Nova Scotia, in what is known as the Great Expulsion, they deported more than 75 percent of the French

Catholics there to a variety of locations, burned their homes, and confiscated their lands. Many perished during the harsh, forced exodus. Survivors were dispersed widely, with large numbers permanently separated from family. Prejudice was pervasive in British-held areas that would become the United States as well: In New England, the presumed cradle of literacy in America, Pope's Day, an annual celebration ridiculing Catholics, ended with burning the Pope in effigy, and the annual Dudleian lecture, Harvard Divinity School's oldest endowment, required the speaker to rotate among four topics, one being an exposure of "the idolatry of the Romish Church, their tyranny, usurpations, damnable heresies, fatal errors, abominable superstitions, and other crying weaknesses" to demonstrate that "the Church of Rome is that mystical Babylon, that man of sin, that apostate church, spoken of in the New Testament" (quoted in Silcox and Fisher, 1934, p. 9).[5] Catholics were persecuted in all English colonies except Pennsylvania (Buetow, 1970, pp. 23–37). Georgia's charter, for example, specifically excluded "papists," and in Maryland, where Catholics were initially most numerous, school attendance for Catholic children became quickly restricted, and other laws similar to the English penal laws imposed.

Recent literacy studies affirm the complex circumstances that influence literacy acquisition and the difficulty in achieving literacy for groups who have been historically relegated to illiteracy and oppressed in other ways. To assume, then, that low literacy rates among North American Catholics resulted from their disinterest is too quick a judgment. Both the hedge schools in Ireland, for which a tremendously impoverished people paid from scant incomes and braved harsh penalties in an effort to educate their children, and US Catholics' willingness to construct and operate their own schools—a financial burden in addition to state-mandated taxes they paid for common schools promoting an anti-Catholic curriculum—suggests that Catholics, too, accepted the literacy myth that schooling was an avenue that ensured an improved socioeconomic status.

If Protestants promoted literacy, a tool for converting and maintaining disciples, Catholics became no less intent on using literacy in countering the Protestant "heresy" and in furthering and maintaining Catholicism. Catholic religious communities had historically provided schools, but numerous Catholic religious orders were founded and proliferated quickly as part of the Counter-Reformation. Ignatius Loyola's Jesuits, perhaps the best-known group, devoted themselves to teaching, but numerous other male groups, such as the Franciscans, the Sulpicians, and the Oratorians, were formed as well and took on teaching missions. Women, too, came to the cause, outnumbering men in religious communities greatly by the beginning of the eighteenth century. Angela Merici, for example, established the Ursuline sisters in Brescia, Italy, in 1535; by the end of the seventeenth century, the community numbered "between ten thousand and twelve thousand Ursulines in some three hundred and twenty communities" across France alone (Rapley, 1990, p. 48). The Ursulines represent just one of numerous communities of women religious involved with literacy. Supported often by the teaching orders who had already created detailed guides for and gained experience with education and assisted by one another, these women's communities established comprehensive curricula for their students and guidelines for training members in becoming effective teachers; the women in these communities placed a lifelong emphasis on literacy for themselves and made their life's occupation the teaching of girls and other women. In addition, the Church also encouraged women's confraternities, which included married women who continued earlier educational quests and became active in their communities. The request for teachers of girls on the part of both Catholic authorities and Catholic parents appears to have been very high and nearly always exceeded the ability of the communities to provide enough teachers for the demand, dispelling notions of Catholics' hostility to literacy (Rapley, 1990, p. 86; *Glimpses*, 1897, p. 73; Friess quoted in Mannard, 1989, p. 158).

After the US Constitution established freedom of religion, European religious communities of women began establishing schools for girls and young women in the young United States, and by the early nineteenth century, US women began founding their own religious communities with the purpose of educating girls; for example, five US teaching communities were founded in just a twenty-year period, between 1809 and 1829. Their numbers grew rapidly. They provided education for tens of thousands of young sisters within their communities and hundreds of thousands of girls and young women in their schools and academies; their schools increased so quickly and became so renowned that Protestant leaders became fearful of the sisters' power. For example, The Sisters of Charity of Nazareth, founded in 1812 near Bardstown, Kentucky, had built a stately academy by 1818 that included 60 sisters with 60 boarders; they had opened three additional schools by 1825. Similarly, the Sisters of Loretto, another central Kentucky community founded in 1812, numbered 100 with 250 girls in six schools by 1824. Both the convent membership and schools continued to grow at this rate well into the twentieth century (Mattingly, 2006, p. 162). The primary purposes of most of the religious congregations were spiritual, educational, and benevolent, but the sisters clearly believed their service to education could make a difference in prejudicial attitudes, reducing the hostility to Catholics and to their religion. For example, chapter 1, article 7, of the *Constitutions of the Associates of Mary at the Foot of the Cross* (Wand and Owens) reads,

> The glory of God and the attainment of one's personal sanctifica-
> tion is the primary and essential purpose of the Society: but the
> special object must never be lost sight of by those belonging to this
> Society which is to devote one's self completely to the education of
> females and implanting in them the principles of our holy religion
> instilling in the minds and hearts of Catholics entrusted to our care
> its teachings and leading their conduct to virtue but, in the case
> of Protestants committed to us, removing the prejudices that may
> have been instilled in them against our religion. (p. 85)

Protestant leaders reacted to such Catholic literacy efforts with fear and persecution.

As the Catholic population grew in the young United States, US Catholic Church authorities expressed concern for providing literacy instruction to the growing Catholic population, including girls. Numerous extant letters between male clergy and the leaders of women's convents attest to efforts to provide schools for girls in Catholic communities, often at the behest of parishioners. By 1829 the Council of Baltimore had proclaimed,

> Whereas very many youth of Catholic parents, especially among
> the poor, have been and still are, in many parts of this Province, ex-
> posed to great danger of losing their faith, and having their morals
> corrupted, from the want of proper teachers, to whom so important
> a trust can be safely confided; we judge it indispensably necessary to
> establish schools, in which youth may be nurtured in the principles
> of faith and morals, while they are instructed in literature. (quoted
> in Silcox and Fisher, 1934, p. 166)

Both Protestants and Catholics saw literacy as an important part of their efforts at converting and maintaining membership, of establishing cultural hegemony. But the unique structure for providing education among Catholics is especially important for our understanding of American women's literacy. The Catholic Church was both hierarchical and paternalistic. In fact, previous to and immediately after the Reformation, the male hierarchy repeatedly curbed religious women's activist efforts, insisting on a clois-tered retirement as sanction for the communal living many sought. Even-tually, however, church leaders gave formal recognition to and supported more fully the efforts of the religious communities of sisters who became educators, as they saw women's literacy as essential to the Church's interests in countering the Protestant threat. The sisters lived apart from men, pursued often very high levels of education, and actively promoted literacy among the women and girls of their communities. The large numbers of literate American Catholic women in religious communities alone calls into question claims that women were always less literate than men, and evidence suggests that their influence spread beyond their convent walls.

Women's Literacy in French American Colonies

Ursuline Sisters began arriving in the New World in 1639. The first Ursulines to Quebec were highly educated, professionally trained teachers. They taught American Indian girls and women as well as the children of French settlers. They learned to speak the languages of the Hurons and Algonquins, and Mother Mary of the Incarnation, one of the original sisters, composed French treatises for the sisters' educational institutions as well as "a sacred history in Algonquin, a dictionary in Algonquin, a catechism in Huron, another catechism and a prayer-book in Algonquin" (*Glimpses*, 1897, pp. 101, 77). The sisters took responsibility for educating a large number of female boarders, both French and Indian, as well as day students. Seminarists, the name given American Indian girls who boarded at the convent, numbered as many as eighty during some years of the first half of the eighteenth century, and the number of French children was even higher (*Glimpses*, 1897, p. 41). The sisters and priests instructed large numbers of adult American Indians as well, both women and men.

The Ursuline rules required sisters to teach "reading and grammar, the Christian doctrine and sacred history, practical arithmetic, penmanship and needlework" (*Glimpses*, 1897, p. 74). According to the early sisters, they gave "religious instructions in three languages, French, Algonquin, and Huron," taught seminarists to read, write, and sew, and taught children of French settlers "all that is necessary to fit them for the station in society to which they belong" (*Glimpses*, 1897, p. 43). Letters written by both Indian and French students attest to the girls' facility in written language.

Another community of Ursuline sisters was begun in what would become part of the United States, in New Orleans in 1727, just nine years after the city's founding. These sisters, too, had expected to work among the American Indians; however, their mission became primarily the evangelization of the African American population and the education of French women and girls, as well as a smaller number of African American and American Indian girls.

These two communities of French sisters throw into question assumptions made about women's education during the colonization of the North

American continent, which are based primarily on the British influence: that women were less literate than men and that "popular culture of the time ridiculed anyone educating a woman" during "the seventeenth and most of the eighteenth century" (Gordon and Gordon, 2003, p. 21). Evidence suggests, rather, that women were supported in literacy efforts in French Catholic communities and that women were often more literate than men.

For example, Allen Greer (1978) reports that signature rates on marriage registers in a number of early-eighteenth-century French Canadian colonies, Riviere-du-Loup, Three Rivers, and Boucherville in Quebec Province, where the Ursuline Sisters taught women and girls, demonstrate that women signed marriage registers more often than men. Greer acknowledges but makes little of this finding, which runs counter to findings in the numerous Protestant communities generally studied—and which have led literacy scholars to assume women's literacy was always lower than that of men.[6]

Similarly, in studying signatures on parish marriage records in eighteenth-century New Orleans, Emily Clark (1998) found women's signature rates to be higher than those of men. In New Orleans marriage registers dated 1760 to 1762, 72 percent of white women signed marriage registers, as compared to 70 percent of white men. The enslaved, both women and men, did not sign the registers, suggesting that the Ursulines' literacy work focused on white women. For those women, however, the change was remarkable. At the time of the arrival of the Ursuline sisters, 36 percent of women and 53 percent of men had signed parish registers (pp. 241–45). The Ursulines also supported a strong laywomen's confraternity in New Orleans. According to Clark,

> [a] devout woman was one who prepared herself to propagate the faith by becoming schooled herself. . . . [G]iven the importance of print and literacy in the advance of Protestantism, the good Catholic woman must also learn to read and write so that she met the enemy with an arsenal of equal strength. (p. 216)

One might reasonably infer that the higher literacy rates for women in both cases resulted from the Ursuline Sisters' efforts at educating women and, equally important, that the approach Catholics took to education, at least in the seventeenth- and eighteenth-century American colonies, offered women opportunities for literacy equal to or superior to those for men and superior to that available for women in British colonies. Women's literacy was almost certainly higher than that indicated by signatures in Catholic settlements, as the often large numbers of literate Catholic nuns would not have signed such legal documents as wills and marriage registers.

Ironically, the very hierarchical and patriarchal nature of the Catholic
Church may have afforded greater literacy opportunities to many women.
The Church, reluctantly accepting women's active role in teaching initially,
came to support the literacy efforts of religious women; women, however,
were restricted to efforts among their own sex. Because education in Catholic countries and communities had been relegated primarily to religious
teaching orders rather than to state-sponsored schools, literacy rates may
have been lower than those where state laws and general funds supported
schools; yet, because the number of sisters in religious communities was
often twice that in men's religious teaching communities, women often had
more opportunities to become literate than men, especially when living
close by convents or other schools staffed by the sisters.

Women's Literacy in Early Nineteenth-Century United States

Knowledge of Catholic literacy efforts places in doubt notions we have held
about women's literacy in the early nineteenth-century United States, as
well, because of the ways it influenced literacy among Protestant women.
While historians of women's literacy have most often cited such women
as Sarah Pierce, Mary Lyon, and Catharine Beecher as pioneers of American women's education, those women, in fact, garnered support for their
operations largely by promoting fear of well-established Catholic convent
academies. Catholics had begun building an impressive network of schools
for both boys and girls in the early United States to provide an education
in rural and frontier areas devoid of schools and to offer an alternative to
state-sponsored schools whose texts were virulently anti-Catholic and whose
curricula generally promoted Protestantism. The teachers in the Catholic
schools, especially in the academies and seminaries, were highly educated,
professionally trained members of religious orders. Sarah Hale's famous
crusade for women's education came in part in response to successful and
well-attended academies run by Catholic sisters. Hale claims, "The only
effective way to prevent the increase of conventual seminaries, is to found
Protestant schools" (1834b, p. 520), as "[t]he convents are now considered the
best and most fashionable places of education [. . .] and there, in all human
probability, many of the future wives, of the pious students of Lane Semi-
nary, are now receiving their impressions" (Hale, 1834a, p. 561). Similarly,
Lyon and Pierce were supported in their promotion of women's literacy by
Protestant leaders, and their promotional and fund-raising materials relied
on anti-Catholic rhetoric, insisting on the need for Protestant schools and
teachers for young Protestant women and capitalizing on fear of a papist
takeover related to Catholic sisters' schools and academies (Mattingly, 2006).

Catharine Beecher, daughter of the blatantly anti-Catholic Lyman Beecher and sister to writers of numerous popular anti-Catholic texts, sought support for her teacher-training schools by insisting on the need to counter the "papist" threat, especially in the West. Catholic women were supported in achieving their own literacy and that of other girls and women partly in response to European Reformation efforts toward literacy. As Catholic women successfully established convents and schools in the Americas, Protestant women's literacy accelerated to a significant degree in order to counter the alleged "popery" threat inherent in Catholic convents and convent schools.

The schools established by the Catholic sisters provide another layer to claims that "[i]n the half-century after the American Revolution, the best-educated women were either self-taught or . . . tutored at home by teachers or relatives. Although institutions offering secondary education for girls were established, many were temporary, underfinanced, haphazard ventures that catered more to society's demands for an 'ornamental education' than to more useful basic literacy" (Gordon and Gordon, 2003, p. 107). Catholic convents, on the contrary, produced large numbers of highly literate teachers, who then provided a useful literacy for other girls and women.[7] Their institutions were impressive, enduring structures, most still in existence. They provided early normal schools with carefully outlined professional guidelines for substantial curricula and effective teachers. The sisters often taught sewing and music, very useful skills for nineteenth-century women and part of a broader, rigorous curricula.[8] Because of their numbers, the sisters were often able to specialize, giving instruction in their area of expertise; many of these academies continue to educate young women today.

I question the notion of Protestantism's superior connection with literacy not to cast doubt on the importance of religion in promoting literacy, to propose the superiority of any other religion in promoting literacy, or to imply that literacy was always a positive force. Nor do I wish to criticize the scholars I have mentioned, who are among our best researchers, and scholars I admire greatly. My purpose is to suggest that by reifying Protestantism's place in promoting literacy, even as we have begun to acknowledge other important influences to literacy, we have neglected sources of information and alternative readings that might provide a more complete narrative. The Protestant Literacy Myth, though flawed, remains so strong that it inhibits our ability to see patterns that run counter to that grand narrative.

In some sense we have hesitated to engage with religious literacy narratives, even though our grandest narrative about literacy remains based on the religious domination of the Puritans. We have comfortably constructed a tale about Puritans' initiation of "common" schools that appear democratic and inclusive, even though those schools have been in many ways extremely exclusionary.[9] We have continued to reify a New England literacy supremacy and largely neglected narratives about areas outside New England, especially the South, for example.[10] As most early nineteenth-century Catholic convents and schools were built outside New England, they can contribute to our understanding of literacy in other, less-studied regions. And, we should be reminded of the need to continue searching for groups whom our grand narratives obscure and to reexamine and question accepted narratives. In a culture that places heavy moral and social values on literacy, groups outside the grand narrative are often left with negative images of the heritage that helps to shape their identities.

As Graff (2010) notes, history allows for "much needed perspective . . . allow[ing] us to reach out for new, different, and even multiple understandings of ourselves." But "[h]istory mandates focusing and refocusing the lenses of time, place, and alternative spaces" (pp. 637–38). Refocusing the lens through which we see the American religious connection with literacy can help to achieve a more accurate history, especially important because, although contemporary beliefs help to construct our narratives about the past, historical representations determine present and future narratives and identities as well. Generations have glorified the literacy accomplishments of the Puritan and Protestant, but it may be difficult for those on the margins of such stories to envision themselves within a tradition of excellent and successful literacy. For example, Jacqueline Jones Royster (2000) has pointed to the importance of identifying and understanding "resonant patterns of engagement with issues of authority, agency, privilege, and entitlement across time" for shaping her own administrative direction as well as for the intellectual identity and engagement of her women students of color (p. 265). While Royster's students have been marginalized in different crucial ways from other marginalized groups, such identification and understanding are, nonetheless, important for all women and all groups whose heritage of literate and intellectual practices has remained largely untold or misrepresented. We have learned that in earlier centuries women were always less literate than men and that Catholics cared little for or were hostile to literacy. We have learned that those in the South valued literacy far less than those in the North. These are all inaccurate, simplistic, and incomplete narratives.

The factual discrepancies about Protestant countries in historical literacy studies also leave many questions unanswered. Why did some Protestant communities advance far more rapidly in literacy than others? Why did Sweden achieve high rates of literacy without institutional schooling? Why did

New England Protestants promote writing and numeracy among men but not women, while Swedish Protestant officials saw to an equal effort among men and women? Many questions about early Protestant literacy practices remain. Perhaps these will be more readily understood as we become more inclusive in our narratives, as we move beyond the Protestant Literacy Myth.

The Catholic Church depended primarily on religious communities of men and women for disseminating and promoting literacy. This approach differed from that of Protestants and appears to have created different results. The Catholic religious orders, numerous though they were both in number of communities and in distribution of members within the communities, appear to have been unable to impart literacy on as massive a scale as state-sponsored and mandated literacy. However, because women taught girls and young women while men taught boys and young men in Catholic communities, the greater number of women in convents appears to have provided equal or greater literacy opportunities to girls and women than to boys and men, at least in some places. Catholic sisters often followed a lifelong pursuit of literacy practices, many becoming highly educated, breaking expectations that women might devote brief periods of their lives to their own education and to that of others but largely relinquish such efforts at marriage. Much of this women's tradition of literacy and intellectual rigor—a tradition in which women excelled at creating community among peers and at successfully building magnificent convents and academies that provided welcoming, literate environments for succeeding generations—has been largely hidden from our narratives. In a culture where women are often taught to compete with one another for the attention of men and, similarly, learn that education and career are more important for men, such a tradition provides one positive alternative. There may be many others.

Notes

1. My grateful appreciation goes to Lisa Arnold, Lindal Buchanan, Jo Ann Griffin, Kimberly Harrison, Annette Powell, and Elizabethada Wright for reading early drafts of this chapter and to editors John Duffy and Nelson Graff for their excellent feedback.

2. Edward Gordon and Elaine Gordon are more inclusive of religions other than Protestantism in their excellent 2003 work on literacy.

3. Early influential works on "American" education, such as those by Bernard Bailyn (1960) and Lawrence Cremin (1970), assume the importance of Protestantism in promoting literacy. Daniel P. Resnick and Lauren B. Resnick review influential scholars who have promoted the importance of Protestantism to literacy in their 1977 *Harvard Educational Review* article, "The Nature of Literacy: A Historical Exploration."

4. Although some Catholics did become literate, the difficulties of gaining more than the most basic literacy were extreme. Edmund Burke describes the penal laws as "a machine as well fitted for the oppression, impoverishment and degradation of a

people, and the debasement in them of human nature itself, as ever proceeded from the perverted ingenuity of man" (quoted in Woodham-Smith, 1989, p. 27).

5. New England Protestants would later demonstrate their hostility toward Catholic sisters and the literacy they provided girls and burn down the Ursuline Convent and Academy in Charlestown, Massachusetts, outside Boston in 1834; the Ursuline Academy was one of the most prestigious academies for girls and young women in New England at the time.

6. Most scholars of literacy in colonial America and the early Republic determine literacy estimates primarily based on signatures on a variety of documents. Distance in time and scarcity of extant evidence in any other form have made signature rate an accepted form of evidence among scholars for determining literacy rates—not an ideal one but one of the few concrete measures available. Such methods have provided important information, such as Lockridge's 1974 study, based largely on signatures found on wills and deeds, and Soltow and Stevens's 1981 study based on records of Philadelphia merchant seamen and army enlistees. Such records are more likely (or only, in the case of Soltow and Stevens's work) able to provide information about or favor higher literacy rates for men.

7. Because of the large numbers of women in convents and the numerous girls and young women they taught, women were likely more literate than men in some communities in the early United States. For example, in central Kentucky, three permanent, early US convents were established between 1812 and 1822 within a fifteen-mile radius of one another; literacy among women may have been especially high here. Marriage records do not provide a source of evidence, as licensing in the United States became a responsibility of the civil government rather than the church, and marriage records were signed by the persons posting bond, usually the prospective groom and a male relative of the bride. As the future bride was not asked to sign, the records are not useful for determining the relative rates of literacy. US census records did not include information on literacy until 1840.

8. In an age of ready-made clothing and easily accessible art prints and decorative tapestries, we sometimes forget the importance for nineteenth-century Americans of the ability to sew for both basic needs and to provide decorative artwork for the home; similarly, our appreciation of the importance of knowledge and ability in music for personal and group pleasure and entertainment may be diminished by the availability of recorded music.

9. Contributing to the notion of Catholics' disinterest in literacy were battles over Bible use in "common" schools. When Catholics sought disuse of the King James Bible in public schools or asked that Catholic students be allowed to use their own Douay translation, Protestant leaders quickly denounced such requests as Catholics' antagonism toward and disrespect for reading Scripture.

10. As David Gold and Catherine Hobbs have begun to demonstrate (in their not-yet-published work), literate practices in the South, especially among southern women and African Americans, have been overlooked partly because their practices often necessarily included different patterns from those we have come to expect.

References

Bailyn, Bernard. 1960. *Education in the Forming of American Society: Needs and Opportunities for Study.* Chapel Hill: University of North Carolina Press.

Barth, Pius J. 1945. *Franciscan Education and the Social Order in Spanish North America, 1502–1821.* Chicago: n.p.

Bizzell, Patricia, and Bruce Herzberg. 2001. *The Rhetorical Tradition: Readings from Classical Times to the Present.* 2nd ed. Boston: Bedford/St. Martin's.

Buetow, Harold A. 1970. *Of Singular Benefit: The Story of Catholic Education in the United States.* London: Macmillan.

Clark, Emily. 1998. "A New World Community: The New Orleans Ursulines and Colonial Society, 1727–1803." PhD diss., Tulane University.

Cremin, Lawrence. 1970. *American Education: The Colonial Experience, 1607–1783.* New York: Harper and Row.

Gallegos, Bernardo P. 1992. *Literacy, Education, and Society in New Mexico 1693–1821.* Albuquerque: University of New Mexico Press.

Gawthrop, Richard, and Gerald Strauss. 1984, August. "Presentation and Literacy in Early Modern Germany." *Past and Present, 104,* 31–55.

Glimpses of the Monastery: Scenes from the History of the Ursulines of Quebec during Two Hundred Years 1639–1839. 1897. 2nd ed. Quebec, Canada: L. J. Demers and Frère.

Gordon, Edward E, and Elaine H. Gordon. 2003. *Literacy in America: Historic Journey and Contemporary Solutions.* Westport, CT: Praeger.

Graff, Harvey J. 1967. *The Legacies of Literacy: Continuities and Contradictions in Western Culture and Society.* Bloomington: Indiana University Press.

———. 1979. *The Literacy Myth: Literacy and Social Structure in the Nineteenth-Century City.* New York: Academic Press.

———. 2010. "The Literacy Myth at Thirty." *Journal of Social History, 43*(3), 635–61.

Greene, Jamie Candelaria. 1994. "Misperspectives on Literacy: A Critique of an Anglocentric Bias in Histories of American Literacy." *Written Communication, 11*(2), 251–69.

Greer, Allan. 1978. "The Pattern of Literacy in Quebec, 1745–1899." *Histoire Sociale, Social History, 11,* 295–335

Hale, Sarah Josepha. 1834a. "Convents Are Increasing." *The Ladies Repository,* 560–64.

———. 1834b. "How to Prevent the Increase of Convents." *The Ladies Repository,* 517–21.

Lockridge, Kenneth A. 1974. *Literacy in Colonial New England: An Inquiry into the Social Context of Literacy in the Early Modern West.* New York: Norton.

Mannard, Joseph Gerard. 1989. "'Maternity of the Spirit': Women Religious in the Archdiocese of Baltimore, 1790–1860." PhD diss., University of Maryland College Park.

Mattingly, Carol. 2006. "Uncovering Forgotten Habits: Anti-Catholic Rhetoric and Nineteenth-Century American Women's Literacy." *College Composition and Communication, 58*(2), 160–81.

Monaghan, E. Jennifer. 2005. *Learning to Read and Write in Colonial America.* Amherst: University of Massachusetts Press.

Rapley, Elizabeth. 1990. *The Dévotes: Women and Church in Seventeenth-Century France.* Montreal: McGill-Queen's University Press.

Resnick, Daniel P., and Lauren B. Resnick. 1977. "The Nature of Literacy: A Historical Exploration." *Harvard Educational Review, 47,* 370–85.

Royster, Jacqueline Jones. 2000. *Traces of a Stream: Literacy and Social Change among African American Women.* Pittsburgh: University of Pittsburgh Press.

Silcox, Claris Edwin, and Galen M. Fisher. 1934. *Catholics, Jews, and Protestants: A Study of Relationships in the United States and Canada.* New York: Harper.

Soltow, Lee, and Edward Stevens. 1981. *The Rise of Literacy and the Common School in the United States: A Socioeconomic Analysis to 1870*. Chicago: University of Chicago Press.

Stone, Lawrence. 1969. "Literacy and Education in England, 1640–1900." *Past and Present, 42,* 69–139.

Wand, Augustin C., and M. Lilliana Owens, eds. 1972. *Constitutions of the Association of Mary at the Foot of the Cross. Documents: Nerincks—Kentucky—Loretto 1804–1851 in Archives Propaganda Fide Rome*, pp. 84–116. St. Louis: Mary Loretto Press.

Woodham-Smith, Cecil. 1989. *The Great Hunger: Ireland 1845–1849.* New York: Old Town Books.

4. Writing the Life of Henry Obookiah: The Sponsorship of Literacy and Identity

Morris Young

The nineteenth-century text *Memoirs of Henry Obookiah* tells a tale somewhat familiar to another nineteenth-century text, *Narrative of the Life of Frederick Douglass, an American Slave, Written by Himself*. While the significant difference is that Henry Obookiah was not subject to the harsh life of slavery or to the denial of the many liberties that we often associate with personhood, his story bears many of the similarities that have led to Douglass's narrative being characterized as a literacy narrative, that is, a story about the acquisition, development, and use of literacy that often results in some transformative state for an individual.[1] In the nineteenth century, a native Hawaiian youth, Henry Obookiah, found himself transported to New Haven, Connecticut. Although he was a "heathen" in the eyes of the residents, it was Obookiah's desire to learn to read and write that persuaded his hosts that he was worthy of being educated and introduced to Christianity. With literacy in hand, Obookiah proceeded to create a dictionary and grammar for the Hawaiian language and translated Genesis into Hawaiian.

After nearly a decade of education in New England and soon after joining the Foreign Mission School, Obookiah was stricken with typhoid fever. While his religious conversion inspired the first Christian mission to Hawai'i, his conversion from illiterate to literate—or, to use Sylvia Scribner's (1988) term, his literacy as a state of grace—also set in motion a cascade of events that changed Hawai'i and its people forever.

Like Douglass's *Narrative*, Obookiah's *Memoirs* did much of the work to institutionalize him. Subsequent celebrations both in Hawai'i and Connecticut to recognize him as the first Hawaiian convert to Christianity and the recognition of Obookiah's contribution to institutionalizing Hawaiian language all mark his historical and cultural significance. As a counterpoint to these significant events, however, we also need to understand the consequences of Obookiah's presence in New England and his conversion, both of which contributed to the first organized mission being sent to Hawai'i to establish Christianity. On one hand, this brought Hawai'i closer to the modern world, bringing Western education and a steady flow of Western culture and capital. Obookiah's development of a Hawaiian grammar and translations of religious texts led to the development of Hawaiian print culture. On the other hand, more substantial Western contact brought the many problems of development and colonial imposition: disease, rapid transformation of indigenous culture, and erosion of self-determination, among other consequences. While Obookiah should not be held responsible for Hawai'i's present-day complex situation regarding indigenous self-determination and nationhood, his life, as both lived experience and symbol, did have a profound effect on him and his homeland. As Native Hawaiian sovereignty activist Haunani-Kay Trask has said about Obookiah's conversion to Christianity: "I think he was trying to understand the very terrible things that were happening to his people. Opukaha'ia was trying desperately to figure out an earlier era. He's actually a very sad figure" (quoted in Tanahara, 1993).

Obookiah's conversion—both religious and educational—did not happen without assistance from many others. In the *Memoirs* and in Obookiah's life, we see many *sponsors* of his literacy and for his conversion to Christianity, providing a powerful and complex example of the function and consequences of literacy described by Deborah Brandt (2001) in *Literacy in American Lives*. Building on Brandt's work, this chapter is organized along two lines of discussion. First, I offer a reading of the *Memoirs* as a literacy narrative, focusing on Obookiah's transformation, both his acquisition of and education in English, and his conversion to Christianity. How does this sponsorship of literacy function in the transformation of Obookiah? And, second, I examine the circulation of the text *Memoirs of Henry Obookiah* and how the text and Obookiah served as a sponsor for the first Christian mission to Hawai'i. Drawing on Brandt's work to inform my framing of the *Memoirs of Henry Obookiah* as a literacy studies project helps us understand how material objects may function to sponsor literacy.

Sponsoring Literacy and Transformation

In her influential study *Literacy in American Lives*, Deborah Brandt offers a conceptual approach that "begins to connect literacy as an individual development to literacy as an economic development." A key concept in Brandt's method is to identify and understand how "sponsors of literacy" function in the lives of individuals. These sponsors are "any agents, local or distant, concrete or abstract, who enable, support, teach, and model, as well as recruit, regulate, suppress, or withhold, literacy—and gain advantage by it in some way" (2001, p. 19). In *Literacy in American Lives*, Brandt builds her analysis on the examination of the life histories of eighty individuals and their experiences with literacy, providing a model for reading the complex relationships between literacy and economic development and unpacking an often undertheorized and uncritically invoked promise of economic and cultural capital in literacy narratives.

In their essay "Reading Literacy Narratives," Janet Carey Eldred and Peter Mortensen (1992) discuss the possibilities of a specific area of rhetorical criticism—literacy studies—in the study of literary texts. Here they suggest that analyzing the tropes of literacy (acts of reading, writing, or the acquisition of education more broadly) within literary texts can help us understand literacy as an element and product of culture (p. 512). Eldred and Mortensen define literacy narratives as

> those stories, like Bernard Shaw's *Pygmalion*, that foreground issues of language acquisition and literacy. These narratives are structured by learned, internalized, literacy tropes (Brodkey 47), by "prefigured" ideas and images (see White 1–23). Literacy narratives sometimes include explicit images of schooling and teaching, they include texts that both challenge and affirm culturally scripted ideas about literacy. (pp. 512–13)

Brandt's reading of life histories as literacy narratives contributes to the rhetorical and literary criticism outlined by Eldred and Mortensen as she identifies experiences of ordinary individuals that both contribute to and are shaped by beliefs about literacy in our culture. Understanding how we acquire and are able to access literacy—who sponsors our literacy—lets us situate literacy within a broader context of social and economic relationships that move beyond the "literacy myths" that value individual acquisition and achievement. Thus, reading for sponsors or sponsorship of literacy helps us to understand the way literacy is both metaphorical and material and is broadly implicated and embedded in our culture as an alternative to the literacy myth that privileges the individual.

Undergirding these discussions of literacy in Brandt and well as in Eldred and Mortensen is how literacy is embodied; that is, how these experiences with literacy are shaped by race, gender, sexuality, culture, and other categories of identity that have material consequences. In this sense the body itself may act as a trope—that is, as a metaphor—for literacy and what literacy may or may not provide. For example, much has been written about the role of literacy in Douglass's narrative and life, and the *Narrative* is often invoked to illustrate the power of literacy and education, especially for people of color or others who have faced oppression through the denial or lack of access to literacy.[2] As Lindon Barrett argues:

> To speak of issues of literacy within the context of the US slave regime and the autobiographical narratives of its ex-slaves is to a very great extent to speak of issues of the body—and of the African-American body in particular. (1995, p. 415)

In my own work, I have argued that literacy has often functioned as a trope for citizenship that itself often limited membership to those who could demonstrate specific levels of education, unaccented speech, or markers of belonging that might exclude people of color, immigrants to the United States, or others deemed "unfit." And as we see in Brandt's work, the role of literacy and what it can deliver has been shaped in great part by gender, race, socioeconomic class, or other dimensions that have clear effect on one's social position and experience. Thus, the person, life, and body of Frederick Douglass and, as I will argue, Henry Obookiah have served as tropes for literacy because of what we believe literacy will deliver: education, freedom, grace despite one's status, and, in fact, often because of one's status as somehow inferior.

Let me turn to the memoir now. For the purpose of this essay, I focus on the parts of the memoir that describe Obookiah's life as he immersed himself in the "west." *Memoirs* functions as a typical developmental narrative somewhat similar to Douglass's *Narrative* and other similar conversion stories, clearly charting a move from uncivilized to civilized and, in the mode of a literacy narrative, from oral to literate culture. *Memoirs* begins with Obookiah's early life in Hawai'i, describing briefly the brutality and uncivilized nature of native life and his desire to escape, to "go to some other country, probably I may find some comfort, more to live there without father and mother. I thought it would be better for me to go than to stay" (Dwight, 1990, p. 6). We do hear about Obookiah's adoption by an uncle who prepared him to become a priest, teaching him native chants and prayers, a sponsorship of literacy in its own right, but the narrative of the text clearly creates a desire and passage for Obookiah to escape to America.

Obookiah finds himself on a ship that first heads for the Pacific Northwest and then returns across the Pacific toward China and then eventually around India and Africa and toward New England. It was during this voyage that Obookiah found a literacy sponsor who would initiate both a literacy and religious conversion.

> Among these men I found a very desirable young man, by name of
> Russel Hubbard, a son of Gen. Hubbard, of New-Haven. This Mr.
> Hubbard was a member of Yale College. He was a friend of Christ.
> Christ was with him when I saw him, but I knew it not. "Happy
> is the man that put his trust in God!" Mr. Hubbard was very kind
> to me on our passage, and taught me the letters in English spell-
> ing-book. (Dwight, 1990, p. 8)

After landing in New York and making his way to New Haven with the ship's
captain, Obookiah found himself in a situation where God and Christianity
as well as education became both more intriguing and more available. In
this setting, Obookiah became a student, as he saw in other students both
spiritual and intellectual awakening, things that he desired.

> In this place I become acquainted with many students belonging to
> the college. By these pious students I was told more about God than
> what I had heard before; but I was so ignorant that I could not see
> into it whether it was so. Many times I wish to hear more about God,
> but find nobody to interpret it to me. I attended many meetings on
> the Sabbath, but find difficulty to understand the minister. I could
> understand or speak but very little of the English language. Friend
> Thomas went to school to one of the students in the college before I
> thought of going to school. I heard that a ship was ready to sail from
> New-York within a few days for Hawaii. The captain was willing that
> I might take leave of this country and go home, if I wish. But this
> was disagreeable to my mind. I wished to continue in this country
> a little longer. I staid another week—saw Mr. E. W. Dwight, who
> first taught me to read and write. (Dwight, 1990, pp. 12–13)

In the above passage is the first appearance of Edwin Dwight, who becomes
Obookiah's next literacy sponsor and perhaps witness to Obookiah's life and
conversion. The next passage is one example of Dwight's narrative as he (in
the third person) describes Obookiah's process of transformation once he
chose to be educated in a Western (New England) manner.

> When Obookiah was first discovered at New-Haven, his appear-
> ance was unpromising. He was clothed in a rough sailor's suit, was
> of clumsy form, and his countenance dull and heavy. His friend had
> almost determined to pass him by, as one whom it would be in vain
> to notice and attempt to instruct. But when the question was put to
> him, "Do you wish to learn?" his countenance began to brighten.
> And when the proposal was made that he should come the next day

to the college for that purpose, he seized it with great eagerness.

It was not long after he began to study, and had obtained some further knowledge of the English language, that he gave evidence that the dullness, which was thought to be indicated by his countenance, formed no part of his character. (Dwight, 1990, pp. 13–14)

In the passages above, Obookiah's role as an eager student certainly is cast in overwhelmingly positive terms. While he is portrayed in some ways as a "heathen," someone from an uncivilized and brutal background, he is also represented as naïve, in search of knowledge and something substantial to fulfill his life. The change in Obookiah's "countenance" from "dull and heavy" to bright suggests an almost physical transformation—that as he became more literate, his physical presence changed from primitive to civilized being.

As the narrative progresses and more examples of Obookiah's acquisition of literacy are detailed, we begin to see another transformation take place as Obookiah develops the tools to access texts that introduce him in more formal ways to Christianity. This initiation into Christianity, although not formally a matter of citizenship (in a juridical sense), certainly can be read as a type of cultural citizenship as Obookiah seeks membership in a community that to him provides a number of rights and sense of identity. The many sponsors of literacy for Obookiah—Russel Hubbard, Edwin Dwight, the church, among others—had begun to provide access to the streams of capital important in nineteenth-century New England. His sponsorship by Dwight gave him entry to some of the highest levels of education available because of Dwight's own training at Williams College and Yale Divinity School. The church itself provided access to New England's elite, including already well-known religious leaders, such as Lyman Beecher, father of Harriet Beecher Stowe. But ultimately these sponsors, while important facilitators of literacy, are secondary to the role an emerging Christian faith plays in Obookiah's life. As the next two passages reveal, Obookiah sees the acceptance and public expression of faith as important to his developing sense of self and the "new" person he has become.

About this time I thought with myself to join with some church. I wished to give every thing up for the glory of God, to give up my whole soul to him, to do with me as he pleaseth. I made known these things to the Rev. Mr. Harvey, and he thought it would be better for me to make a profession of religion. He wished me to go and see the Rev. Mr. Mills and the people whom I have been acquainted with, and talk the matter over with them; for I longed to be. I therefore went and conversed with my good friend and father Mills concerning my case. All the matter seemed to him well. He wished me to come over on the next Sabbath and attend my examination. I staid at Goshen until the approaching of the Sabbath which was appointed, and then went over to Torringford. I thought while I was traveling, that I was going home to New Jerusalem—to the welcome gate. As I walked along I repeated these words, "Whom have I in heaven but thee? And there is none upon earth that I desire besides thee." I was received into the church of the Christ in Torringford, on the ninth day of April, in the year 1815. (Dwight, 1990, p. 36)

And then Obookiah turns his view to returning back to Hawai'i to bring back the Word.

I was now taken under the care of the Board of Commissioners for Foreign Missions, with a view to my future employment to be as a Missionary to my poor countrymen—who are yet living in region and shadow of death—without knowledge of the true God and ignorant of the future world—have no Bible to read—no Sabbath—and all of these things are unknown to them. (Dwight, 1990, p. 37)

The conversion of Obookiah certainly was facilitated by literacy as he learned to read and write, which allowed him to participate both in civic and religious communities. Literacy allowed Obookiah to become a public figure, not someone who remained isolated and certainly not someone who shied away from developing relationships among the important figures of the era, including Timothy Dwight, then the president of Yale College.

Obookiah became so accomplished that Edwin Dwight described him "perhaps as perfect as most young men of our own country" (1990, p. 78). As this next passage illustrates, Obookiah's literacy and conversion placed him comfortably among the elite of New England society.

When Obookiah became a member of the Foreign Mission School, he had attended to all the common branches of English education. In reading, writing, and spelling, he was perhaps as perfect as most young men of our own country, of the same age and with common opportunities. He wrote a legible manly hand, and had acquired the habit of writing with considerable rapidity. He had at this time studied the English Grammar so far as to be able to phrase most sentences with readiness. He understood the important rules in common Arithmetic, and had obtained considerable knowledge of Geography. He had studied also one book of Euclid's Elements of

Geometry, and of his own accord, without a regular instructor, had acquired such knowledge of the Hebrew, that he had been able to read several chapters in the Hebrew Bible, and had translated a few passages into his native language. He had a peculiar relish for the Hebrew language, and from its resemblance to his own, acquired it with great facility; and found it much less difficult to translate the Hebrew than the English into his native tongue.

The winter before he came to the school he commenced the study of Latin. This he pursued principally after he became a member of the Institution. (Dwight, 1990, p. 78)

The developmental character of the narrative is perhaps best illustrated by the development of Obookiah's language. Although Obookiah began with no ability in English, moving to very rudimentary English (perhaps best described as childlike), by the end of *Memoirs*, the quality of his English reaches the level of oratory. Even on his deathbed, Obookiah continues to advocate for Christianity, especially for what it could provide to his people in Hawai'i.

My dear countrymen, I wish to say something to you all—you have been very kind to me—I feel my obligation to you—I thank you. And now, my dear friends, I must beseech you to remember that you will follow me. Above all things, make your peace with God—you must make Christ your friend—you are in a strange land—you have no father—no mother to take care of you when you are sick—but God will be your friend if you put your trust in him—he has raised up friends here for you and for me—I have strong faith in God—and I am willing to die when the voice of my Savior call me hence—I am willing, if God design to take me. But I cannot leave you without calling upon the mercy of God to sanctify your souls and fit you for heaven. When we meet there we shall part no more. Remember, my friends, that you are poor—it is by the mercy of God that you have comfortable clothes, and that you are so kindly supported. You must love God—I want to have you make your peace with God. Can't you see how good God is to you? God has done a great deal for you and for me. Remember that you must love God, or else you perish for ever. God has given his Son to die for you—I want to have you love God very much. I want to talk with you by and by—my strength fails—I can't now—I want to say more. (Dwight, 1990, p. 89)

Throughout *Memoirs* we see how Obookiah acquired and developed his literacy not only for personal improvement and expression of faith but also in the belief that literacy would facilitate sharing the gospel with his people. Literacy in this sense is a communal act, bringing together a community around a common text and set of beliefs. And in this sense, Obookiah completes his transformation as he imagines himself as a sponsor of literacy by communicating his faith in God. However, Obookiah's acquisition and application of literacy were only possible because of the many sponsors who chose to actively engage this Hawaiian youth, whom many may have dismissed as primitive, impossible to educate, or even simply as an example of a "savage" to place on display. Rather, from his first experience on the ship leaving Hawai'i to his final days in Connecticut, Obookiah found himself surrounded by people who facilitated both literacy and faith, first acting as sponsors for Obookiah but then becoming the sponsored, inspired by his life, death, and belief that Hawai'i would welcome Christianity.

The *Memoirs* and Obookiah as Sponsor: Circulating Literacy and Identity

As my discussion above about *Memoirs* as literacy narrative makes clear, the story told here was meant to inspire, persuade, and provide evidence that someone like Obookiah could be both educated and converted. For this message to be successful, however, meant that *Memoirs* needed to find an audience and generate a readership who would take up the mission to bring Christianity to Hawai'i. Thus the circulation of *Memoirs* is key in understanding how the text itself could serve as a sponsor of literacy, that is, as a material object taken up by individuals to inspire their own actions. *Memoirs of Henry Obookiah* was first published in 1818 by the *Religious Intelligencer* in New Haven, and a second printing occurred in 1819. The American Tract Society printed two editions, one in 1831 and the other in 1847. A Hawaiian language edition was published by the American Tract Society in 1867. There have been subsequent editions, notably one that commemorated the 150th anniversary of Obookiah's death (Dwight, 1968) and the most recent edition printed in 1990, just three years before his repatriation to Hawai'i. A children's story version, *Ka Mea Ho'ala: The Awakener: The Story of Henry Obookiah Once Called Opukaha'ia*, written by Cecily Kikukawa, who used the *Memoirs* as her primary source material, was published in 1982.

To call Obookiah's text a memoir perhaps fits in with our modern sensibilities about authorship and authenticity, since *Memoirs* often feels multivoiced and is perhaps more acutely aware of the self-construction taking place here. In fact, it (and other memoirs of the period) functions rhetorically as testimonial and as a declamation of the acceptance and joy of a Christian life. While the text does include what is purported to be the narrative of Obookiah, including diary entries and letters written by him but also much reported and recorded dialogue, there is also the presence of a sort of coauthor, Edwin W. Dwight, who was Obookiah's friend and early teacher. While Obookiah does tell his own story, Dwight provides a third-person narrative and even commentary about Obookiah's life without ever becoming anything more than a character in the story referred to as "Mr. Dwight." This presence of Dwight does raise a question about the authenticity or, perhaps more accurately, the authority of Obookiah's narrative. A "note" in the 1990 edition remarks that "the first editions of the *Memoirs of Henry Obookiah* gave no author's name, but later editions listed 'the Rev. E. W. Dwight, First Instructor of the Foreign Mission School' as the author" (p. 98). The clearest statement on the "authorship" of the narrative appears early on in chapter 1, "History before Reaching America," when the unnamed narrator says,

> His feelings on the subject, with some account of his situation while he remained upon the island, of his departure for America, and his reception in this country, are found in a history of his past life written by himself several years before his death. As this, to all the readers of these memoirs, will doubtless be interesting, considered a production of a heathen youth, the greater part of it will be inserted, with but few slight alterations. His own ideas, and, in general, his own language will be preserved. The history commences at the time of his parents' death. (Dwight, 1990, p. 3)

Here we see another type of sponsorship where the unnamed narrator, presumed to be Dwight, acts to sponsor Obookiah's literacy by attesting to the authenticity of the story and to Obookiah's "ownership" of his own ideas and language. This proclamation of authenticity by another party is a convention seen in nineteenth-century slave narratives and again raises interesting and important questions about how literacy and identity are intertwined in expressing personhood and value as a full human being.

We see a similar phenomenon with Obookiah and his *Memoirs*. Certainly, his *Memoirs* served as an example to and sponsor of those who signed on with the American Board of Commissioners for Foreign Missions, illustrating both the possibility for conversion and the state of grace that could be achieved by those heathens in the Pacific, and the "good works" that could be done by the missionaries. Tracing the textual and circulation history of the text, *Memoirs of Henry Obookiah* can offer a clear idea of the cultural significance of the text and how it "sponsored" the work of various individuals and groups, including the missions to Hawai'i. Let me address the circulation history first. There is a pretty clear publication history of the text, from its first edition published by the *Religious Intelligencer* in 1818, later editions published by the American Tract Society in the mid-1800s, and the most recent editions published by the Woman's Board of Missions for the Pacific Islands since the mid-twentieth century. However, tracking down publication numbers can offer a wealth of information: How many books were published with each edition? Who was buying these books? How was the *Memoirs* circulating and being consumed?

Book reviews of *Memoirs* suggest both the cultural context and cultural capital of the text. These few book reviews, however, are ones published in religious periodicals and often are not much more than summaries, even advertisements for *Memoirs*. This itself suggests something about the marketing of the book and its target audience, but situating this text in a broader context illustrates the impact of this text beyond expressions of Christian faith. Considering the genre of the memoir during this period—and in particular how it is related to other American narrative traditions, such as the conversion narrative, the travel narrative, the captivity narrative, and the slave narrative—may help us to understand the function of the memoir and the cultural work it performs. Work by scholars Mary Cayton (2010) and Lisa Shaver (2012) examines the memoir genres of women missionaries and Methodist women of the same period as Obookiah. In her study of nineteenth-century American evangelical writing and publishing, Candy Gunther Brown (2004) argues that the memoir was a genre privileged by evangelicals because they "considered example a powerful tool to mold Christian 'character'" (p. 88). In particular, memoirs of "less prominent Christians, including African Americans, women, and children," were viewed as having particular value because these subjects were seen as being especially "near to Christ" because of what Harriet Beecher Stowe had characterized as their "lowly status" in *Uncle Tom's Cabin; Or Life among the Lowly* (p. 89). Additionally, Brown argues, memoir subjects were understood to be models for emulation and thus led editors to more directly shape these figures for public consumption in order to achieve the transmission of a Christian message (p. 93). Thus, in this sense, memoirs serve to both document and declaim, to provide examples of ordinary and exemplary lives of those who have been touched by Christianity.

If memoirs in these cases are instructional and rhetorical and not simply biographical, then Obookiah himself may be considered not only the subject of the text but perhaps inextricably a part of the text. That is, *Memoirs* itself can be understood as the material embodiment of Obookiah, where

Obookiah is both subject and object and understood more as a literary figure rather than as an individual with a full life history. What I have discussed here and much of the scholarship on Obookiah have focused on the rhetorical Obookiah, the person whose life and power exists in the way he has been constructed through a variety of texts. The biography of Obookiah that has been constructed has been based primarily on *Memoirs* and other published accounts of his life, such as reviews of *Memoirs*, accounts of his death, and descriptions of him in documents related to the Foreign Mission School and the American Board of Commissioners for Foreign Missions. These materials are highly mediated by their ideological purposes and employ rhetoric very well, as they are used to confirm Christianity and to argue for moral and material support in sending missions to the Pacific or other foreign lands in order to spread the gospel.

However, who is the material Obookiah? What are the other facts of his life—not necessarily disarticulated from what is clearly an important part of his life, his conversion to and belief in Christianity—that create a more complete portrait of his time in New England? What I am particularly interested in is his status as a Pacific Islander in early nineteenth-century New England. What role did his racial condition play during this period when slavery was still prominent and complex interactions with Native Americans still active? Was the fact that he was a converted Christian enough to offset other aspects of his person that may have been disadvantageous? To return to the analogy of Frederick Douglass, how is Obookiah's body, as well as his soul, connected with issues of literacy and citizenship?

Additional materials, including individual letters and correspondence from Obookiah, may confirm and complement the content of the letters and diary entries reported in *Memoirs* or in other publications so that there is little suspicion about the authenticity of Obookiah's experiences, especially since Edwin Dwight remains such a strong presence in the text. Just as there were questions put to the authenticity of Douglass's literacy and accomplishments and the writing of his narrative, there have been doubts about Obookiah as well. In 1814 and 1815, a letter written by Obookiah was published in two religious periodicals—four years before *Memoirs* appears—as evidence that the achievements of Obookiah are indeed true. The editorial note introducing the letter reads,

> For the purpose of enabling our readers to judge more accurately respecting Obookiah's acquirements, we present them his letter without correcting some obvious inaccuracies—Neither the capitals, nor the spelling is varied in a single instance. We have made some corrections in the punctuation, and omitted one article, but

in other respects we give the original without erasing, inserting or altering a word, nor a letter. Some of the inaccuracies were evidently made through inadvertency. And most of the rest are such as might be expected from a person, who was writing in a language, with which he was not perfectly familiar. ("Letter," p. 329)

Obookiah's letter to his friend then follows. The content of the letter is a description by Obookiah of his devotion to God and the church. The context for this letter remains unclear to me, or more important, for the editorial note that argues for the authenticity of Obookiah. And I find this a bit odd given that this occurred four years before *Memoirs* was even published. This suggests that Obookiah was already living a public life, of having a celebrity that warrants a discussion about the authenticity of his achievements and deeds. For example, Obookiah and his *Memoirs* also entered into American literary culture when Mark Twain (1872) referred to him in *Roughing It*, describing Obookiah as weeping on the steps of a church because his people did not have the Bible.

That incident has been very elaborately painted in many a charming Sunday-school book . . . and told so plaintively and so tenderly that I have cried over it in Sunday school myself, on general principles, although at a time when I did not know much and could not understand why the people of the Sandwich Islands needed to worry so much about it as long as they did not know there was a Bible at all. (p. 461)

Additionally, it is interesting to see how Obookiah has operated as a trope in the more recent past. For example, in Cornwall, Connecticut, where Obookiah lived, died, and was laid to rest, he remains a beloved figure, so much so that there was a "sense of loss" when his descendants in 1993 decided to have his remains returned to Hawai'i (Clark, 1993, July 24; Chamberlain, 1993). Though Obookiah was moved to Hawai'i, he remains a figure of interest in Connecticut and is even included in local historical literature there. Obookiah's return to Hawai'i was received with much interest by the local community. On August 15, 1993, Obookiah was buried in the graveyard of Kahikolu Church at Napoopoo in Kona. His family formed an association, Ka 'Ohe Ola Hou ("The bamboo lives again"), that has four goals:

- That indigenous Hawaiians can take "full ownership of this Hawaiian son and all he envisions . . . so that the true history of Hawaii can be made."
- To see that students have "access in their schools and libraries to sufficient curriculum and materials so that Opukaha'ia's story can help bring self-esteem, future and hope."

- To promote "a second great awakening—a contemporary release of native Hawaiians to launch Opukaha'ia's vision of sharing the gospel of Jesus Christ to the Pacific peoples and beyond."
- "To recognize our place in Hawaii history in seeking the events of Opukaha'ia's return and attempt to restore the monarchy." (Clark, 1993, November 6, p. A7)

For Obookiah's family, his return signaled more than just a return to his ancestral home. His return marked both his educational and spiritual achievement as well as brought Obookiah home to preach the gospel to his people, continuing his legacy as a sponsor of literacy and Christianity. In this sense, Obookiah continues to act as sponsor for the continued development of the Hawaiian people.

The Consequences of Literacy

What I have discussed above is a preliminary exploration of *Memoirs of Henry Obookiah* as a literacy studies project, primarily situating *Memoirs* as a literacy narrative and examining how it illustrates and develops Brandt's concept of literacy sponsorship. Brandt's *Literacy in American Lives* provides a useful frame for understanding how life narratives, whether contemporary or historical, can provide deep texture to theorizing the way literacy is thoroughly embedded in lives and culture. I have read *Memoirs* to illustrate how the sponsorship of literacy functioned to provide Obookiah access to both texts and Christianity. Like many literacy narratives, Obookiah's *Memoirs* illustrates quite strikingly Sylvia Scribner's (1988) three metaphors for literacy. While I have spent much of this essay addressing literacy as a state of grace for Obookiah, it's very clear that Obookiah acquired literacy as an adaptation strategy for his new life and new opportunities in New England, and it is also clear that literacy provided access to power, both spiritual and material, as he moved among New England's elite and even became a literary figure in Mark Twain's *Roughing It*.

We also see the material effects of literacy in this project, from the documentation of a life and production of a material text, and then the subsequent circulation of this text to a very specific audience and public, an audience that the American Board of Commissioners for Foreign Missions hoped to persuade in order to win support for their missions to other nations. Sponsorship as a specific trope of literacy reveals the complex relationships that exist between the way literacy functions in people's lives and the hope such sponsorship implies. In this sense, sponsorship, while challenging the literacy myth of individual achievement, still reinforces a myth that literacy itself provides access to power and state of grace. Earlier in this essay, I briefly discussed the direct personal sponsors of Obookiah's literacy, from his first interaction with Russel Hubbard on his initial sea voyage, to Edwin and Timothy Dwight, to the many individuals with whom he lived and interacted. But I do not think we can underestimate the power of religion and the church as an institutional sponsor of literacy. Faith is ever-present in Obookiah's writing and in reports of his interpersonal communication. Were it not for this faith, this state of grace achieved through the acquisition, use, and belief in literacy as a means to accept and practice Christianity, would *Memoirs of Henry Obookiah* have been written, published, and sustained through today? And finally, we cannot look past both *Memoirs* and Obookiah himself as sponsors of literacy and conversion. Although the consequences of literacy and Christianity for Hawai'i are mired in the complexities of modernity, indigeneity, and culture, it is undeniable that Obookiah has functioned as a symbol of faith. For some this has meant a belief in what Christianity can provide; for others this has meant a return of a native son. As the cover of the 1968 edition accurately proclaims, Obookiah and the *Memoirs* are "[t]he boy, the book . . . that changed the course of Hawaii's history."

Notes

1. In this chapter I use the Anglicized and Christian name for Henry Obookiah. Though his Hawaiian name was Opukaha'ia, I choose to use the Anglicized form as a way to indicate the constructed and institutionalized self of Obookiah.

2. For example, see Lindon Barrett (1995), "African-American Slave Narratives: Literacy, the Body, Authority," and Henry Louis Gates Jr. (1995) "A Dangerous Literacy: The Legacy of Frederick Douglass."

References

Barrett, Lindon. 1995. "African-American Slave Narratives: Literacy, the Body, Authority." *American Literary History*, 7(3), 413–42.

Brandt, Deborah. 2001. *Literacy in American Lives.* New York: Cambridge University Press.

Brown, Candy Gunther. 2004. *The Word in the World: Evangelical Writing, Publishing, and Reading in America, 1789–1880.* Chapel Hill: University of North Carolina Press.

Cayton, Mary Kupiec. 2010. "Canonizing Harriet Newell: Women, the Evangelical Press, and the Foreign Mission Movement in New England, 1740–1840." In *Competing Kingdoms: Women, Mission, Nation, and the American Protestant Empire, 1812–1960,* edited by Barbara Reeves-Ellington, Kathryn Kish Sklar, and Connie A. Shemo, 69–93. Durham, NC: Duke University Press.

Chamberlain, Frances. 1993, May 9. "A Village Senses the Loss of a Hero Long Held as Its Own." *The New York Times*, p. CN2.

Clark, Hugh. 1993, July 24. "185 Years Later, A Devoted Isle Lad Is Coming Home." *The Honolulu Advertiser*, p. A3.

———. 1993, November 6. "Family of Opukuhaia Founds Group to Keep Convert's Story Alive." *The Honolulu Advertiser*, p. A7.

Dwight, Edwin W. 1818/1968. *Memoirs of Henry Obookiah*. Honolulu, HI: Woman's Board of Missions for the Pacific Islands.

———. 1818/1990. *Memoirs of Henry Obookiah*. Honolulu, HI: Woman's Board of Missions for the Pacific Islands.

Eldred, Janet Carey, and Peter Mortensen. 1992. "Reading Literacy Narratives." *College English, 54*(5), 512–39.

Gates, Henry Louis, Jr. 1995, May 28. "A Dangerous Literacy: The Legacy of Frederick Douglass." *The New York Times Book Review*, pp. 3, 16.

Kikukawa, Cecily H. 1982. *Ka Mea Hoʻala: The Awakener: The Story of Henry Obookiah Once Called Opukahaʻia*. Honolulu, HI: Bess Press.

"Letter from Henry Obookiah, a Native of Owhyhee, to a Friend in Middlebury." November 1814. *The Adviser, or Vermont Evangelical Magazine*, pp. 329–30. Reprinted in *The Columbia Magazine*, April 1815, pp. 237–38. Citations are to the *Adviser* letter.

Scribner, Sylvia. 1988. "Literacy in Three Metaphors." In *Perspectives on Literacy*, edited by Eugene R. Kintgen, Barry M. Kroll, and Mike Rose, 71–81. Carbondale: Southern Illinois University Press.

Shaver, Lisa. 2012. *Beyond the Pulpit: Women's Rhetorical Roles in the Antebellum Religious Press*. Pittsburgh: University of Pittsburgh Press.

Tanahara, Kris. 1993, July 31. "Return of Opukahaʻia Inspires Hope." *The Honolulu Advertiser*, p. B4.

Twain, Mark. 1872/1972. *Roughing It*. Vol. 2. Berkeley: University of California Press.

PART TWO

Looking Now at Literacy: A Tool for Change?

5. Sponsoring Education for All: Revisiting the Sacred/Secular Divide in Twenty-First-Century Zanzibar

Julie Nelson Christoph

> Conservative in nature but often ruthlessly demanding of change, sponsors carry within their material and ideological orbits multiple aspects of literacy's past and present, receding and emerging traditions that accumulate as part of a history of contact and competition. Even within single institutions, the uses and networks of literacy crisscross through many domains, potentially exposing people to multiple sources of sponsoring powers—secular, religious, bureaucratic, legal, commercial, technological. It is these characteristics of the sponsors that give contemporary literacy its demanding qualities of complexity, multiplicity, and stratification, its sense of surplus and its volatility.
> —Deborah Brandt, *Literacy in American Lives*

In 2010, while describing the reading and writing activities in which he had engaged in the past twelve months as part of his professional activities, a forty-five-year-old man explained that he does not read "[b]ecause I am a businessman" and that he does not write because "[i]n business, there is nothing to write."[1] Similarly, a forty-nine-year-old man who works in agriculture said, "My work has nothing to do with reading and writing"; a female farmer, age thirty-eight, said, "I don't write goods that I produce; I keep records in my mind." A fifty-two-year-old woman reported that there is no need to engage in reading or writing activities with her family because "[m]y whole family knows how to read [and] how to write."

These respondents are citizens of Zanzibar, a semi-autonomous republic of Tanzania—one of the 164 countries that committed in 2000 to accomplishing the UNESCO goal of achieving Education for All (EFA). All of these respondents report being able to read and write materials they encounter in their daily lives and would thus likely be included among the literate adult population in Zanzibar in measures of EFA achievement. And yet, their descriptions of their literacy practices demonstrate a different valuation and use of literacy than EFA might predict.

UNESCO often depicts literacy as an essential step on a unidirectional pathway to success, as the catalyst that will transform economic systems and empower women and families. A UNESCO pamphlet on EFA, for instance, makes these unequivocal claims: "Education is a fundamental human right. It provides children, youth and adults with the power to reflect, make choices and enjoy a better life. It breaks the cycle of poverty and is a key ingredient in economic and social development. Mothers' education has a strong impact on health, family welfare and fertility" (n.d.a, p. 2). As Brian Street (1984) has argued of the UNESCO literacy campaigns of the 1960s through 1980s, such campaigns value literacy as a socially transformative good—one that not only leads to predictable ends but that also can be "reduced to statistical measures and economic functions" (p. 13). This autonomous understanding of literacy suggests that once the measures have been attained, the social transformation will follow suit. In keeping with earlier UNESCO initiatives, EFA aims to effect "positive social transformation, justice, and personal and collective freedom" as assessed through six measurable goals, including an improvement in adult literacy levels by 50 percent by 2015.[2]

In contrast, the literate Zanzibaris quoted above describe reading and writing as tools—useful in some contexts, perhaps, but not necessarily essential to or transformative of every element of daily life. These responses from Zanzibari citizens illustrate the difficulty of attempting to control from above something as unstable as contemporary literacy. Even where the statistical measures suggest that international literacy goals are being met, individuals' daily literacy practices may undermine or complicate the goals of the literacy campaign. Using Brandt's understanding of literacy as a fundamentally volatile entity that is facilitated through messy, complex, and even contradictory sponsorship networks can help illuminate why literacy is the way it is in Zanzibar—why it is that the very people who seem to be fulfilling EFA goals undervalue and often fail to benefit from literacy as EFA envisions it. Brandt's model can also suggest ways that discussions of literacy and development might move beyond the autonomous model.

In this essay, I draw from my survey of adult literacy practices in Zanzibar, exploring this disconnect between the official objectives of international literacy initiatives and the uses to which individuals' literacy is put—with a special focus on the role of Islam as an important but largely unacknowledged sponsor of literacy in Zanzibar.[3] Large literacy campaigns like EFA operate from the assumption that literacy learning facilitates predictable development outcomes and that it is possible to disseminate and measure literacy from a centralized location. In contrast, I argue that the growth of communication technologies and global influences in the twenty-first century are creating increasingly diverse and decentralized literacy networks—networks that are increasingly difficult to understand or control from a centralized model, especially when that centralized model overlooks the role of religion in twenty-first-century life.

Zanzibar: A Literacy and Development Success Story?

Zanzibar is a semi-autonomous republic of Tanzania—a nation that formed in 1964 when the newly decolonized nations of Tanganyika and Zanzibar joined together. According to the most recent census, in 2002, Zanzibar has a population of approximately 982,000, the vast majority of whom are Muslim.[4]

Zanzibar's location has facilitated its long history as a trading post and cultural meeting point between Africa and the Arab world. It is an archipelago in the Indian Ocean, about twenty miles from the east coast of Africa, comprising two large islands and many islets. Modern Zanzibar is a place of great contrast. Its pristine beaches and rich blend of Islamic and Swahili architecture have increasingly landed it on lists of must-visit international travel sites. It is included, for instance, in the *New York Times'* "41 Places to Go in 2011," with the tagline, "On an African isle, luxury lures the après safari set." But the après safari experience of Zanzibar is very different than that of most Zanzibar residents; a single night's stay in the rooms recommended by the *Times* would cost up to ten times the $120 mean per capita annual household income of Zanzibar residents.

Though transportation is reasonably easy, via paved roads and local "dala-dala" buses, many people in Zanzibar live their entire lives without spending extended time far from their home villages. The strong sense of local identity develops, at least in part, from the uneven distribution of infrastructural features (e.g., schools, electricity, and broadcast signals) along with varied environmental features (e.g., soil types, fresh water sources, and plant life). Though the islands are small and villages are relatively close together, the experience of daily life is quite different in fishing villages versus in farming villages versus in urban environments versus in tourist destinations.

Swahili is the home language for the majority of Zanzibaris, and it is the language of instruction in public primary schools; English and Arabic are taught as foreign languages up until secondary school, when English becomes the language of instruction. As has been the case since the formation of Tanzania, public education on the islands is administered through the Zanzibar government, through a separate administrative structure from that on the mainland.

But, to some degree, Zanzibar has benefited from Tanzania's nationwide literacy campaign in the 1970s and 1980s. During the years shortly after the formation of Tanzania in 1964, Tanzania achieved worldwide fame, both for the leadership of former teacher President Nyerere and for the rapid spread of adult literacy (Unsicker, 1987; Kassam, 1983; Mbakile, 1979).[5] For Nyerere, universal literacy was essential to the vision of the new country and the development of his people, and this insistence on education was reflected widely in his administration. Nyerere—perhaps the only head of state ever to publish an article in *Harvard Educational Review*—wrote in 1985 that the efforts between 1971 and 1985 had succeeded in raising the level of adult basic literacy from 25 percent to 85 percent (pp. 48–49).

The self-reported literacy rates from the most recent three census reports in Zanzibar show steady growth in Swahili literacy levels, from 46.3 percent adult literacy in 1978, to 58.8 percent in 1988, to 72.5 percent in 2002. But attaining reliable numbers for literacy rates is challenging—not only because of the practical challenges of assessing literacy in any context but also because of the specific linguistic, cultural, and political challenges in Zanzibar. Numbers for Zanzibar are only sometimes disaggregated from numbers from Tanzania as a whole, and many of the existing numbers available on literacy rates are not truly comparable because of measurement methods: Some are derived from tests given by the Ministry of Education, whereas other data come from population and housing census reports. Further complicating the matter is that in the 1978 and 1988 censuses, literacy was self-reported and only in Swahili. In 2002, in recognition that there continue to be many citizens who are literate in languages other than Swahili, census data included self-reported literacy in both Swahili and other languages.[6]

Zanzibar's status as a semi-autonomous, developing republic presents special rhetorical and political challenges when it comes to reporting literacy rates. In theory, the Zanzibar Ministry of Education is responsible for all educational programs on the islands and is thus credited with the successes and failures of literacy initiatives. As the EFA Country Report of 2000 notes, "The education system of Zanzibar is centrally managed and administered by the Ministry of Education. The management council of the ministry is responsible for policy decisions regarding the implementation of all education activities including EFA." In practice, though, the management and administration of education is more complex. As the report states, "external [foreign development aid] financing is particularly important to the financing of the education system" in Zanzibar, but "donor's priorities not all the time matches [sic] with government preference" (UNESCO, n.d.c).

The competing priorities can lead to very different assessments of literacy. For instance, in 2000, just before the large jump in literacy rates reported in the census, UNESCO's EFA country report on Zanzibar stated, "[T]he percentage of adults who are literate [in Zanzibar] is not known. . . . However, illiteracy seems to be on increase [sic]." (UNESCO, n.d.c). In contrast, in a speech in October 2009 to the General Conference of UNESCO, Zanzibar's then-president Amani Abeid Karume reported,

> In the 1970s Tanzania attained [an] adult literacy rate of 90%. Due to numerous challenges this has dropped to 69.4% in 2006 [on the mainland] though it is a positive case in Zanzibar where it stands at over 85%. Tanzania has embarked on a comprehensive education development programme to improve access and quality of education. With respect to attaining Education for All goals, Tanzania is making good progress. (2009, p. 4)

From these two perspectives—both with some standing in UNESCO but with very different positions in relation to funding—literacy in Zanzibar is either on the rise or on the decline.

Beyond Literacy Rates: Literacy Practices in Zanzibar

Most assessments of literacy in Zanzibar have been interested in the binary question of whether adults are literate or not, but—as the responses from the Zanzibari residents quoted above indicate—even if valid numbers were available, knowing whether a person is "literate" does not reveal much about what literacy means for that person. Is literacy perceived as being key to social mobility? Is literacy understood as giving the power of reflection? What role do literacy practices play within family life? How is literacy used on a daily basis, and through what technologies?

From March through May 2010, a team of Zanzibari researchers and I attempted to answer these and other questions by surveying adults throughout Zanzibar about their literacy practices and attitudes towards literacy. In an hour-long session with each adult, we asked eighteen questions in Swahili, including open- and close-ended questions about respondents' use of communication technologies (radio, television, mobile phones, and Internet), as well as about their use of newspapers and libraries and their reading practices in the domains of recreation, paid employment, religious practice, and family activities. The questionnaire included a series of Likert-type scale questions about attitudes toward the importance of literacy in daily life—using language from the International Adult Literacy Survey's definition of literacy (Kirsch, 2001, p. 6)—and concluded with open-ended questions about literacy in Tanzania.[7]

We surveyed adults in each of Zanzibar's regions, a total of seventy-five adults.[8] In each district, a research assistant and I spoke with the district administrator, asking him to work with local shehas (neighborhood government representatives) to select fifteen respondents from the district, representing a diverse group of people with respect to age (eighteen and over), sex, educational level, literacy level, disability, socioeconomic status, profession, marital status, and religion.[9] Respondents were surveyed at central locations in the district, and each was given an honorarium sufficient to cover bus fare plus the cost of a soda and snack, and district administrators were given about four times that amount as an honorarium. Because the shehas' involvement in the selection process introduced a potential bias, we were vigilant about balancing the population that we surveyed and sought to make corrections when necessary.[10] Though my aim was not to interview a strictly representative sample of Zanzibaris, our sample was diverse and, as it happened, closely approximates the census trends for adult literacy, with a 77 percent literacy rate among respondents (as determined by self-reporting of not engaging in particular literacy activities because of an inability to read or write).

Two Zanzibari research assistants independently translated the completed surveys, and then I combined the translations into idiomatic English, talking with the translators to reconcile discrepancies between the translations. The English translation was then interpretively coded independently by me and by a Zanzibari research assistant.

Belief in the Value of Literacy

Respondents espoused a nearly unanimous belief in the power of literacy—in language not unlike that expressed in the EFA literature. In answering the Likert-type scale questions, the median answers for nearly every question about the value of literacy attested that respondents "agree strongly" (the most positive response) that literate people are "more knowledgeable," "more successful," "better parents," and "happier" than those who are not literate. Respondents also agreed strongly, "All people should be literate," "One aspect of basic human rights is access to education," and "Free, compulsory and high quality primary education is important." The only exception to that strongly positive sense of the value of literacy is that the median response was "neutral" about the statement "One cannot earn a living without being literate."

Here is a snapshot of one respondent who upholds the belief that literacy can lead to "a better life" but who does not yet have access to that life (UNESCO, n.d.a, p. 2). Mtumwa is a fifty-two-year-old married woman, a farmer from rural northern Unguja (the larger, more developed island).[11]

She did not attend any secular schooling and went to a Qur-an school only, where she memorized portions of the Qur-an in Arabic. She lives about a mile away from the village where she grew up and lives within about one hundred feet of a main road, about a 120-minute bus ride from the capital city and from a public library. Her main connection to the world outside her village is the radio; she listens to the radio daily at her home for news and for information on agricultural practices, and she talks with her husband and neighbor about "dangerous things" and about agricultural issues reported on the radio.

Mtumwa expressed dissatisfaction with her inability to access more communication technologies. She does not watch television because the few televisions in her village are in spaces informally designated for men only. She reports that she has no writing utensils or blank paper, that she does not own or use a mobile phone, and that she "doesn't know" the Internet. She does not know how to read newspapers or books for herself, and the only texts she encounters are her recitations of the Qur-an and the prayers and religious lessons that others read to her.

Mtumwa is among the twelve women and five men in our survey sample who are illiterate, and her situation embodies problems that EFA was created to remedy—including poverty and gender (in)equity in education. In her district, 48.3 percent of the population is below the basic-needs poverty line, and 12.06 percent is below the food poverty line; 7.9 percent of households have electricity, and 38.2 percent have modern and waterproof metal roofs, as opposed to thatched palm leaves. In Mtumwa's district, 60 percent of women are literate (Office of the Chief Government Statistician, 2008). When she was of primary school age, the primary schools in her district were far enough apart that some children had to walk a mile or more to the nearest school—a short distance but enough to be seen as too dangerous by parents and especially parents of girls (Christoph, 2010). Mtumwa and other girls of her generation were thus kept home from school, ostensibly for their protection.

Mtumwa's assessment of her literacy abilities is in keeping with those of the respondents as a whole—as well as with many of the assumptions behind EFA. Like Mtumwa, respondents who reported not engaging in particular literacy activities because of an inability to read or write "disagreed strongly" with the statements, "I know how to read [or write] well enough to function in society, to achieve my goals, and to develop my knowledge and potential." Those who could read and write "agreed strongly" with those same statements.[12] These responses and the life of restricted literacy that Mtumwa has lived demonstrate the validity of some of the assumptions inherent in EFA and other international literacy campaigns; while Mtumwa and others feel neutral about the correlation between literacy and the ability to earn a living, she and others express the belief that literacy corresponds with a better life.

The (Ir)relevance of Literacy to Daily Life

Though our respondents affirmed a link between literacy and a better life, the second most common reason that our respondents gave for not participating in reading and writing activities was that such activities were not relevant to them personally—as in the agricultural worker who said, "My work has nothing to do with reading and writing," or the woman who saw no reason to read or write together with family members because they were already literate. If literacy is highly valued—if the respondents so unanimously and positively affirm claims about the power of literacy to affect lives—then why are literate activities seen as irrelevant to so many concrete aspects of their daily lives? The following snapshots of two individual respondents' literacy practices help to flesh out the diversity of literacy practices that exist in Zanzibar and illustrate how literacy can be seen, on the one hand, as highly valuable and, on the other hand—even among literate individuals—as irrelevant to the ideals of economic progress and personal fulfillment that inspire EFA and other UNESCO initiatives.

Maryam

Maryam is an unmarried, twenty-year-old woman living in Pemba (the smaller major island in the archipelago) in a rural area very close to the airport and one of the island's two major cities. She attended all seven years of primary school, in a town about two miles from where she now lives.[13] Maryam does not have electricity where she lives and so does not watch television, but she does listen to the radio every day, often tuning in to readings of the Qur-an. She does not own a mobile phone herself, but she uses one more than once a week to make voice calls. As she had learned to do in school, she reads Swahili textbooks, both by herself for pleasure and with family, and she reads the Qur-an and a variety of religious texts; however, she chooses not to engage in many other literacy practices that are available to her. She says she does not have time to read newspapers, and although she lives within three miles of one of Zanzibar's two public libraries, she does not go there because she does not know where the library is and does not feel she has any reason to go. She says she does not read or write anything for her job with a small business related to schools: "I don't have a reason" to do so. Maryam—as a young, single, professional woman who affirms the value of literacy, has completed her primary education and has easy access to libraries and newspapers—would seem to be well situated to engage in many literacy activities. However, she chooses in the vicissitudes of her daily life not to engage in the kinds of civic and professional literacy activities that UNESCO holds up as activities that can transform lives in developing countries.

Juma

Juma is a forty-six-year-old married businessman who lives within two miles of Pemba's other major city. He attended school through the end of junior secondary school, about three miles from where he currently lives. He does not use the Internet because he neither knows how to use nor has access to it, but he does attend to news and religious programs on the television and radio at his home more than once a week, and he uses a mobile phone daily for voice and text messaging. He reads the Qur-an and other religious texts but otherwise does not engage on a regular basis with text. He chooses not to purchase newspapers himself, but he does read from a newspaper about once a week if someone passes one along to him. He normally does not go to the library: "I am not a reader—I don't normally read such things as books and magazines for pleasure." He claims that he does not read because he is a businessman, and he does not write because "[i]n the business of sales, there is nothing to write."

Maryam's and Juma's responses encapsulate the ambivalent attitude toward literacy expressed by many of our literate respondents. On the one hand, literacy is perceived as valuable and necessary, and many respondents concluded their interviews with such statements as these by Maryam and Juma, respectively: "We should learn a lot. We shouldn't quit learning. Let's keep on learning," and "The level of literacy has increased in comparison to the past; however, it needs to be increased due to its importance now and in future days." On the other hand, few respondents could give examples of reading and writing that they had done for pleasure, at work, or with their families in the past year. Some literate respondents—like Maryam and Juma—expressed the belief that literacy is, in fact, irrelevant to those very realms of career and family life that are seen as key to UNESCO initiatives.

Silent Sponsorship

The literacy practices of the respondents we surveyed indicate that there is a vibrant literacy culture in Zanzibar, but this literacy culture and its sponsorship look quite different than the literacy culture envisioned in EFA's centralized, secular, economic development model. Our respondents' descriptions of their own literacy practices suggest that the achievement of such measurable goals as improved literacy rates and access to education has little predictive value in relation to international literacy campaigns' larger goals for secular economic and social development. Though Maryam and Juma do read and write on a regular basis, their reading and writing activities do not serve development concerns in any direct way. And though the Zanzibar Ministry of Education is the official sponsor responsible for seeing that EFA goals are met, such secular sponsorship is relatively absent in respondents' day-to-day activities after formal schooling has ended.

Reading for religious purposes was by far the most common literacy activity, both in terms of the percentage of respondents who reported engaging in literacy for these purposes and in terms of the range of texts and uses to which literacy was put. *All* respondents reported engaging in some form of religious literacy activity—either reading and writing themselves, or having others read or write for them as part of religious activities. Respondents reported engaging in literacy activities in about equal numbers in Arabic and Swahili.

The extent of religious literacy activities in Zanzibar is more striking in light of how *much* our respondents reported reading and writing. In response to the prompt "Please give some examples of materials that you have read for X in the past twelve months," respondents overall gave nearly three times the number of specific examples of religious reading they had done as they did of reading for entertainment, work, and family literacy activities. For pleasure reading, for instance, respondents generally could not recall any specific examples of reading they had done but sometimes mentioned one or two broad genres they had read (e.g., "stories" or "school books"). For religious reading, respondents were able to recall readily the specific genres they had read—such as prayers for the dead, Fiqh, and Hadith—as well as titles of specific books, such as "Grandfather" and "Boat" or works by specific Islamic scholars.[14] These and other low-cost extended prose are available in the Islamic bookstands that are ubiquitous in markets and outside mosques.

Respondents thus reported engaging with a greater quantity and variety of religious texts than with texts in any other domain of literate activity. The most commonly read text for religious purposes was the Qur-an. All but thirteen respondents (two of whom are Christian) reported either having read the Qur-an to themselves, having it read to them, or reading it to someone else. Respondents also reported engaging with the Qur-an in ways that are not, strictly, "reading" but that indicate the importance of this one text in Zanzibari life. Of the seventeen respondents who reported not being able to read other kinds of texts, nine reported reciting the Qur-an—a practice that they viewed as reading rather than as recitation.

Access to the text of the Qur-an is available in a variety of formats. In addition to print copies of the Qur-an, television and radio programs are available that solely broadcast readings of the Qur-an; respondents reported watching and listening to these programs, as well as watching televised Qur-an recitation competitions. Phone customers with a bit of disposable income can purchase daily text messages of verses from the Qur-an. Two respondents reported writing Qur-an verses as Kombe (or medicine made by washing written verses with water and drinking the resulting infusion). And though none of the respondents reported engaging in such practices, there are many syncretic practices in Zanzibar that meld use of the Qur-an with indigenous ritual; for instance, it is a common syncretic practice in Zanzibar to wear amulets made of verses of the Qur-an, or to engrave verses in the door of one's home or place of business, or to hang verses from the ceiling to ward off evil spirits. The Qur-an is *the* text in Zanzibar, and there are numerous modes through which residents in Zanzibar can engage with the text on a daily basis. In terms of literacy practices and—to a lesser extent—literacy education, Islam is a significant sponsor of literacy and one that is almost completely unacknowledged by UNESCO.

When I say that Islam is a sponsor of literacy, I mean Islam in the sense of an abstract agent that serves to "enable, support, teach, and model" literacy (Brandt, 2001, p. 19). Islam is not a sponsor of literacy in the official sense that the Ministry of Education is—and could not be a sponsor in that official sense because of the complex and decentralized structure of the various branches of Islam represented in Zanzibar. Muslims in Zanzibar are, of course, diverse, comprising Shias and Sunnis, as well as representatives of divisions therein. But while Zanzibari Muslims disagree on a number of issues, they agree on the five pillars of Islam. Islam is central to the uses to which many Zanzibaris' literacy is put on a daily basis, and reverence for and familiarity with the Qur-an are essential, especially to the daily prayers that shape the rhythm of life in schools, businesses, families, and government in Zanzibar.

Islam as Complex Literacy Sponsor

Despite the pervasiveness of Islamic religious literacy, the official sponsor of literacy in Zanzibar—the sponsor that is held accountable through EFA for the successes and failures of literacy education efforts—is the Zanzibar Ministry of Education. This official, centralized, exclusive sponsorship of literacy masks the ways in which, as Brandt writes, "the uses and networks of literacy crisscross through many domains, potentially exposing people to multiple sources of sponsoring powers—secular, religious, bureaucratic, legal, commercial, technological" (2001, p. 70).[15] In Zanzibar, as elsewhere, the uses and networks of literacy in the twenty-first century are untraceably complex, bearing the marks of relatively new influences, such as the Internet, along with much older influences like Islam and indigenous religion.

Literacy practices in Zanzibar demonstrate the volatility that comes with these crisscrossing and conflicting networks of sponsorship. The relatively high literacy rates and the rising levels of schooling in Zanzibar appear to show progress toward EFA goals numerically. Moreover, respondents readily voice the kinds of beliefs in the essential and transformative value of literacy. But the antipathy of our literate survey respondents toward many secular literacy activities shows that success in schooling and even recall of literacy campaign-style slogans do not necessarily equate with the use of literate skills in ways that EFA and many other international literacy campaigns envision. Literacy is not so easily disseminated and controlled.

The intractable nature of literacy sponsorship ironically has benefits for overall literacy learning. There are many ways in which the literacy currently being sponsored by Islam in Zanzibar is giving people in Zanzibar a reason not only to become literate but also to continue engaging in literacy activities well into adulthood—even though these activities might not seem to be in concert with EFA goals. Examples of individuals reading for religious practice are abundant and offer models for how literacy might be used, in a climate in which, as one respondent put it, "I have never seen anyone else writing."

But, as Brandt notes, sponsors not only "enable, support, teach, and model" but also "regulate, suppress, or withhold, literacy" (2001, p. 19). There are other ways in which Islam as sponsor may also withhold or discourage the literacy of the twenty-first century, and it is for this reason that international literacy campaigns like EFA need to think beyond the centralized economic model and binary measures of literacy if they are to intervene successfully in economic development through education initiatives. The literacy practices of people in Zanzibar are much more complex than the numbers might suggest.

One example of literacy that promises to be increasingly important and increasingly contentious between the official and unofficial sponsors in the coming years is computer literacy and, specifically, Internet literacy. Though the information technology infrastructure in Zanzibar is not yet well developed, there are Internet cafés in the urban centers in Zanzibar, as well as increasingly reliable and affordable cell phone modems, and there are many initiatives by the government, businesses, and nongovernmental organizations to create even more information technology infrastructure.[16]

Among the respondents, however, only five out of seventy-five respondents reported having used the Internet in the past year. Twenty-two respondents reported not using the Internet because they didn't know what it was (including a twenty-year-old and a twenty-six-year-old), though some of them had heard of it; one woman said, "I just hear people saying 'Internet, Internet'; I don't know what it is." Fourteen people said they don't use it because they don't know how. Twenty-six said they didn't have Internet access and/or couldn't afford it. One woman said that she was "not encouraged to use the Internet."

The limitations of the questionnaire format prevent our knowing whether that respondent feels actively discouraged or merely "not encouraged." However, the Internet is viewed by a sizeable segment of the population in Zanzibar with suspicion—and, specifically, because of its perceived threat to Islamic values. Bjørn Furuholt and Stein Kristiansen (2007) conducted a survey of five hundred respondents in Indonesia, Zanzibar, and mainland Tanzania and learned that Internet usage is stigmatized because it is associated with pornography and lewd behavior—a finding that is consistent with my experiences of living in Zanzibar and reading such claims in my students' papers as "internet is a bad place," "people use more time on the internet and forget other duties that is praying, working as well as domestic duties," and "having internet cafes in Zanzibar is the sources of destruction of culture" (Student papers, 2010).[17]

This fear of "destruction of culture" is an important way in which Islam as silent sponsor has the potential to undermine the literacy purposes of EFA and other secular literacy initiatives. The interchange of ideas has been the hallmark of life in Zanzibar since the late 1400s, but as Simon Turner (2009) notes in his article on Islamic revival in Zanzibar, globalization has enabled turns both outward and inward in Zanzibar. In facilitating Zanzibar's role in international tourism, Zanzibar has opened up in a big way to the outside world, and the influx of tourists from around the world has brought dollars, euros, and yen to the local economy. At the same time, Zanzibar has also reconnected with the rest of the Islamic world, bringing home new versions of Islam, some of which denounce involvement with non-Muslims and promote a fundamentalist attitude towards the Qur-an—as exemplified by one respondent's observation that there is no need to write anything in religious practice because "the books have already been written."

Revisiting the Sacred/Secular Divide in the Twenty-First Century

Work in the New Literacy Studies has examined religion's central role in providing the means and purpose for literacy learning in a variety of settings, but the role of religion as an integrated part of modern daily life does not receive enough attention.[18] In national literacy programs, George Ladaah Openjuru and Elda Lyster note that "religious literacy practices are often overlooked," as well, plausibly suggesting that such practices may be ignored "because they do not relate directly to national development concerns and can also be negatively associated with colonialism and evangelism" (2007, p. 97). Katherine Marshall (2010) argues that international literacy development initiatives like EFA presume that governments and secular international organizations are and should be responsible for meeting international literacy goals, writing that the religious context is "poorly reflected in policy analysis and decision-making" (p. 280).

But does there need to be a bright line between sacred and secular literacy? Might the crisscrossing networks of sponsorship provide opportunities for EFA and other development initiatives? There is evidence that Arabic literacy initiated for religious purposes can extend into secular uses. Sylvia Scribner and Michael Cole's (1981) research in Liberia is best known for countering the Great Divide view of literacy through identifying the different functions of Vai versus Arabic versus English script; however, *The Psychology of Literacy* also records nonreligious uses of Arabic script for letter-writing, family record-keeping, and financial record-keeping (p. 83). Brian Street (1984) similarly reports that merchants in Iran adapted Arabic literacy learned in the *maktab* Islamic schools to new commercial functions. In Zanzibar and throughout East Africa into the twentieth century, Swahili itself was originally written in Arabic script because it was first recorded by people who were literate enough in Qur-anic Arabic to be able to adapt it to new purposes. EFA has largely steered clear of affiliation with religious organizations, but, given the crisscrossing "uses and networks of literacy," this strategy is likely not the most effective.

In Zanzibar, Islam is an important sponsor of literacy not only as a motivating force but also as a source of education and reading materials. This sponsorship might provide opportunities for cooperation between international and local interests. Of the seventy-three Muslim respondents we surveyed, fifty-four had attended *madrasa* (Islamic religious school), in comparison to fifty-six of seventy-three who had attended state-supported secular school. In a typical day, a Zanzibari child will go to secular school in the morning, then to madrasa in the afternoon and on Saturdays, and then, perhaps, to tuition school in the evenings to prepare for standardized grade-level exams. For these students attending school from morning to evening, madrasa and secular schooling are, at best, duplicative and, at worst, competitive—diluting the time, effort, and money that can be devoted to either.

A more cooperative approach might be something like the partnership forged through the Madrasa Resource Center (MRC), a program funded by the Aga Khan Foundation and the US Agency for International Development (USAID) to promote early childhood education through a curriculum that integrates religious and secular education. The MRC provides in-service teacher training that builds awareness of the needs of children, modeling flexible and improvisatory teaching methods, rather than rote learning. The MRC-supported preschools are popular with parents because the fees are low and because the teachers come from the local communities and thus understand community norms. In just the year after the MRC was founded, the number of preschool madrasas doubled (UNESCO, n.d.d).

There are indications that many of our adult respondents, too, have an interest in ongoing learning and do engage with readily available literacy materials—sometimes in ways that literate people in resource-rich environments would normally not do. Several respondents, for instance, reported reading their children's schoolbooks for pleasure reading, and three respondents reported listening to a program called *Tucheze Tujifunze*, a radio program using the open airwaves but designed for broadcast to the specific audience of rural preschool classes.[19] The thirst for ongoing study could be supported through more robust religious study. For many, madrasa is already an important part of lifelong Islamic learning. Indeed, five respondents—the oldest of whom was fifty-five—reported currently attending madrasa as adult students, and opportunities for more advanced levels of madrasa study would present opportunities for a deeper understanding of Arabic as a language than is currently common in Zanzibar. With that deeper understanding could come opportunities not only for religious practice but also for transfer to other domains, perhaps especially if such opportunities are perceived as being locally inspired rather than disseminated from a central (and, especially, foreign) location.

Mtumwa and others of our respondents expressed a strong desire to gain access to literacy learning and economic opportunities, and the desire to fill those very real needs is in large part what motivates EFA and other international literacy campaigns. But working from a centralized model that ignores the complexities of local culture and religious resources is not effective. Local and international organizations that seek to facilitate economic mobility through literacy learning would do well to consider the contact, competition, and accretion inherent in the sponsorship networks that Brandt describes in the epigraph to this essay: Literacy is not docile or easily managed. Religion continues to be an especially volatile and powerful sponsor of literacy, one that is rarely considered central to international development work related to literacy; my research in Zanzibar exemplifies, though, that it is not enough to attempt to teach and measure literacy accomplishment from a central, singular, secular perspective when the literacy cultures of the present moment are so multilayered.

Notes

1. I am grateful for Fulbright's support of this research and to the many people who helped me during my year in Zanzibar, especially research team members Mussa Hassan, Haroun Maalim, and Fatma Kombo.

2. For more information on EFA, see UNESCO, n.d.b.

3. For a definition of *literacy sponsor*, see Brandt, p. 19.

4. No census data on religion have been gathered since 1967, but published estimates for Zanzibar are at 90+ percent. The CIA World Factbook states that the population in Zanzibar is "more than 99% Muslim." Central Intelligence Agency.

5. Known popularly as "Mwalimu" (teacher) and "Baba wa Taifa" (father of the nation).

6. The 2002 census in Zanzibar reports a literacy rate of 72.5 percent in Swahili and 73.4 percent in all languages.

7. The IALS defines *literacy* as "using printed and written information to function in society to achieve one's goals and to develop one's knowledge and potential." Kirsch, 2001, 6. Survey respondents in my survey were asked to identify what of a range of reading and writing tasks they considered necessary to "function in society, to achieve my goals, and to develop my knowledge and potential" and were asked to what extent they agreed with the statement, "I know how to read [or write] well enough to function in society, to achieve my goals, and to develop my knowledge and potential."

8. Because of Zanzibar's strong local cultures and its concomitant administrative system, we recruited survey respondents through local government leaders. Zanzibar's government is divided into five administrative regions, which are, in turn, divided into two districts each, for a total of ten districts. Within those districts, there are many she-hias—236 total for Zanzibar as a whole. Each of those shehias has a head administrator, called the sheha, who is an appointed official and is responsible for a variety of tasks, including keeping records on individuals living in the shehia, settling disputes among residents of the shehia, and implementing government laws. A shehia is a socially as well as administratively meaningful designation, like a neighborhood, and the sheha is a person of importance who keeps tabs on what is happening in his shehia and who knows quite a bit about the background of each resident. Gaining access to respondents in rural areas necessitates working through local government; consequently, our purposive sample of respondents was selected by local government officials.

9. To avoid inconveniencing respondents because of the length of the survey and to avoid selection bias, we requested that the district administrator choose three random shehias from the district and to ask the sheha from those shehias to select five adults from the shehia.

10. For example, one entire set of data had to be replaced when we realized in the course of our analysis that a district administrator had chosen only illiterate adults involved in a local adult basic literacy program (we later learned that the administrator had an official role in adult literacy programs and hoped for some professional advantage through our research). To replace those fifteen interviews, we gathered data at the other district in that region. In another district, the first five respondents who arrived to be surveyed were men, and we learned that only men had been invited to participate. To respect the time of the people who had been selected, we surveyed that morning group of men but asked the district administrator to ensure that the respondents later that day included more women than men.

11. All names are pseudonyms.

12. For literate respondents, the median answers were "agree strongly," and the averages were "agree somewhat."

13. Zanzibar has a 3-7-3-2-2 education system, consisting of three optional years of preschool, followed by ten years of government-supported basic education: seven years of primary school (beginning at around age seven) and three years of junior secondary school. At the end of junior secondary school, students take an exam to be among the 40 percent who pass into two years of senior secondary school, which is followed by another exam for entry into advanced secondary school.

14. Fiqh is interpretation of proper Islamic practice, involving matters on which the Qur-an is silent. A hadith is an extra-Qur-anic story attributed to the Prophet Mohammed.

15. In fact, when I presented an early version of this chapter to an audience in Zanzibar, a representative of the Ministry of Education in Zanzibar objected to my finding that Zanzibaris are engaging in religious more than other kinds of literacy practices, observing that the ministry is a secular organization and does not promote religious literacy. Mjasiri, 2010.

16. For example, see the press release for a partnership among USAID, Zanzibar's Ministry of Education and Vocational Training, and several international information technology companies. US Department of State, 2010.

17. These comments are in the original English.

18. See, for example, Lathan (chap. 2) and Mattingly (chap. 3), the current volume.

19. Let's play, let's learn.

References

Brandt, Deborah. 2001. *Literacy in American Lives*. New York: Cambridge University Press.

Central Intelligence Agency. 2013. "World Factbook: Africa: Tanzania." *Central Intelligence Agency*. https://www.cia.gov/library/publications/the-world-factbook /geos/tz.html

Christoph, Julie Nelson. 2010. Field notes.

"41 Places to Go in 2011, The." 2011, January 9. *The New York Times*, New York ed., sec. Travel.

Furuholt, Bjørn, and Stein Kristiansen. 2007. "Internet Cafés in Asia and Africa—Venues for Education and Learning?" *Community Informatics: A Global e-Journal*, 3(2). http://ci-journal.net/index.php/ciej/article/viewArticle/314/320

Karume, Amani Abeid. 2009. "Address by the President of Zanzibar, H. E. Dr. Amani
    Abeid Karume, to the 35th Session of the General Conference of UNESCO
    on 19th October 2009, Paris—France." Documents/35VR_PDF/Official_visits
    /Zanzibar-E-35-VR-13.pdf

Kassam, Yusuf. 1983. "Nyerere's Philosophy and the Educational Experiment in Tan-
    zania." *Interchange, 14*(1), 56–68.

Kirsch, Irwin. 2001, December. *The International Adult Literacy Survey (IALS): Under-
    standing What Was Measured.* Princeton, NJ: Educational Testing Service. http:
    //www.ets.org/research/policy_research_reports/publications/report/2001/hsfn

Marshall, Katherine. 2010. "Education for All: Where Does Religion Come In?" *Com-
    parative Education, 46*(3), 273–87.

Mbakile, E. P. R. 1979. "Motivation in Non-Formal Education (Tanzania's Experience)."
    Indian Journal of Adult Education, 40(7), 9–18.

Mjasiri, Jaffar. 2010, July 7. "Zanzibar Lacks Literacy Sponsorship." *DailyNews, online
    edition.* http://www.dailynews.co.tz/home/?n=11507

Nyerere, Julius K. 1985. "Education in Tanzania." *Harvard Educational Review, 55*(1),
    45–52.

Office of the Chief Government Statistician. 2008, May. *Zanzibar Statistical Abstract
    2007.* Zanzibar: Revolutionary Government of Zanzibar.

Openjuru, George Ladaah, and Elda Lyster. 2007. "Christianity and Rural Community
    Literacy Practices in Uganda." *Journal of Research in Reading, 30*(1), 97–112.

Scribner, Sylvia, and Michael Cole. 1981. *The Psychology of Literacy.* Cambridge: Harvard
    University Press.

Street, Brian V. 1984. *Literacy in Theory and Practice.* Cambridge: Cambridge Univer-
    sity Press.

Student papers. 2010, May 19. "Diploma-Level Communication Skills." State University
    of Zanzibar, Semester 2.

Turner, Simon. 2009. "'These Young Men Show No Respect for Local Customs'—Glo-
    balisation and Islamic Revival in Zanzibar." *Journal of Religion in Africa* 39
    (3): 237–61.

UNESCO. n.d.a. "Education for All: An Achievable Vision." *UNESCO.* http://www.
    unesco.org/education/efa/global_co/policy_group/EFA_brochure.pdf

———. n.d.b. "Education for All Movement." *UNESCO.* http://www.unesco.org/new
    /en/education/themes/leading-the-international-agenda/education-for-all/

———. n.d.c. "EFA 2000 Assessment: Country Reports: Tanzania (Zanzibar): Part I:
    Descriptive Section." *UNESCO.* http://www.unesco.org/education/wef/coun-
    tryreports/zanzibar/rapport_1.html

———. n.d.d. "Tanzania (Zanzibar): Report: Part III: Prospectives." *UNESCO.* http:
    //www.unesco.org/education/wef/countryreports/zanzibar/rapport_3.html

Unsicker, Jeff. 1987. "Tanzania's Literacy Campaign in Historical-Structural Perspec-
    tive." In *National Literacy Campaigns and Movements,* edited by Robert F.
    Arnove and Harvey J. Graff, 219–44. New Brunswick, NJ: Transaction.

US Department of State. 2010, June 9. "Public-Private Consortium Signs MOU to Enhance
    Technology for Education in Zanzibar." http://zanzibar-tanzania.usvpp.gov
    /zpr_06092010.html

6. Connecting Literacy to Sustainability: Revisiting *Literacy as Involvement*

Kim Donehower

When Deborah Brandt's *Literacy as Involvement* (1990) was first published and reviewed, it was considered mainly in terms of what it might offer classroom pedagogy. Reviewing the book for the *Journal of Advanced Composition*, Patricia Bizzell worries that "[while] I share Brandt's sense that the best position is one drawn against E. D. Hirsch[. . . .] Brandt's pluralism is a weak alternative to, and hence a weak defense against, Hirsch's canonicity. She says little about how the opening of standards in the academy is to be accomplished" (1991, p. 319). Masahiko Minami, reviewing the work for the *Harvard Educational Review*, describes it as "a thought-provoking book that demonstrates the need for educators . . . to consider the significance of a plurality of literacies" (1991, pp. 232–33). But as Bizzell notes, getting this kind of change to happen in the minds of educators, particularly K–12 educators, is difficult—perhaps even more so in the current educational climate.[1] In this essay, I argue that *Literacy as Involvement* deserves a second life for what it might say about literate life not in classrooms but in the "extracurriculum" (Gere, 1994) and, more specifically, the ways that extracurricular literacies can influence sustainability.

Brandt's project in *Literacy as Involvement* is to repudiate what she calls the "strong text" view of literacy, which she attributes primarily to Walter J. Ong and to the earlier works of Jack Goody, David R. Olson, and Deborah Tannen. The name "strong-text" comes from a privileging of texts over the actual processes of reading and writing. Brandt states, "Literacy, from [the strong-text] perspective, is said to entail a suppression of ordinary social involvement as the basis of interpretation and a reinvestment in the logical, literal, message-focused conventions of language-on-its-own" (p. 13). In proposing "literacy as involvement" as an alternative, Brandt privileges the processes of reading and writing over texts: "From a process perspective, literacy does not take its nature from texts. Rather, texts take their natures from the ways that they are serving the acts of writing and reading" (p. 13). Instead

of dialing social involvement down, Brandt argues that message and involvement are inextricably linked: "[M]essage originates in involvement. . . .
[It] is, inescapably, an embodiment of involvement. . . . In fact, the other
partner on [Tannen's] seesaw with involvement is not message but silence
or inaction" (p. 68). Brandt's is an active, activist literacy, a literacy that does
things—social things. In *Literacy as Involvement*, she offers an instrumen-
talist view of literacy not as a tool for individual achievement but as a means
"to sustain the processes of intersubjective life" (1990, p. 103).

This vision is particularly useful for considering literacy's role in rural sustainability. Literacy levels have long been considered markers of the
health of a community. But the benefits of literacy for the survival of rural
towns have generally been described in terms of economic development
and the ways that mastering new technologies of literacy can "bring rural communities into the 21st century" and allow them to "compete on a
global stage." While reading and writing can certainly contribute in these
areas, this view of literacy-as-mastering-a-technology is a strong-text vision.
Brandt's work lets us make other kinds of claims about the role of literate
practices in sustaining rural communities.

Making these other kinds of claims is my goal as I work with literacy
data I collected in the town of Hammond, North Dakota, in 2008–9.[2] As
rural communities go, Hammond is doing pretty well, managing to keep
its population at a fairly stable level and its residents mostly employed. Local leaders assert that Hammond could easily increase its population were
there more housing stock—homes, not jobs, are the problem of the moment.
Other communities in the area are not faring so well. A short drive to Virgil,
eighteen miles away and once a hub for the region, shows empty buildings,
lifeless streets, and a diminished population—a sharp contrast with Hammond's tidy homes, large, well-kept school, and active main street.

I chose Hammond because, in addition to its success at sustaining itself,
it has unusually high levels of literate activity for a town of its size. There are
numerous book clubs, religious-study groups, an active association of local
historians, a reading incentive program for children, and a school library,
town library, and private library. While there is some direct support for
enhancing literacy-for-economic-development, in the form of a community
center that includes a free computer lab and has offered e-literacy classes
for residents, most of the literate activity in Hammond seems to be making
some other kind of contribution to the continued vitality of the community.
In what follows, I demonstrate how Brandt's *Literacy as Involvement* offers
a method for analyzing community reading and writing activities to better
understand their role in community sustainability. I also consider possible

connections between Brandt's work and that of political theorists who work on issues of social capital and associational democracy.

Bowling Together:
Reading Groups, Involvement, and Associational Democracy

On May 5, 2009, I attended one of Hammond's book-club discussion groups, this one housed in a self-described "women's clubhouse" in a defunct café in nearby Blomgren. Darla James, of Hammond, purchased the café on impulse at an auction, wanting to create a space for women to meet and do needle crafts, particularly quilting. The group also formed a book club that meets monthly and reads a variety of fiction and nonfiction. Since my visit, Darla has purchased a larger building in Hammond and moved the group there.

On the night I attended, the featured book was comedian Steve Harvey's *Act like a Lady, Think like a Man: What Men Really Think about Love, Relationships, Intimacy, and Commitment.* The participants were myself, Darla, Mae Gallmeyer, Amy Kjelland, Donna Evans, and Janet Langland—all of us married and ranging in age from our early forties to early sixties. We sat surrounded by traditional signifiers of rural femininity: The group meets in a large front room full of glass-fronted cabinets filled with colorful fabrics. An antique Singer sewing machine stands in the corner. Janet, introducing herself to me, called herself a "farmwife"—a bit of an anachronism, since she is really a farmer who is married to another farmer.

The book under discussion has a distinctly urban sensibility, springing from a segment of Harvey's radio show, syndicated primarily to hip-hop, R&B, and "urban contemporary" radio stations in the eastern and southern United States. Harvey's advice seems directed at twenty- to thirty-something African American single mothers to help them secure a good marriage to a good man. One might expect some awkwardness in discussing Harvey's message within the stark contrast of the book club's assertively "rural" surroundings, in a former small-town café filled with quilting fabric in a tiny prairie community (population sixty-two in the 2000 US Census) inhabited entirely by the descendants of northern European settlers. But, aside from briefly acknowledging the obvious differences between Harvey's target audience and ourselves in the middle of the conversation, the discussion focused on how applicable Harvey's descriptions were—and were not—to our own lives and relationships, with an emphasis on the connections we saw between his observations and advice and what we had discovered in our own lives.

We were able to have this sort of conversation, in part, because of the way Darla ran the group, exemplifying Brandt's notion that expert readers "attempt . . . to determine what an author [is] trying to do, especially what the author [is] trying to do to them[. . . .] Expert readers know how to transform a text into an episode in which they are centrally involved" (1990, pp. 89–90). Her copy marked with bookmarks, Darla called our attention continually back to the text, having preselected the segments with which she felt we could form some connection.

In *Literacy as Involvement*, Brandt "puts intersubjectivity (the mutual recognition of the presence of the other) at the core of interpretation and meaning in literate as well as oral exchanges. [. . .] Writer and reader are together in that they are, at any moment, at the same 'place' in a text, a right-here, right-now social reality of their mutual making" (pp. 30–31). When we book-club members discussed our own versions of Harvey's man-manipulating tactics and the ethics of these maneuvers, the disparity in our physical and cultural locations and Harvey's target audience periodically receded. We found that not only did Harvey have something to say to us but also that we had something to say back. Brandt writes that "literate knowledge is fundamentally . . . knowledge about how people use written-down language to sustain ad hoc involvement in order to arrive at meaning" (1990, p. 100). Over the course of two hours, we were able to sustain our involvement with a text that seemingly did not target us. (It is, after all a manual on how to catch a husband, and we had all already caught one.)

Political scientist Robert Putnam (2001) notes that Americans' participation in activities that "sustain ad hoc involvement" are on the decline.[3] Putnam's concern is that this represents a weakening of social networks and, therefore, of social capital whose value he describes as "fostering sturdy norms of reciprocity [. . . and a] society characterized by generalized reciprocity is more efficient than a distrustful society" (pp. 20–21). Hammond has many of what Putnam calls "networks of engagement"—nearly sixty different official "groups" in a town of five hundred—and they are likely a key factor in the community's continued development. But Brandt's work suggests why the fact that such a significant proportion of these groups are literacy based makes them particularly good at doing the sorts of work Putnam values.

Putnam distinguishes two categories of social capital, bonding and bridging; social scientist Michael Woolcock (2001) adds a third. Using Woolcock's definition, these are as follows.

> Bonding [. . .] denotes ties between people in similar situations, such as immediate family, close friends and neighbours[.] Bridging [. . .] encompasses more distant ties of like persons, such as loose friendships and workmates[.] Linking [. . .] reaches out to unlike people

> in dissimilar situations, such as those who are entirely outside of
> the community, thus enabling members to leverage a far wider
> range of resources than are available in the community. (pp. 13–14)

Essentially, each type is distinguished by the proximity and similarity of
the people it works to connect.

The book club described here was engaged in all three efforts, using
its discussion of the text to connect, and distinguish, the perspectives of
the people in the room, the perspectives of Harvey-as-authority-advis-
ing-young-women-on-relationships (at least two participants said that if
she had a teenage daughter or granddaughter, she would give her Harvey's
book to read, or at least the first seventy pages), the perspectives of Harvey's
audience as the text represented its mindset, values, and aspirations, and
the perspective of Harvey-as-representative-man-speaking-for-all-men.[4]
Brandt (1990) notes that this negotiation of, and ability to see, these sorts of
multiple perspectives in a text is a hallmark of advanced literacy.

> The problem for readers is not usually puzzling out the formal re-
> lationships among adjacent parts but keeping track of the compli-
> cated perspectives that are often laid side by side in a text with only
> the subtlest indications of change. As a text progresses it develops
> a certain relationship to a topic, may at the same time be report-
> ing the relationships of others to the topic, while simultaneously
> maintaining the writer-reader relationship through which the entire
> discussion is being managed. (p. 91)

Brandt shifts literacy from the work of understanding a text as a decontextualized linguistic object to the work of "keeping track of perspectives" and
relationships and understanding how to use a text to sustain involvement.
This shift allows us to attribute much more power to the kind of group
reading activity described here. Brandt explains that in a strong-text view,
"we are said to deal not directly with each other in literate exchanges but
deal, on this side or the other, with language. Alignment of consciousness
in writing and reading is not with the other but with the language on the
page" (p. 24). But in Brandt's formulation, we do indeed, in some way, "deal
directly with each other," through what she calls "the tenuous enterprises
of reading and writing, making literacy not the narrow ability to deal with
texts but *the broad ability to deal with other people as a reader or writer*" (pp.
13–14, italics mine). Brandt's view suggests that literacy work is well-suited
to creating the bonding, bridging, and linking forms of social capital that
Putnam and Woolcock describe and to doing these simultaneously.

This simultaneity is important given the potential negatives of groups that create high levels of bonding social capital. Putnam notes, "Sometimes 'social capital,' like its conceptual cousin 'community,' sounds warm and cuddly[. . . .] [T]he external effects of social capital are by no means always positive" (2001, p. 21). Other political theorists elaborate on this point: Amy Gutmann (1998) contrasts the Ku Klux Klan with Putnam's discussion of reciprocity and points out, "Among its members, the Ku Klux Klan may cultivate solidarity and trust[. . . .] But [these] cannot be characterized as fostering 'sturdy norms of generalized reciprocity.' Quite the contrary" (p. 6). Yael Tamir similarly notes, "Some associations . . . threaten social cohesion, erode the social capital, frustrate social equality and equal opportunity, and violate individual rights" (1998, p. 215). Left unchecked by mechanisms for bridging or linking, bonding-focused groups can directly destroy the very civility they are supposed to promote—"good will, fellowship, and sympathy" (Hanrihan quoted in Putnam, 2001, p. 19). As Tamir describes,

> [e]ven soccer associations, which Putnam claims are a major vehicle for democracy in Italy, can induce violent, racist, and uncontrolled behavior[. . . .] We should then be careful *not* to presuppose that the very existence of civic associations will necessarily support democracy and foster civic virtues. (1998, p. 219)

To assess the positive potential of civic groups, Gutmann focuses our attention on the "reciprocity" part of Putnam's explication of the core benefits of social capital, and it is in this notion that Brandt's depiction of expert literacy's "requir[ing] heightening awareness of how language works to sustain intersubjectivity" proves intriguing. Brandt writes, "Learning to read is learning that you are being written to, and learning to write is learning that your words are being read"—a discovery, in other words, of how literacy both reveals and enacts reciprocity (1990, p. 5). The potential is there when proficient readers, such as Darla, Amy, Mae, Donna, and Janet, get together, to bond, bridge, and link in complex ways.

Brandt repeatedly uses the phrase "the state of the we," arguing that a text "will always carry a message of involvement along with its propositional message, a message about the state of the we" (1990, pp. 63–64). But this "we," for Brandt, is not a simplistic, us-versus-them "we," as with Gutmann's example of the Klan. It is instead an explicit reflection on multiple "we's"—on the linkages of Darla, Amy, Mae, Donna, and Janet to each other but also their collective and individual connections to the women whose perspective is implied in Harvey's text, to the Harvey persona in the text, to "men" as a group represented by Harvey, and so on. At one moment in the discussion,

Darla's unique relation to Harvey's target audience emerged, as she took issue with his advice that women should introduce men they are dating to their children early in the relationship. (Darla was the only member of the group who had been divorced and begun dating her second husband while her children were young.) As Darla talked out her position, group members brought up instances they had known of single-parent women dating, and these individual contexts, and the perspectives they led to, became the topic of the talk.

Charlotte Hogg, Eileen E. Schell, and I (2007) argue in *Rural Literacies* that a key aspect in rural sustainability is promoting reflection on the complicated material, psychological, and cultural connections among urban, rural, and suburban people. This involves bonding, bridging, and, especially, linking work, and in this particular instance, we can see all three being promoted through literate activity. Any work that can desimplify "we," "us," and "them" can begin to erode the ways of thinking about the rural (in both rural and nonrural communities) that consign rural places and people to "other" status.

Writing Local History: Beyond the Archival Function

It is useful to consider a written literacy artifact to see how bonding, bridging, and linking involvements might be signaled in a text. James Rundberg's self-published history of Blomgren, North Dakota, 1910–2010, provides an interesting contrast to the literacy work done in Darla's book group, just as Blomgren contrasts sharply with Hammond. Hammond is, by local standards, thriving; Blomgren is dying. The status of Blomgren as a dying town can be seen in the proportions by which Rundberg's history engages in bonding, bridging, and linking work, and the groups whose perspectives the text is managing and privileging.

On the surface, Rundberg's text seems occupied only in bonding work, performing as an archive for descendants of the town's inhabitants. This seems logical, given Blomgren's status as a dying town; we would not expect a history of Hammond to be so predominantly archival. But Brandt (1990) cautions us not to see any text as solely an archive.

> [T]exts obviously serve archival purposes[. . . .] But it is [. . .] equally important to the understanding of literacy, that texts are the way they are because they facilitate the work of writing and reading. They are not merely the objects of outcome for writers nor the objects of consumption for readers. They are the means by which present-tense literate acts are carried out. (p. 99)

On first glance, it is hard to see how Rundberg's text could function as anything other than an archive. It is an assemblage of photographs and narratives about a seemingly disparate list of aspects of Blomgren's history, listed on a table of contents at the back of the book: "History of Blomgren, Prairie Fire, Bank, Bars . . . Beauty Shop . . . Electricity . . . Hardware Store . . . Lumber Yards . . . Telephone . . . School, Café, Radio Shop . . . Human Interest Stories . . . Baseball . . ." and the like. Were the list alphabetized, it would read similarly to the list of "What Literate Americans Know" at the end of E. D. Hirsch's *Cultural Literacy*. Yet, Brandt would have us reconsider the notion that a text such as Rundberg's functions only as a strong-text inscribing of what Blomgren-literate people know (or ought to know or might find interesting).

This is made clear when a total community outsider, such as myself, attempts to make sense of Rundberg's text. Just as with the list at the end of *Cultural Literacy*, context and relationship are everything in understanding not only what is being presented but also why it is considered to be important. As I reskimmed Hirsch's list in 2010, I had to actively banish my first mental associations with the word *Nirvana*—an image of singer Kurt Cobain—and consider both the date of the edition I was using (1988) and my knowledge of Hirsch's project and his commitments. (He does, after all, include The Beatles in his list, so it is not completely impossible that a later edition of the book might include another influential rock band.) To arrive at Hirsch's intended associations for *Nirvana*, I had to "keep . . . track of who is involved with whom, how, and when" (Brandt, 1990, p. 82) by understanding the relationships among Hirsch's commitments and the needs of Hirsch's presumed readers at the time the book was written and my own perspective on canonical and popular culture at the present time.

If the history of Blomgren is designed to "facilitate the work of writing and reading" (Brandt, 1990, p. 99) and thereby be a way for "people [to] use language to sustain the processes of intersubjective life" (Brandt, 1990, p. 103), Brandt says the evidence will be in the text itself. One of the most impressive moments in *Literacy as Involvement* is when Brandt performs a reading of a seemingly "archival" newspaper article reporting on a baseball game to reveal what she calls the "'undertalk' that speaks of a developing involvement between writer and reader-in-the-act" (1990, p. 9). She contends that to sustain the act of writing, effective writers must constantly think how the demands of their context might allow them to best communicate with their readers, and that the evidence for this is present in the texts themselves (1990, p. 37).

The history of Blomgren begins this way: "My intent of putting together [these] pictures and writings [. . .] was to preserve those memories of a town so dear to many people throughout the short time period of a hundred years of its existence. All happenings, of course, are not given, but I hope it to be enough to give one a sense of the town and the people who lived in and around it."[5] Brandt might note a number of features here that signal an involvement focus demanded by both writer and readers who participate in this text. First is the obvious metacommentary about the writing process itself, as the writer speaks about both his overall goal ("intent") for the writing and some of the writerly decisions he had to make ("all happenings . . . are not given").

Second, Brandt describes the newspaper article she analyzes as "depend[ing] for its tenses, reference, coherence, and significance largely on the assumption that readers are involved in some real time, some of which they share with [author] and [subject of story] and some of which they do not" (1990, p. 84). In the Rundberg excerpt, readers must determine their relationship to those whose "memories" are represented in the text, to the "many people" who hold the "town so dear," to the "one" who is the reader-as-envisioned-by-the-writer, and to "the people who lived in and around it." These represent four distinct, though potentially overlapping, groups. Any reader of the Blomgren history must "mak[e] sense of this . . . [by] depend[ing] heartily on keeping track of who is involved with whom, how, and when" (Brandt, 1990, p. 82).

To read Rundberg's history of Blomgren with attention to these details reveals the ways in which the production and consumption of this text might perform bonding, bridging, and linking work, addressing three groups at various removes from the town itself. One of these groups is supremely local—those who still live in Blomgren or nearby. The second is at a physical remove but with a previous or current proximate connection to the town—those who lived there once, or whose families did, or those who live nearby, such as in Hammond, and know of the existence of Blomgren (which doesn't appear on maps) but never had any relatives who were part of the Blomgren community. It is this group with whom Blomgren residents must affiliate as their own community ceases to exist; they must be absorbed into "greater Hammond" once Blomgren ceases to be. The third group is those who have no historical connection to Blomgren and live at a proximal remove from it.

The first group is the one most clearly addressed throughout the Blomgren history, primarily in Rundberg's use of indexical expressions, which Brandt describes as one type of evidence of writer/reader involvement in the shared process of literacy:

Indexical expressions essentially say "you fill it in." The reference is less to a specific set of events or things than it is to the knowledge that those events or things *are already shared* [. . .] by virtue of a common experience. (1990, p. 74)

In other words, indexical expressions perform a bonding function, identifying and cementing the "we" who is closest to a topic. A passage such as this one, from the "Plot Map [Blomgren]" section of the book, is so filled with indexical expressions that it might make very little sense to a reader who is not part of this supremely local "we":

City Hall or [Blomgren] Hall was built in 1925 by stockholders on shares. Legion bought some shares and balance donated for its ownership. Roof collapsed and was taken over by township. Legion retained storage privileges. (Better built now than ever.)

Elsewhere in the text, some acronyms are not explained, and certain names are given with the apparent assumption that readers will know the people and personalities involved. Other families who have not had descendants living in the area for a while are described in more detail.

The book's bridging function can be seen in its signals to the second group, those in the proximate area with no highly detailed knowledge of Blomgren. One of the most curious sections in the book is the one-page "History of Blomgren" right after the author's preface. It is written not by Rundberg himself but by a contributor to the volume, and it elides tremendous portions of the town's history. Of thirteen paragraphs, the first eleven deal almost entirely with events from the founding of the town in 1910 to the year 1913. The emphasis is on when key elements of the community—the initial homesteads, the post office, the grain elevator, the lumber yard—were established—what those at a remove from the town would need explained to them. The only hint in this section that Blomgren is now, essentially, a dying town, comes at the end of the next-to-last paragraph: "The school closed in 1968 and the children are now being bussed to [Maynard]." Those in the area with experience of the trajectory of dying towns will understand the import of this sentence; total outsiders might not. Rural sociologist Thomas Lyson, quoting Alan Peshkin, notes, "Viable villages generally contain schools; dying and dead ones either lack them or do not have them for long" (2002, p. 131). When the school closed, the fate of Blomgren was sealed. It doesn't need to be elaborated on further to those in the area.

It is harder to see the history of Blomgren as performing linking work between its most local audience and those who are at the farthest remove from Blomgren. There is, however, on the final page of the text, a curious juxtaposition of images and captions that suggests a complex relationship of an "us" to a truly outsider "them." A collage of four black-and-white photos takes up most of the page. At the top are images of a neatly kept local house in summer and another tidy home and outbuilding in deep snow. At the bottom are two smaller photos of small, prefabricated, unadorned buildings. There are two paragraphs of accompanying text.

> In the spring of the year one can walk by the home of [Nora Johansen] and [Marie Jensen] and smell the new lilac bush flowers giving off their interesting fragrance. Or in the winter one can walk in the deep snow accumulated and admire the home of [Steven Lindsay] and [Ellen Slane]. Either day can be an enjoyable one in [Blomgren].
>
> At the bottom of the page are some very new additions to the town of [Blomgren]. Owned by some out of state people, these "cabins" (as some locals call them) are used and enjoyed as vacation spots whether it is to just relax or to enjoy the fishing and hunting of North Dakota.

What might this closing page say about "the complicated perspectives that are often laid side by side in a text with only the subtlest indications of change" (Brandt, 1990, p. 91)? One option is the insider/outsider perspective that sees the world in terms of us versus them—we who live here and smell the lilacs and walk in the snow, who have names and personalities and stories that have been described in this book, versus "some out of state people"—the sort of dangerous bonding isolationism that Gutmann, Tamir, and others deplore. Another interpretation splits the "us," noting the phrase "'cabins' (as some locals call them)." Here the author divides the locals into those who call the out-of-staters' lodgings "cabins" and those who have some other name for or way of thinking about them. The use of "some" and the quotes around "cabins" suggest that the author is not a member of this group, and the entire phrase implies that locals are split on their opinion of the presence of these outsiders in the community. Last, the phrase "enjoy the hunting and fishing of North Dakota," the final one of the entire volume, suggests a link between locals and out-of-staters who both appreciate the local environment for the hunting and fishing it offers. As wetlands have lessened in other parts of the country, this region has seen an increase in hunting and fishing tourism and the resultant bump to local economies. This final phrase suggests that perhaps a future in which the cabins of out-of-staters gradually coexist with, outnumber, or even replace the tidy homes in the other two photos might not be an entirely terrible thing. It would, at least, "leverage a far wider range of resources than are available in the community," as Woolcock attributes to linking forms of social capital (2001, p. 14).

Linking People and Places

I wish to return to Putnam's caveat (quoting Xavier de Sousa Briggs) that we not see associational activity solely through "a treacly sweet, 'kumbaya' [lens] of social capital" (2001, p. 21). In considering rural communities, this edges far too close to stereotypical, nostalgic depictions of rural neighborliness versus urban selfishness; such depictions suggest that rural communities must survive by relying on their bootstrapping heritage to "pull together" and somehow be self-sustaining. This implies that activities that bond rural people only to themselves and their discrete local places should be prioritized in working for rural sustainability.

On the other hand, attempting to align rural people with urban and suburban norms also poses a danger to rural sustainability. In *Membership and Morals: The Personal Uses of Pluralism in America*, Nancy L. Rosenblum argues that some associational groups "reinforce rather than replace individualist norms. These groups facilitate mobility [and] loosening of familial and community attachments" (1998, p. 360). She uses addiction support groups as her example, arguing that they can loosen local attachments because they focus on helping individuals conquer personal difficulties (rather than dealing with communal issues) and emphasize interactions and structures (e.g., the twelve steps) that remain the same regardless of a particular group's local context. In other words, such groups, in their similarity, effectively "de-place" the potential of group activity to create specific bonds among people and places. It would not be a stretch to say that Rosenblum sees these kinds of groups as being "associated with no particular place, no particular dialect, no particular social groups, except for those who can forsake commitment to locale, dialect, and clan to cross over to the universal, standard ways," as Brandt argues that strong-text proponents see literacy (1990, p. 116).

Rural communities who wish to sustain themselves in the current economic, political, and cultural climates must enact a delicate balance, stemming outmigration by solidifying local identity and pride-of-place while not isolating themselves from the rural, urban, and suburban communities with which they must be interdependent. They must bond, bridge, and link. They must push back against the kinds of de-placing Rosenblum describes, retaining a distinct local identity while "reaching out to unlike people [. . .] to leverage a far wider range of resources than are available in the community" (Woolcock, 2001, pp. 13–14). *Literacy as Involvement* suggests that literate activity may give groups a way to achieve this balance. If literacy is inherently about "sustaining the processes of intersubjective life" (Brandt, 1990, p. 103), distinctive, home-grown literacy groups and activities, such as the ones described here, have great promise for rural sustainability.

Notes

1. *Literacy as Involvement* has had some influence in K–college pedagogy, literary analysis, and community literacy. See, for example, Doty, 2002; Royer, 1994; Grabill, 2001.

2. All place and personal names are pseudonyms.

3. There is much critique of Putnam's (2001) assumptions in *Bowling Alone* and social capital theory in general; these are categorized by Michael Woolcock (2010) as "social capital spans too many units of analysis; inadequately engages with questions of power and inequality; uses tautological reasoning; fails to accommodate the fact that harmful consequences can flow from cooperation and trust; shoehorns distinctive social concepts into economic neo-liberal theory; and is unclear as to whether it is a cause or effect." Labeling social capital an "essentially contested concept," Woolcock notes that such concepts still "do their work through the fruitful public debates they facilitate, not the clean, unambiguous, consensual path they chart" (p. 482). Concurring with Woolcock, I find the interpretive frame of social capital and the bonding/bridging/linking distinction useful to explicate my data.

4. It is unclear what actual experiences the book-club participants had with the urban African American women who make up Harvey's audience and to what extent each person's sense of Harvey's audience was based on actual relationships or contacts with urban African American women and to what extent each participant had to invent or construct her notion of Harvey's audience based on general cultural knowledge, assumptions, and Harvey's text itself.

5. *Blomgren* is a pseudonym, and the original text does not have page numbers, so no page numbers are cited here.

References

Bizzell, Patricia. 1991. "Professing Literacy: A Review Essay." *Journal of Advanced Composition, 11*(2), 315–22.

Brandt, Deborah. 1990. *Literacy as Involvement: The Acts of Readers, Writers, and Texts.* Carbondale: Southern Illinois University Press.

Donehower, Kim, Charlotte Hogg, and Eileen. E. Schell. 2007. *Rural Literacies.* Carbondale: Southern Illinois University Press.

Doty, Tim. 2002, November 21–24. "What's Wrong with Papa Bear's Chair: Toward Literacy as Involvement in the Second Grade Classroom." Paper presented at the Annual Meeting of the National Communication Association, New Orleans, Louisiana.

Gere, Anne Ruggles. 1994. "Kitchen Tables and Rented Rooms: The Extracurriculum of Composition." *College Composition and Communication, 45,* 75–92.

Grabill, Jeffrey T. 2001. *Community Literacy Programs and the Politics of Change.* Albany: State University of New York Press.

Gutmann, Amy. 1998. "Freedom of Association: An Introductory Essay." In *Freedom of Association,* edited by Gutmann, 3–32. Princeton: Princeton University Press.

Hirsch, E. D. 1988. *Cultural Literacy: What Every American Needs to Know.* New York: Vintage.

Lyson, Thomas A. 2002. "What Does a School Mean to a Community? Assessing the Social and Economic Benefits of Schools to Rural Villages in New York." *Journal of Research in Rural Education, 17,* 131–37.

Minami, Masahiko. 1991 "Book Notes: *Literacy as Involvement: The Acts of Readers, Writers, and Texts*." *Harvard Educational Review, 61*, 232–33.

Putnam, Robert. 2001. *Bowling Alone: The Collapse and Revival of American Community*. New York: Simon and Schuster.

Rosenblum, Nancy L. 1998. *Membership and Morals: The Personal Uses of Pluralism in America*. Princeton: Princeton University Press.

Royer, Daniel J. 1994. "The Process of Literacy as Communal Involvement in the Narratives of Frederick Douglass." *African American Review, 28*(3), 363–74.

Tamir, Yael. 1998. "Revisiting the Civic Sphere." In *Freedom of Association*, edited by Amy Gutmann, 214–38. Princeton: Princeton University Press.

Woolcock, Michael. 2001. "The Place of Social Capital in Understanding Social and Economic Outcomes." *Isuma: Canadian Journal of Policy Research, 2*, 1–17.

———. 2010. "The Rise and Routinization of Social Capital, 1988–2008." *Annual Review of Political Science, 13*, 469–87.

7. Toward a Labor Economy of Literacy: Academic Frictions

Bruce Horner and Min-Zhan Lu

Increases, and demands for further increases, in the volume and velocity of global traffic in peoples, goods, services, capital, and information are forcing literacy scholars and teachers to revise their models of literacy and literacy instruction. In this chapter, we review the ways in which two dominant models of literacy now circulating address the challenges such traffic poses: a "foundationalist" model of literacy and an "accommodationist" model. These two models, we argue, treat language difference and the labor of communicative activity in ways that preclude the possibility, and ignore the reality, of the transformation of language(s) and knowledge that recent scholarship on translingual literacies, English as a lingua franca (hereafter, ELF), and world Englishes demonstrates to be the case.[1] Drawing on that scholarship, we argue instead for a model of literacy as translation that highlights the necessity and contribution of the labor of readers and writers for the production and transformation of meaning. We identify this labor with the concept of "friction" introduced by Anna Lowenhaupt Tsing (2005) as a corrective to dominant conceptions of the global "flow" of capital. Tsing's concept of friction reintroduces agency to language users by highlighting the necessity of their labor to the (re)construction of meaning out of language in reading and writing. By treating translation as a constant and inevitable feature of language use, such a model of literacy recognizes and makes visible the necessity of readers' and writers' concrete labor to the production of meaning and hence to the economy of reading, writing, and knowing, the friction necessary to the work of academic literacy.

We begin by identifying and comparing the language assumptions, curricula, and pedagogies of two dominant models of "academic literacy" circulating within composition studies, the field most directly charged with producing such literacy. A comparison of these models shows that despite significant differences in their assumptions and in the curricula and pedagogies to which they lead, they are aligned in their valuation of communicative efficiency and language commodification and, concomitantly, their elision of readers' and writers' labor in the production of meaning. This alignment, we show, supports a technocratic view of academic literacy aligned with fast capitalist, neoliberal ideology's valuation of speed in the "flow" of information, goods, services, and capital. Within that ideology, difference is treated as a problem to be overcome rather than a condition for meaning insofar as it impedes the speed of that "flow."

The Foundationalist Model of Academic Literacy

What we are terming the "foundationalist" model treats academic literacy as a universal, uniform, and fixed set of linguistic and notational conventions and procedures that writers are to follow. Adherence to these is, in this model, the necessary and sufficient means by which thought is to be represented and communicated. Conversely, any deviation from these is linked to the production of reader confusion (associated with the writer's confusion represented by such deviation) and thus to be eliminated. Language difference thus constitutes a problem to be overcome through adherence to universal conventions and practices of academic literacy.[2] Agency is located precisely in such adherence, and hence in the conventions and practices themselves, rather than in writers or readers. Power relations operating among readers and writers are denied; instead, literacy is deemed a politically neutral technology by which meaning is transmitted, and any difficulties experienced are thus treated as technical failures.

Those accepting this model of academic literacy adopt a pedagogy of transmission. Whether through direct instruction or apprenticeship/immersion, that pedagogy aims to transmit the conventions and practices thought to be universal attributes of academic literacy to students, and to eradicate deviations from these. In this model, writing and reading are conceived of entirely in terms of meaning transmission, smooth or interrupted. While it is recognized that there is a process whereby students develop fluency with academic literacy, it is assumed, drawing from cognitivist theories of language acquisition, that this process is uniform and linear in direction.[3] This approach takes curricular form in requirements for all college students to pass a single course or set of courses to prepare them to meet the demands for academic literacy in the rest of their subsequent academic careers. Although there are few advocates for this view of academic literacy in current literacy and composition scholarship, it inheres in the design of many composition curricula and is prevalent in the mass media and among academics outside the fields of composition and literacy studies, hence our inclusion of it in this chapter. Such curricula purport to provide students the literacy skills—including knowledge of how to produce a specific set of linguistic, generic, and notational forms—thought to be necessary, adequate, and required in academic reading and writing generally.[4]

The Accommodationist Model of Academic Literacy

The accommodationist model of academic literacy differs from the foundationalist model in its recognition of the presence of a plurality of different sets of linguistic and notational conventions and procedures for academic reading and writing, each associated with a different discipline, often deemed "practices." Deborah Brandt (2001, p. 9) has observed of this model that it is, in fact, now common "to consider literacy in the plural, as sets of social practices, diverse routines that must be understood in relationship to the particular social aims and habits associated with their context of use." While this model rejects the foundationalist notion of a single, universal set of such conventions and procedures, it retains that model's assumption of the static character of each such set. Thus, it retains a transmission model of academic literacy and literacy pedagogy. Nonetheless, its recognition of a plurality of different sets of linguistic and notational conventions and procedures requires that linguistic and notational differences are no longer identified strictly with technical failure, as in the foundational model. Instead, while some such differences may be identified as instances of technical failure, others are seen as evidence of the existence of a plurality of distinct disciplinary literacy practices and hence to be accommodated through code-switching: the need for writers (and their readers) to "switch" from one code and to another, depending on the specific discipline within which the communicative act is located. Errors are typically attributed to "interference," imagined as the failure to "switch" to the code appropriate to that given discipline.[5] As in the foundationalist model, power relations are typically occluded: What is "appropriate" to any particular discipline is not questioned.[6] When power relations are acknowledged, they are viewed as fixed sets of relations about which there is nothing to be done. Agency itself is located in the specific sets of conventions and procedures identified with particular disciplines. Hence, in this model, to "empower" students requires transmitting these conventions and procedures to students (see, for example, Delpit, 1988, 1993).

In the accommodationist model, the task of the writer and reader is to identify the specific set of conventions and procedures appropriate to the discipline within which one is located. The set defining each discipline is thus to be "accommodated" rather than overwritten or challenged (or eradicated). Conflicts across and power relations sustaining hierarchies and divisions among the disciplines remain unexamined. The pedagogy is a pedagogy of transmission: The sets of linguistic and notational conventions and procedures for reading and writing of different disciplines are transmitted, whether through direct instruction or apprenticeship in a "community of practice," with the aim of enabling students to achieve mastery of one or more of these sets of types of academic literacy. Academic literacy is thus pluralized (to academic literacies), and the aim of instruction, ideally, is to add one or more of these to any literacies students may be identified as having already mastered. The most common curricular form for this model is an array of "writing in the disciplines" courses, each of which transmits the academic literacy conventions of a specific discipline to students pursuing that discipline.[7] But efforts to accommodate disciplinary differences can take other forms, including individual, but mandatory, courses to introduce all students to a range of types of literacy practices associated with particular disciplines or writing courses "linked" to work in specific disciplines.

Despite their differences, both the foundationalist and accommodationist models of academic literacy accept a reified conception of academic literacy, hence their commitment to a transmission model for literacy itself and literacy pedagogy: Academic literacy is conceived as either a fixed entity, or a fixed set of entities, to be used and transmitted. Difficulties are seen to arise from failure to use academic literacy or the appropriate sort for a given occasion. The task of the writer and reader is simply to use the given set of conventions and practices—the possibility of changing or challenging these is not considered (Canagarajah, 2002, p. 35). The two models are further aligned in excluding the possibility of communication across differences. Instead, communication is imagined as operating only within a homogeneous community ("of practice"), whether that community is envisioned as a single monolithic "academic" or "literacy" "club" or the community of fellow members of a specific academic discipline (Harris, 1997). The task of pedagogy is to somehow bring students into that community, whether through a single course or set of courses. Doing so, it is believed, will ensure efficiency in communication through the elimination of any potential differences.

There is a telling parallel here to approaches in US language education to language differences. In an explicitly monolingualist and specifically English-only approach, English language learners are expected to shed any previous language abilities in exchange for learning English, which itself is imagined as a discrete, uniform, and static code, the "target" language. English alone, it is thought, is or ought to be the universal language of communication within the nation state, at least in the "public" sphere. (Of course, equivalent approaches for other languages obtain elsewhere.) The

dominant "multilingual" approach posed as an alternative, while acknowledging the legitimacy for purposes of communication of multiple languages,
retains a monolingualist view of all languages as discrete, uniform, and
static entities. That is to say, despite the explicit allegiance of that approach
to multilingualism, it effectively offers simply to pluralize monolingual
approaches to language, with each language (or language variety) assigned
a specific and discrete place and purpose, and language users expected
to switch to the language deemed appropriate to that place and purpose.
This "silo" model of multilingualism, like the accommodationist model of
academic literacy, accommodates difference in language practices through
eliding what critics have termed "traffic" between sites and among people
and practices, whereby people travel among various sites and exchange,
mix, intermingle, and transform language practices available (Kramsch,
2006; Pennycook, 2008). We attribute the domination of this silo model of
multilingualism to its alignment with monolingualist tenets.

Translation Models of Literacy: Residual and Emergent

A translation model of literacy is distinct from both foundationalist and
accommodationist models in its attention to communication across differences. In these, communication across language and literacy differences—
that is, "traffic"—is, in fact, not only acknowledged but taken as the norm.
Thus, in place of a model of discrete linguistic monolingual "utopias," we
have Pratt's (1987) linguistics of contact among and across differences. At
issue for those pursuing a translation model of literacy are the questions of
who, or what, is to be translated, how, under what conditions, to what ends,
and with what effects. However, residual notions of language and literacy
as reified, and the concomitant disposition of accommodation to these notions, pose a challenge to those attempting to address these questions. As
Pennycook (2008, p. 40) has warned, debates on language difference typically "leave uncontested . . . how we can understand diversity outside those
very frameworks that are part of the problem," for example, the concept of
languages as discrete, objectifiable entities.

    To work past and through models of translation that seem to leave such
frameworks uncontested, we begin our discussion of translation models of
literacy by reviewing those models that seem to manifest just such frameworks: models calling for a "neutral" set of language and literacy practices
for global communication across differences, models for code-switching
between practices still seen as discrete, and models that fetishize code-meshing. Against all of these, we pose a translation model of all language use
as inevitably involving the concrete labor of translation across differences,

with the work of translation in cross-language practices representing simply more readily visible instances of work necessary to all communication.

"Neutral" Models of Translation Literacy

Arguments for a separate, "neutral" set of language practices assume both that users' language affiliations are exclusively monolingual and discrete and that a single, neutral set of language practices might, nonetheless, be abstracted for use across these.[8] In the most common variant of this type of argument, English itself is identified as the universal and global lingua franca of communication, at least for purposes of commerce. This effort is best exemplified by attempts to codify a discrete form of ELF for use by those for whom English is not a primary language.

These efforts have, however, run into serious difficulties. In the case of ELF, researchers have discovered that "[ELF] is intersubjectively constructed in each specific context of interaction . . . negotiated by each set of speakers for their purposes" and thus "never achieves a stable or even standardized form" (Meierkord, 2004, p. 129; quoted in Canagarajah, 2007, p. 925). Indeed, as Friedrich and Matsuda (2010) have observed, ELF is best thought of not as a form at all but, rather, as a function. Thus, while it might be possible to abstract and teach a grammar and lexicon from a particular instance of ELF, that very abstraction would work against students' ability to participate meaningfully in the multilingual languaging that continually reconstitutes "ELF." As Nicos Sifakis explains,

> [V]ariability in the communication between different N[on] N[native] S[peaker]s renders any attempt at codifying the various uses of English in [ELF] situations difficult, since we would have to know in advance many things that are situation-specific and user-dependent. (2006, p. 155)

In the case of "general writing skills instruction," it has, likewise, been difficult to identify what these might be; it turns out that writing practices posited as "general" are, in fact, typically those general only to participants of particular variants of specific disciplines (see, for example, Miller and Cripps, 2005, pp. 130–31).

Models of Translation as "Code-Switching" or "Code-Meshing"

Models of translation as code-switching forgo the attempt at forging a common, "neutral" code for all to learn in interacting across differences. They, nonetheless, reiterate reifications of language practices by positing these as discrete "codes" that writers might switch to and from. As we discussed earlier, this model either obscures the power relations dictating which code a writer is to use or treats these as fait accomplis (Horner and Lu, 2007). But this model is also problematic in its assumptions about the effect of translation. First, while it does not pose a separate, "neutral" code for use in communication across differences, it does assume that in switching from code to code, the meaning will not be transformed; hence neutrality is ascribed to the codes themselves in their effect on meaning. Second, it assumes that the process of switching from code to code does not alter the codes themselves, which are seen as stable, discrete, and uniform: That is to say, the concrete labor entailed in switching is not seen as in itself contributing to meaning through revisions of "encoding" practices but simply as a means of accommodating its transmission, a purely "technical" or "mechanical" matter. Hence the question posed for writing instructors adopting this model is limited to whether or not students are to be allowed to write in one code/language or another (see, for example, Bean et al., 2003), a question to which the answer will always be yes insofar as no change to the codes or their meaning is imagined to arise. Occluded from these considerations are both the labor of such translation and the labor of (re)writing (in) "code." In other words, this model of translation, like the model of cross-language work through a "neutral" code, is one claiming to be "friction free."

Recent efforts to combat these limitations of code-switching as a model for translation have posed "code-meshing" as an alternative (Canagarajah, 2009; Young, 2009). Code-meshing highlights the agency of language users to alter both the "codes" employed and the meanings communicated through "meshing." It thus works against residual notions of language and literacy practices as discrete and static entities and against the practice of attributing agency to these entities in themselves rather than to the writers using them. Writers are seen as not only "shuttling" between languages but also revising these: They compose not just texts but the languages of these texts out of whatever linguistic and literacy resources are available (Canagarajah, 2006a, 2006b, 2009; Lu, 2006). Further, those adopting code-meshing as a model reject the monolingualist treatment of individuals and social groups affiliated with specific language "codes" as being themselves discrete, uniform, and in hierarchical relation to one another (Young, 2004, 2009). Instead, they recognize both the fact and necessity of code meshing in language use: the "traffic" in languages and among and even within language users.

Despite these advances, those adopting code-meshing as a model have had to confront the power of residual notions of language and literacy practices as discrete, static, and uniform to render code-meshing itself a discrete set of practices (known as "code-meshing") that writers have the option of choosing to employ or not. In this regressive step, the option of code-meshing, so defined, becomes one limited to those writers and speakers recognized as multilingual in the terms set by "additive" accommodationist models of language and literacy. That is to say, those attempting to advance a "code-meshing" model have had to confront the temptation to fetishize code-meshing as itself a finite and stable practice available only to those in possession of what are recognized as multiple "codes," who can then produce recognizable "meshings" of these for aesthetic or other purposes. Through such fetishizing, recognition of the agency (and the labor) involved in putting "codes" to various uses is bestowed on a very limited number of writers, just as the legitimacy of "experimental" or "alternative" forms of literacy is recognized as the purview only of those already assigned the status of being "Authors" (Lu, 1994).

The telling parallel here can be found in debate on so-called alternative or hybrid discourse as something to be pursued in composition. We have argued elsewhere that this tends to the hypostatizing of hybridity itself (Horner and Lu, 2007). As Patricia Bizzell has warned, the concept of a "hybrid" discourse "relies on a reified notion of academic discourse that obscures institutional dynamics of power" and suggests, inaccurately, that "traditional academic discourse [is] a fixed and unchanging entity" (2002, p. 3). The hypostatizing of hybrid discourse thus risks making a fetish out of what is simply recognized as, in fact, hybrid and thereby reinforces belief in the "purity" of other discourses. In this way, discourse hybridity, like the "meshing" of codes, may come to be pursued for its own sake rather than as a strategy enacted in the context of particular needs, desires, and conditions. This tends toward the aestheticization of discoursal forms that ignores the contextual and contingent understanding of what is "hybrid" and not.

Further, the hypostatizing of hybrid discourse leaves reified notions of academic and other mainstream discourse unchallenged. That is to say, in seeking to insert or "mesh" elements of other discourses into mainstream discourse, the always already "mixed" character of the privileged, mainstream varieties goes unrecognized, contributing to support their status as "pure." Alternatively, it would seem necessary to interrogate both that discourse "marked" as alternative and also discourse that would not appear to be so marked to demonstrate the "hybrid" linguistic (and other) character of mainstream discourse rendered invisible through canonization.

Toward an Emerging Model of (All) Literacy as Translation

In terms of writing, we can combat such fetishizing by recognizing that any and every use of every and any language(s) is always already an act of translation, and any "language" the abstraction of a mesh (Pennycook, 2008). That is to say, rather than conceiving of writers engaged in the act of meshing otherwise discrete codes, the "meshed" character of the "codes" themselves can be assumed. This should have as a consequence the de-exoticization of meshing by granting the labor of ordinary writers in any act of writing: Writers do not simply write "in" a particular language, code, or discourse but, rather, write (or rewrite) the language in every act of writing. To claim otherwise is to occlude language users' concrete labor with and on language and the necessity of the contribution of their labor to sustaining language and literacy. Concomitantly, to recognize writers' labor is to recognize all writing as involving translation insofar as language is the "process of meaning-construction" (Spivak, 1993, p. 179). For, as George Steiner has observed, "inside or between languages, human communication equals translation. A study of translation is a study of language" (1975, p. 47; quoted in Pennycook, 2008, p. 40). Thus, as Pennycook observes, "communication between languages presents not so much the central process of translation but rather a special case: all communication involves translation," including communication "within" "the same" language (2008, p. 40).

To recognize the necessity of translation even within "the same" language is to recognize the fact of semiodiversity, the multiplicity of meanings, the complexity of choosing from among them, and the inevitability of the necessity of the labor of doing so in reading and writing—that is to say, the "friction" of reworking meaning in translation that conduit/transmission models of language and literacy take to be an interference in, rather than integral to, the communicative act. We take the notion of friction from Tsing (2005), who introduces it to name and account for the interactions by which "cultures are continually co-produced . . . the awkward, unequal, unstable, and creative qualities of interconnection across differences" (p. 4). In contrast to narratives of global mobility as an unimpeded "flow of goods, ideas, money, and people" proceeding "entirely without friction," she notes, "In fact, motion does not proceed this way at all" (p. 5).

In place of such a model of movement, she reminds us of the importance of interaction in defining movement, cultural form, and agency:

> Friction is not just about slowing things down. Friction is required to keep global power in motion. It shows us . . . where the rubber meets the road. . . . Roads create pathways that make motion easier and more efficient, but in doing so they limit where we go. (2005, p. 6)

As Tsing subsequently explains, as universals "travel across difference," they "are charged and changed by their travels" (2005, p. 8). This charging and changing is the work of translation. As Michael Cronin (2003) observes, contrary to facile (if common) notions of translation, translation involves, in fact, "the effort, the difficulty and, above all else, the time required to establish and maintain linguistic (and by definition, cultural) connections" (p. 49). Attempts at translation that overlook these lead, Cronin warns, not to transmitting knowledge but simply to the "physical transfer of information" (p. 20). In short, attempts to overlook such effort ultimately reduce travel to what Michael Byram (1997), in a study of intercultural communicative competence, critiques as "tourism," distinct from "sojourns." As Byram observes, whereas "the tourist hopes . . . that what they have traveled to see will not change . . . and . . . that their own way of living will be enriched but not fundamentally changed," the sojourner "produces effects on a society which challenges its unquestioned and unconscious beliefs, behaviours, and meanings, and whose own beliefs, behaviours and meanings are in turn challenged and expected to change" (p. 1). While the image of travel as tourism is dominant in considerations of cross-language and cross-cultural movement,

> [t]he experience of the sojourner is potentially more valuable . . . both for societies and for individuals, since the state of the world is such that societies and individuals have no alternative but proximity, interaction and relationship as the conditions of existence. (1997, p. 2)

That is to say, however challenging and labor-intensive the work of the sojourner, such work is both inevitable and necessary in life. Tourism, alternatively, remains the "friction-free" fantasy, which inevitably eludes wannabe tourists' grasp as their travels confront them with difference.

Labor in Translation Literacy

We can see both the myth of friction-less, labor-free translation literacy and the contradiction to that myth in Brandt's recent account of the experience of "workaday" writers (2009). As Brandt notes, the courts have decided that unlike literary authors, these writers—people who are required to write for, and as, their employers or clients—are "willingly coerced [sic] corporate voices" who, at least officially, "don't write as themselves at work," "are not individually responsible for what they are paid to say," and "[c]onsequently, . . . don't really mean what they say [and in fact] . . . can't really mean what they say" (2009, p. 166). In theory, then, (they and) their writing should serve as a friction-less conduit for and translation of their employer's ideas, beliefs, positions, and so on. For example, a municipal employee whom Brandt interviews describes his/her writing as an act of ventriloquism:

I have to convey the [agency's] policy. It's not me. It's not my policy. It's not my position. It's the [agency's] position. . . . It's not my role to give my personal opinion. I have to convey the policy of the city. (2009, p. 175)

This ventriloquism is in accord with legal strictures. Brandt explains, "Under law, those who employ people to write for them take full responsibility and full credit for the work produced" (2009, p. 177).

But friction emerges nonetheless. As Brandt observes further, "for those tasked with word production, neither credit nor responsibility seems able to be completely lent nor relinquished" (2009, p. 177). There is a "stickiness" to the translation of self, a friction, that seems impossible to avoid, what Brandt describes as an "inevitable intermingling of self and corporate interest" in which "adding, borrowing, and lending (of power, knowledge, integrity, experience, selfhood and efficacy) are major elements" (2009, p. 177). As another of Brandt's interviewees acknowledges, though s/he "really can't share my certain opinions on certain things . . . I have to stick between certain guidelines. . . . But I believe I am in there" (quoted in 2009, p. 176). This intermingling can lead the writers to a sense of satisfaction and pride in the writing, despite the fact that it is (legally) not "theirs," though it can also lead to conflicts and threaten their sense of integrity (again, despite the fact that the writing remains legally not "theirs").

Officially, of course, no such intermingling is to take place. As Brandt observes, "[workaday writing's] creators are considered interchangeable (their personalities being irrelevant to the creation)," the value of what they produce "utterly instrumental": In fact, "[o]nce a piece of writing does its immediate job (conveys a message, wins a case, implements a policy, seals a deal, etc.) it has no residual value to worry about or protect" (2009, p. 178). This is the technocratic perspective par excellence on writing, translation, and literacy more generally that dominates the present-day teaching of writing, the same technocratic perspective that demands, and expects, literacy to constitute smooth, friction-free translation, a complete and unadulterated "transfer" of the "message" from writer to reader, speaker to listener through language. Indeed, the continuing power of foundationalist and accommodationist models of academic literacy and their residual presence in at least some of what we have termed "translation" models of literacy, despite what we have identified as their monolingualist roots and despite their failure to address communication across differences in language, can be understood as manifestations of not just conceptual inertia but also of an ideology of technocratic literacy aligned with neoliberalism. It is an ideology that views labor and difference as a cost of rather than a contributor to, a drag on rather than a means of, communication and the construction of knowledge, something to be overcome rather than a necessity.[9]

But literacy, Brandt observes elsewhere, "is often jumping its tracks" (2001, p. 9). She introduces the concept of literacy sponsors as a way to "connect literacy as an individual development to literacy as an economic development," a connection she identifies as pressing in light of the "tightening associations between literacy skill and social viability, the breakneck pace of change in communications technology, persistent inequities in access and reward" (2001, p. 19). Each of the three models of academic literacy discussed in this chapter can be understood as a competing response, at the level of individual literacy development, to shifts in the tasks assigned literacy consequent on economic developments. And if, as Cronin has argued, translation is "not simply a by-product of globalization but is a constituent, integral part of how the phenomenon both operates and makes sense of itself" (2003, p. 34), then competing models of literacy as translation, as well as other, competing models of literacy, will shape both the operation and understanding of all that attends globalization, economic and otherwise.

Brandt identifies sponsors of literacy broadly as "any agents, local or distant, concrete or abstract, who enable, support, teach, and model, as well as recruit, regulate, suppress, or withhold, literacy—and gain advantage by it in some way." They are "delivery systems for the economies of literacy, the means by which these forces present themselves to—and through—individual learners" (2001, p. 19). Despite, or rather because of, its breadth, her definition of literacy sponsors is helpful in allowing us to consider the academic site itself for its potential uses as well as threats to the kinds of literacy and beliefs about literacy that the academic site, and we as its agents, might sponsor. Against technocratic notions of literacy, we can call on our and our students' everyday experiences of "friction" in reading and writing to posit and pursue an alternative—the normality of friction itself and the labor it entails, often derided and denigrated as confusion, difficulty, misunderstanding, even opacity.[10] To do so would be to grant students agency as contributors, through their labor in reading and writing, to the production of meaning and thus knowledge. As we have argued, this would require replacing a transmission model of both pedagogy and writing with a model of both as translation. In writing classes informed by such a model, the friction and labor of meaning construction arising from difference would be recognized as the cultural norm, a resource for knowledge production requiring due consideration in the ways time, and occasions for rereading and rewriting, are allocated in the design of coursework.[11]

Despite the statistical normality of such experiences of difference, they are all too often viewed as obstacles, evidence of the inabilities of specific readers or writers to "process" what should, it is believed, be effortless, friction-less, labor-free.[12] Viewed, however, as normal, these experiences—ordinarily derided as unnecessary confusion and difficulty, even incomprehension—can be viewed as resources for examining the actual and necessary labor of literacy as translation, a laborious working across and through differences, rendering our students' experiences as manifestations of their normality and positioning to contribute to knowledge.

While there are powerful voices demanding a continuation of literacy as "foundational" in the sense of representing a universal and monolithic set of practices with language, and other voices, also powerful, offering accommodation of a plurality of literacy practices in ways that allow for continuation of status quo relations and the denial of the labor and contribution to meaning and knowledge inherent in the everyday writing of everyday writers, there is also a long, even proud, if sometimes neglected tradition within the academy of valuing "difficulty," a tradition we find often expressed in teachers' injunctions to students to "complicate" their perspectives, arguments, interpretations by consideration of alternative perspectives, arguments, interpretations, and even language practices (as in the common requirement, however moribund in practice, that students have at least some familiarity with a second language). In our work as academics, we can sponsor—"enable, support, teach, and model"—in our courses an alternative model of writing that values experiences of difficulty, confusion, and difference as both inevitable and as resources upon which writers and readers, through their labor, create and re-create meaning. We can sponsor a literacy in which the labor of translation is always already a visible and recognized part of and necessary contributor to the academic economy of reading, writing, and knowing, the friction necessary to the conduct of academic work.

Notes

1. The scholarly literature on these is vast and growing. For a sampling, see Horner et al. (2011); Rubdy and Saraceni (2006); Mauranen and Ranta (2009); Makoni and Pennycook (2007). For analyses of language difference in composition on which we draw here, see Canagarajah (2009); Horner and Lu (2007); Horner, Lu and Matsuda (2010); Horner and Trimbur (2002); Lu (2009).

2. This is, of course, aligned with what Brian Street (1985) has identified as an "autonomous" model of literacy conflating a particular set of literacy practices, for example, academic "essayist" literacy, with all literacy.

3. On the cognitivist (aka "telementational") model of language acquisition, see Firth and Wagner (2007).

4. Compare Petraglia's (1995) notion of "General Writing Skills Instruction" (GWSI).

5. In this sense, it is opposed to what linguists characterize as code-switching, that is, the introduction of terms associated with different languages within the same utterance (see Klimpfinger, 2009).

6. On the politics of invoking "appropriateness," see Fairclough (1992). Compare Canagarajah's discussion of the approach to academic discourse informed by contrastive rhetoric. 2002, pp. 34–36.

7. An alternative curricular form parallel to this is the Sydney "genre" school of literacy instruction aiming to empower students through giving them access to specific genres (see Luke, 1998).

8. Compare the New London Group's call for states, schools, and literacy pedagogy to become "neutral arbiters of difference." 2000, p. 15.

9. On the demand for "zero drag" labor, see Hochschild (1997), quoted in Bauman (2007, p. 9).

10. On valuing opacity and miscomprehension, see Bernabé, Chamoiseau, and Confiant (1989, pp. 52, 113); Prendergast (2010).

11. For accounts of pedagogies emphasizing such difficulty, see Bartholomae and Petrosky (1986); Horner (2000); Lu (1994); Lu (2009); Miller (1994); Salvatori (1996).

12. For a recent review of this myth and its prevalence in composition teaching, see Barnard (2010).

References

Barnard, Ian. 2010. "The Ruse of Clarity." *College Composition and Communication,* 61(3), 434–51.

Bartholomae, David, and Anthony R. Petrosky. 1986. *Facts, Artifacts, and Counterfacts: Theory and Method for a Reading and Writing Course.* Upper Montclair, NJ: Boynton/Cook.

Bauman, Zygmunt. 2007. *Consuming Life.* Cambridge, England: Polity.

Bean, Janet, Robert Eddy, Rhonda Grego, Patricia Irvine, Ellie Kutz, Paul Kei Matsuda, Maryann Cucchiara, Peter Elbow, Rich Haswell, Eileen Kennedy, and Al Lehner. 2003. "Should We Invite Students to Write in Home Languages? Complicating the Yes/No Debate." *Composition Studies, 31*(1), 25–42.

Bernabé, Jean, Patrick Chamoiseau, and Raphaël Confiant. 1989/1990. *Éloge de la Créolité* [In praise of Creoleness]. Trans. M. B. Taleb-Khyar. Paris: Gallimard; Baltimore: Johns Hopkins University Press. Citations are to the 1990 edition; page references are to a passage in the original French version, followed by the location of the passage in the English translation.

Bizzell, Patricia. 2002. "The Intellectual Work of 'Mixed' Forms of Academic Discourse." In *ALT/DIS: Alternative Discourses and the Academy,* edited by Christopher Schroeder, Helen Fox, and Patricia Bizzell, 1–10. Portsmouth, NH: Boynton/Cook.

Brandt, Deborah. 2001. *Literacy in American Lives.* New York: Cambridge University Press.

——. 2009. "When People Write for Pay." *JAC, 29*(1–2), 165–97.

Byram, Michael. 1997. *Teaching and Assessing Intercultural Communicative Competence.* Clevedon, England: Multilingual Matters.

Canagarajah, A. Suresh. 2002. "Multilingual Writers and the Academic Community: Towards a Critical Relationship." *Journal of English for Academic Purposes, 1,* 29–44.

———. 2006a. "The Place of World Englishes in Composition: Pluralization Continued." *College Composition and Communication,* 57(4), 586–619.

———. 2006b. "Toward a Writing Pedagogy of Shuttling between Languages: Learning from Multilingual Writers." *College English,* 68(6), 589–604.

———. 2007. "Lingua Franca English, Multilingual Communities, and Language Acquisition." *Modern Language Journal,* 91(5), 923–39.

———. 2009. "Multilingual Strategies of Negotiating English: From Conversation to Writing." *JAC,* 29(1–2), 17–48.

Cronin, Michael. 2003. *Translation and Globalization.* London: Routledge.

Delpit, Lisa D. 1988. "The Silenced Dialogue: Power and Pedagogy in Educating Other People's Children." *Harvard Educational Review,* 58(3), 280–98.

———. 1993. "The Politics of Teaching Literate Discourse." In *Freedom's Plow: Teaching in the Multicultural Classroom,* edited by Theresa Perry and James W. Fraser, 285–96. New York: Routledge.

Fairclough, Norman. 1992. "The Appropriacy of 'Appropriateness.'" In *Critical Language Awareness,* edited by Norman Fairclough, 33–57. London: Longman.

Firth, Alan, and Johannes Wagner. 2007. "On Discourse, Communication, and (Some) Fundamental Concepts in SLA Research." *Modern Language Journal,* 91(5), 757–72.

Friedrich, Patricia, and Aya Matsuda. 2010. "When Five Words Are Not Enough: A Conceptual and Terminological Discussion of English as a Lingua Franca." *International Multilingual Research Journal,* 4(1), 20–30.

Harris, Joseph. 1997. *A Teaching Subject: Composition Since 1966.* Upper Saddle River, NJ: Prentice Hall.

Hochschild, Arlie Russell. 1997. *The Time Bind: When Work Becomes Home and Home Becomes Work.* New York: Holt.

Horner, Bruce. 2000. *Terms of Work for Composition: A Materialist Critique.* Albany: State University of New York Press.

Horner, Bruce, and John Trimbur. 2002. "English Only and U.S. College Composition." *College Composition and Communication,* 53(4), 594–630.

Horner, Bruce, and Min-Zhan Lu. 2007. "Resisting Monolingualism in 'English': Reading and Writing the Politics of Language." In *Rethinking English in Schools: A New and Constructive Stage,* edited by Viv Ellis, Carol Fox, and Brian Street, 141–57. London: Continuum.

Horner, Bruce, Min-Zhan Lu, and Paul Kei Matsuda, eds. 2010. *Cross-Language Relations in Composition.* Carbondale: Southern Illinois University Press.

Horner, Bruce, Min-Zhan Lu, Jacqueline Jones Royster, and John Trimbur. 2011. "Language Difference in Writing: Toward a Translingual Approach." *College English,* 73(3), 303–21.

Klimpfinger, Theresa. 2009. "She's Mixing the Two Languages Together—Forms and Functions of Code Switching in English as a Lingua Franca." In *English as a Lingua Franca: Studies and Findings,* edited by Anna Mauranen and Elina Ranta, 348–71. Newcastle-upon-Tyne, England: Cambridge Scholars.

Kramsch, Claire. 2006. "The Traffic in Meaning." *Asia Pacific Journal of Education,* 26(1), 99–104.

Lu, Min-Zhan. 1994. "Professing Multiculturalism: The Politics of Style in the Contact Zone." *College Composition and Communication,* 45(4), 442–58.

———. 2006. "Living-English Work." *College English,* 68(6), 605–18.

———. 2009. "Metaphors Matter: Transcultural Literacy." *JAC,* 29(1–2), 285–93.

Luke, Allan. 1998. "Genres of Power? Literacy Education and the Production of Capital." In *Literacy in Society: Language Description and Language Education,* edited by Ruqaiya Hasan and Geoffrey Williams, 308–38. New York: Longman.

Makoni, Sinfree, and Alastair Pennycook, eds. 2007. *Disinventing and Reconstituting Languages.* Clevedon, England: Multilingual Matters.

Mauranen, Anna, and Elina Ranta, eds. 2009. *English as a Lingua Franca: Studies and Findings.* Newcastle-upon-Tyne, England: Cambridge Scholars.

Meierkord, Christiane. 2004. "Syntactic Variation in Interactions across International Englishes." *English World-Wide,* 25, 109–32.

Miller, Richard E. 1994. "Fault Lines in the Contact Zone." *College English,* 56(4), 389–408.

Miller, Richard E., and Michael J. Cripps. 2005. "Minimum Qualifications: Who Should Teach First-Year Writing?" In *Discord & Direction: The Postmodern Writing Program Administrator,* edited by Sharon James McGee and Carolyn Handa, 123–39. Logan: Utah State University Press.

New London Group. 2000. "A Pedagogy of Multiliteracies: Designing Social Futures." In *Multiliteracies: Literacy Learning and the Design of Social Futures,* edited by Bill Cope and Mary Kalantzis, 9–38. London: Routledge.

Pennycook, Alastair. 2008. "English as a Language Always in Translation." *European Journal of English Studies,* 12(1), 33–47.

Petraglia, Joseph, ed. 1995. *Reconceiving Writing, Rethinking Writing Instruction.* Mahwah, NJ: Erlbaum.

Pratt, Mary Louise. 1987. "Linguistic Utopias." In *The Linguistics of Writing: Arguments between Language and Literature,* edited by Nigel Fabb, Derek Attridge, Alan Durant, and Colin MacCabe, 48–66. New York: Methuen.

Prendergast, Catherine. 2010. "In Praise of Incomprehension." In *Cross-Language Relations in Composition,* edited by Bruce Horner, Min-Zhan Lu and Paul Kei Matsuda, 230–35. Carbondale: Southern Illinois University Press.

Rubdy, Rani, and Mario Saraceni, eds. 2006. *English in the World: Global Rules, Global Roles.* London: Continuum.

Salvatori, Mariolina. 1996. "Conversations with Texts: Reading in the Teaching of Composition." *College English,* 58(4), 440–54.

Sifakis, Nicos. 2006. "Teaching EIL—Teaching *International* or *Intercultural* English? What Teachers Should Know." In *English in the World: Global Rules, Global Roles,* edited by Rani Rubdy and Mario Saraceni, 151–68. London: Continuum.

Spivak, Gayatri. 1993. *Outside in the Teaching Machine.* New York: Routledge.

Steiner, George. 1975. *After Babel.* Oxford: Oxford University Press.

Street, Brian. 1985. *Literacy in Theory and Practice.* Cambridge: Cambridge University Press.

Tsing, Anna Lowenhaupt. 2005. *Friction: An Ethnography of Global Connection.* Princeton: Princeton University Press.

Young, Vershawn Ashanti. 2004. "Your Average Nigga." *College Composition and Communication,* 55(4), 693–715.

———. 2009. "'Nah, We Straight': An Argument against Code Switching." *JAC,* 29(1–2), 49–76.

8. The Unintended Consequences of Sponsorship

Eli Goldblatt and David A. Jolliffe

> Sponsors of literacy [are] any agents, local or distant, concrete or abstract, who enable, support, teach, and model as well as recruit, regulate, suppress, or withhold literacy—*and gain advantage by it in some way.*
> —Deborah Brandt, *Literacy in American Lives* (added emphasis)

Deborah Brandt's well-known definition of a literacy sponsor has been used to explore and analyze learning situations inside and outside academic settings. This formulation sensitizes us to the benefits that flow to institutions offering classes or tutelage of any sort. By Brandt's light we recognize any education or training serves not only the students but also the donors, corporations, nonprofits, and governments that create and fund systems through which learners pass from literacy to literacy. Her focus on the economic history of mass literacy has provided an operational method for performing a Foucauldian power analysis of educational opportunities in America over the last hundred or more years. And yet, the last phrase of her definition—the word *gain* ringing out, conjuring the rise and fall of housing values in a suburb as funding levels fluctuate for its local school district—has always bothered us as incomplete and overstated. Certainly, county governments fund community colleges to make their workforce more attractive for outside investors, but "gain advantage" does not exhaust the story of sponsorship. Sponsors take risks, too. Indeed, sponsors can be harmed, altered, or even transformed by the population and pedagogy they contract to teach.

We raise this question because we are both involved in community literacy projects that require significant sponsorships from institutions with vast investments in the economic development of under-resourced areas. David works with primarily rural populations in Eastern Arkansas, and Eli pursues projects in the stressed neighborhoods of North Philadelphia. Over the years we have come to recognize that the people we know in our respective communities share remarkable similarities despite the obvious differences of geography and history: Children and adults possess great talents, but, discouraged by poor teaching and underfunded schools, they expect too little from their literacy lives. Both areas offer great possibilities for potential employers, but the jobs do not come, partly because companies can get sweeter deals in places where they will not have to spend so much to train the workforce. Both have potential or actual sponsors—universities and colleges, churches, hospitals, immigration services, and corporations in addition to public school systems in crisis—capable of creating many additional literacy opportunities for the people of the place. Much depends on these institutions undergoing the sort of challenge to their current forms that would allow their sponsorship to succeed *for the sake of those not now adequately served.* If institutions and their backers take the risk, both sponsors and learners might benefit, but sponsors may have to undergo transformations they neither expect nor welcome in the process of engaging groups not originally included in their charters or missions.

Community Learning Network in an Urban University

Temple University sits squarely in the middle of North Central Philadelphia. On one side of majestic old Broad Street, the proud but stressed African American community stretches fifteen blocks to the park, ten blocks south, and twenty blocks north. On the other side of Broad, the residents are primarily African American for another five or eight blocks east, and then the Latino community begins—largely Puerto Rican but also increasingly Mexican, with Colombians in the northern margin and Dominicans here and there. Outside the campus the people are haunted by the usual urban ills of near Depression-era unemployment, poor schools, high food prices, vacant lots, violence accompanying drugs exacerbated by easy access to guns. And yet, this area contains neighborhoods rich with small nonprofits trying to serve ex-offenders, new mothers, elders and kids; the churches host literacy centers and food banks; the schools have their share of teachers who care passionately about their students; and cops who are often portrayed as villains can also show compassion and creativity to protect the communities they patrol. North Philly might be characterized as a rich country with tragically inadequate infrastructure. The greatest treasure, the human beings, cannot develop themselves well enough to transform their circumstances or shake the government on their behalf.

Our university libraries and lecture rooms and laboratories lie within yards of inadequate housing and dangerous outside basketball courts. Our theaters offer plays and host recitals while only blocks away people cook their dinners and hope to pay the rent. But this is not a pity story; the university itself is in grave danger because of major state budget cuts. The general society grows unwilling to pay taxes for common services like higher education, and traditional American wariness of intellectual pursuits raises suspicions that Temple's research agenda is merely a luxury for a city and state in financial crisis. Leave the research to rich private institutions like Penn and Princeton, some critics say. Turn Temple back into a teaching college where anyone can get an education that will get them better pay and higher status. But then research, and the elite education associated in this country with research institutions, will only be carried on in precincts removed from city streets and urban rhythms. The most challenging social and environmental problems facing us today are not susceptible to solutions devised in isolation from the lived texture of those problems, nor are the most compelling arts coming from high conservatories as much as they are from local studios in abandoned areas or small drama troupes teaching children in the neighborhoods. Meanwhile, college students plagiarize and turn off in large lectures or even small seminars where they see no compelling reason for their study or substance to their assignments.

In short, a new metropolitan university with a vibrant research agenda needs its city as much as its city needs its university, but in order to take hold of this new role in relation to the region and its people, it must reimagine every phase of its practice, from tenure decisions and teaching hierarchies to tuition financing and administrative duties. If students learn through community-based experiences in schools and literacy programs and senior centers, shouldn't the neighborhood partners be paid for their supervision burdens and the cooperation they give teachers and researchers? If faculty members serve on boards for the nonprofits that act as collaborators on their projects, shouldn't board membership count in a tenure or promotion file? If an executive director from a community development center gives lectures to students on sustainability, shouldn't she be consulted by the university administration on new building projects in her community development corporation (CDC) catchment area? As faculty members design creative courses to involve their students and local residents in mutually beneficial learning projects, the university is increasingly challenged to defend or transform its traditional policies.

One example from work in North Philadelphia indicates both the potential benefits and challenges that a network of partnerships offers an urban university. At Tree House Books, a small neighborhood literary center only a few blocks from Temple's central library, more than thirty students a semester work with elementary school students after school on homework assignments as well as creative writing, visual arts, theater, and gardening projects throughout the year. Some college students are enrolled in a class, such as Eli's "Literacy and Society" course in the English department or his architecture colleague's general education course called "Guerrilla Altruism." Others find their way to Tree House through college clubs, word-of-mouth publicity, or a sorority campaign. The kids, ages six to fourteen, come from the local elementary school or other nearby schools. Parents have signed waivers to allow their kids at Tree House each afternoon, and some parents have begun to take an active interest not only in the children's programs, such as the literary magazine called *The Ave*, but also in evening programs Tree House sometimes offers on violence prevention or documentary movies about Philadelphia. Not only do the youngsters become fiercely devoted to Tree House but college students regularly report that the experience of interacting with children from stressed Philadelphia neighborhoods changed their attitudes toward education, city life, and career opportunities.

Temple pays a small amount for a user's fee to help defray the cost of rent at Tree House, but Temple students receive tremendous benefits from the staff time and attention they receive. Tree House is run by two staff members —one full-time, one part-time—with the assistance of a few devoted older women from the neighborhood and some college students who have taken on leadership roles. Eli serves on the board, and other colleagues have attended board meetings but have been unable to maintain a commitment to the board. Administrators and faculty have, in recent years, expressed more and more interest in the organization, and some have given generous donations. The neighborhood would be warier of Tree House if it were an outright project of the university, but eventually some shared sponsorship arrangement should form between the nonprofit and the university to support the volunteer coordination and training Tree House provides Temple students. Students who work at Tree House have already won university research awards for their work, but university departments should recognize teaching and faculty research done through an organization like Tree House as meritorious as well.

If we multiply this one instance many times over, we see the necessity for at least one centrally supported academic unit to develop and maintain relationships with nonprofits and even some profit-based companies in the area that both benefit the neighborhoods and serve the Temple population. At Temple, we have many projects that involve truly collaborative efforts between university and community programs. The nationally recognized Inside/Out program, developed by Lori Pompa of the criminal justice department, educates undergraduates alongside incarcerated students at penal institutions in the Philadelphia area and trains instructors from across the country in the model's unique pedagogy. The University Community Collaborative of Philadelphia, established by political scientist Barbara Ferman, works with youth on building leadership and research capacities in local public schools. These and other outstanding community-university projects have attracted millions of dollars of foundation and donor funds to address social issues, but until recently the university had no central way to support these efforts and connect them to the mission of the university. The new Community Learning Network fosters shared sponsorship for literacy and other disciplinary-based projects that link academic programs with neighborhood partners. Its mandate goes beyond the traditional service-learning center because it not only places students with groups or centers but also actively seeks projects motivated by community partners. It thus has a community organizing function without being a full-fledged advocacy agency. Whether the funding continues for this venture is, of course, an open question, but the Network represents a choice about direction the university must make.

Schools like Temple can choose to ignore contemporary challenges and become irrelevant to the civic life of their specific locations, or they can shift their focus and priorities to establish a regional leadership role for themselves that will attract new sources of funding and public interest. Like a monolingual writing program doomed to punish and indoctrinate its students to little effect because of a flawed basic philosophy of knowledge transmission (see Horner and Lu, chapter 7, this volume), large, state-related urban universities must maintain their academic aloofness with greater and greater desperation if they do not recognize that the complex and multilayered environment of a city offers a rich model of literacy for both students and faculty. In order to obtain the "gain" of literacy sponsorship in this environment, a university must lose at least some of its traditional power by sharing resources with a network of partners who offer their fraught and unpredictable learning landscape as an alternative to the seemingly safe but illusory vision of standardized classroom knowledge.

Rural Literacy Comes to the Flagship University

The heavily agricultural region of the Arkansas Delta—the eastern part of the state where the counties either have a border with the Mississippi River or sit on one side or the other of Crowley's Ridge, a 150-mile, crescent moon–shaped geological feature—may seem a world removed from North Philadelphia. In significant ways, however, the challenges of negotiating literacy sponsorship in the two locales are similar. The development and growth of the Arkansas Delta Oral History Project (ADOHP) substantiates this proposition.

The ADOHP is an educational outreach program sponsored by the Brown Chair in English Literacy at the University of Arkansas. (David is the initial occupant of the Brown Chair, having been appointed to it in 2005.) In the ADOHP, the Brown Chair initiative works every year with four or five high schools from the Delta. Once the economic breadbasket of the state, the Delta is now, by all measures, a region in decline as the family agriculture industry has morphed into the corporate agribusiness enterprise.

In each of the participating schools, a teacher agrees to use oral history as a teaching method in one of his or her classes. During most of the second semester, the high school students work on projects that require them to identify and do background research on a topic from local legend or lore; find someone with an informed perspective on the topic to interview; plan, practice, conduct, and transcribe the interview; and then, on the basis of that interview, produce a substantial final project: an academic essay, a piece of historical fiction, a series of poems, a play, a website, a brochure, and so on. At the same time the high school students are working on their oral history projects, a group of University of Arkansas undergraduates—frequently English, history, and anthropology students—is enrolled in the ADOHP course, in which they study the history, politics, economics, and literature of the Delta; work individually on their own Delta oral history projects; and serve as mentors, both face-to-face and in electronic writing groups, to four or five of the participating high school students. The project begins with a daylong meeting in January, when all the U of A student mentors travel to Helena, Arkansas, a central location in the Delta, where the U of A and high school students meet, writing groups are formed, and the logistics of the program are covered in a series of workshops. Back at their home schools for the next seven or eight weeks, all students work on their projects, following a schedule established at the opening meeting, and everyone logs on to the electronic conferencing site at least once a week to share drafts and comments about the evolving project with their writing group. Around midsemester, all the participating high school students come to Fayetteville for a weekend of cultural activities, fun, and work at the University of Arkansas. Then, back at their home schools, they work on their projects and confer in the electronic writing groups, bringing their final projects to completion in time to travel again to Helena for a day of celebration and performance, with all the U of A student mentors and high school students in attendance.

The final products of the ADOHP have been astounding: a narrated video about the great Mississippi River flood of 1927; a set of poems, with water-color illustrations, about Friday night football in McGehee, Arkansas; a play about the desegregation of businesses in downtown Pine Bluff,

Arkansas; a short story about the writer's parents' participation in the civil rights movement; a documentary video about the first substantial farm ever run by a woman in the Delta; and so on and so on. Collectively, the ADOHP projects represent the most creative, most engaged student work that David has seen in his nearly four decades of teaching.

The University of Arkansas administration seems genuinely to admire the ADOHP. In its efforts to diversify the student body, faculty, and staff at the university—a concerted initiative under way for the past decade—the university almost always mentions the ADOHP. University publications have featured photo spreads of U of A students working with the students from the small, generally rural, frequently African American–majority schools. Officials from deans upward in the administration praise David for "your work in the Delta," a region of the state from which the university would like to recruit more students as part of its diversity initiative.

On paper, the ADOHP looks very much like a straightforward strategic initiative designed to foster high school–college articulation, to provide U of A undergraduate students the opportunity to learn about a part of the state that needs economic and educational support, to instill a sense of pride about the region by celebrating its past, and to show high school students from the Delta something about the demands of designing and carrying out a rigorous academic project, similar to ones completed by university students just a few years older than they are. It would be a mischaracterization, however, to cast the ADOHP as a conflict- and trouble-free enterprise. The ADOHP has also fleshed out several lessons that the University of Arkansas in general and the Brown Chair and his associates in particular need to heed if the institution truly wants to welcome students from the Delta, African American and otherwise, to the university.

First of all, the university (and higher education in general, no doubt) needs to realize that high school–college articulation programs, particularly those that might contribute to diversifying the institution, are often as much about issues of class and experiential dissonance as they are about academics. Instructors and U of A mentors who have led the ADOHP writing groups have discovered three points related to this idea. First, each year we have noticed—and consciously tried to mitigate—an odd power dynamic that shows up in the online writing group discussions: The Delta students invariably treat the U of A mentor not as an equal participant in the group work but instead as a teacher figure, a power authority who must orchestrate all conversations and pass judgment on all in-progress activities. It has taken considerable effort to get the Delta students to comment on each other's work and offer ideas about student-to-student collaboration, rather than simply to seek the approval of the mentor-cum-teacher. Second, try as we might to keep the online discussions to the agenda of selecting a topic, doing background research, and then planning, practicing, conducting, and transcribing the interviews and creating the final project, the Delta students more than occasionally seek to divert the discussions to "college life" issues. They are wont to ask the mentors questions about what kinds of parties they go to, what kinds of food and drink they consume at college, what kinds of friends they have and how they make them. Third, we have learned that it is no simple matter to require the Delta students to log on and participate in online discussions once a week. In many of our sites, students have access to Internet connectivity only at school, and even access there might be restricted by the high student population–to–computer terminal ratio. Moreover, while most of the Delta students have had ample experience surfing the Internet and visiting a range of noninteractive sites, relatively few of them have ever gone beyond simple e-mail to correspond with another person on the Internet. The prospect of interacting with four, five, or six people on an electronic platform is quite daunting to them.

Finally, the university (and, again, higher education in general) needs to be aware of the substantial difference in the size and scope of academic projects that students in high school generally do and the ones they are asked to take up in college. The ADOHP challenges the Delta high school students and the U of A mentors to take ownership of their work in a way that almost all of the high schoolers and a substantial number of the university mentors have never experienced before. The oral history project is theirs from beginning to end. Though their teachers might suggest some broad parameters, the students must essentially take charge from the initial proposal to the final project: They pick the topic, do the background research, find someone to interview, do all the interview subtasks, select the genre for the final project, complete it, and present it to a public audience. For a novice, a project of this scope can be overwhelming. Lots of scaffolding and support—more than we realized at the outset—are required to help students succeed.

Challenging the Sponsor

We recognize the immediate benefits our respective institutions receive for their sponsorship of community literacy projects. Both of us have seen official university publications run compelling photos of neighborhood kids in our programs, allowing the higher-education institution to claim a level of engagement and concern for disenfranchised people that is not always wholly warranted. We have met graduate and undergraduate students who chose our schools because they wish to work with populations our projects serve, even though both of us have our doubts that those students will be fully supported by some of our colleagues. Indeed, we ourselves have gained advantages by writing about our community engagements, although in our generation, both of us needed to establish ourselves as scholars and teachers before we could venture into this new field. Given our positions, we are quite willing to carry water for our institutions as long as we continue to have space for our work and can quietly encourage the unintended changes that community engaged sponsorship inevitably brings.

The ADOHP experience offers a model lesson on how the sponsoring institution—the University of Arkansas and its Brown Chair in English Literacy—needs to change if it hopes to gain from the literacy sponsorship it offers to the schools and students from the Delta. The ADOHP can go a long way toward helping the U of A recruit students, minority and otherwise, from this economically challenged region. To help them matriculate and eventually graduate from the university, the institution will need to take substantial steps toward supporting the transition. But the striking products of the ADOHP program also represent a challenge to traditional practices within the university. Student-generated projects that draw on contemporary interviewing and observation offer compelling alternatives to the usual end-of-the-semester college research paper or final exam. The way the ADOHP students relate to each other and their teachers—face-to-face or online—raises questions about usual power hierarchies associated with the transmittal of knowledge from certified knowledge professionals to uninitiated academic novices. As is the case with Tree House Books and other agencies in the Community Learning Network in North Philadelphia, the ADOHP points to directions in which the literacy sponsor, not just the literacy sponsored, must change in order to gain a new student population and social approval for "reaching out" and "giving back."

Brandt's observation that sponsors of literacy "gain advantage" by their sponsorship remains convincing, but our experience suggests that we cannot afford to define gain narrowly or quickly. Yes, in order to argue for a new program, we must always highlight the way it addresses the self-interest of the institution; that is good community organizing as well as good rhetorical practice. At the same time, some of the largest gains for a sponsoring institution may come in unexpected forms, changing old practices and confronting attitudes toward what constitutes knowledge or what might be a suitable subject for study in a research university. As oral histories from the Delta and vibrant poetry from the students at Tree House demonstrate, the neighborhoods we serve also have much to teach us about bringing knowledge and action together through literacy.

9. Making Literacy Work:
A "Phenomenal Woman" Negotiating Her Literacy
Identity in and for an African American Women's Club

Beverly J. Moss and Robyn Lyons-Robinson

> She keeps us informed. . . . Ever since Niki has been teaching at Columbus
> State, she's always telling us about something that is going on down on that
> campus and is always inviting us.
>
> —Charlene, PWI

> We've watched her grow, and it's just been such a blessing to have her as
> president. She's brought a lot to the group.
>
> —Veronica, PWI

The sentiments above, spoken about Robyn Lyons-Robinson by fellow club members, were shared by many club women during the sixteen months of the ethnographic study for which Beverly J. Moss collected data. "Keeping us informed," "always telling us about something that's going on down on that campus and inviting us," and "bringing a lot to the group" are statements that provide insight into Robyn's literate life within Phenomenal Women Incorporated (PWI), the Columbus, Ohio, club that is the subject of Beverly's ethnography. In this essay we examine how Deborah Brandt's concept of literacy sponsorship fits (or not) Robyn's literacy role and identity within the club. Foundational to our attempts at describing her literacy role in PWI is Robyn's discomfort with the concept of being a literacy sponsor. In locating the root of the discomfort, we extend Brandt's concept. To do so, we examine how the blurring of boundaries among family, professional, and community domains that characterizes Robyn's literacy practices in the club provides Robyn with an opportunity to make literacy work in specific ways in PWI. She uses resources from her academic space—the community college where she teaches—to advance the mission of a community space—the club—while she invites the club to share her academic space. In this essay, we turn our gaze toward what these blurrings of boundaries and spaces mean for how Robyn's literacy identity is established and operates within the club.

A word about our process: We present both of our perspectives in a kind of back-and-forth commentary-narrative approach. We do not pretend to have a conversation so much as to use each other's narrative and analysis as prompts. To distinguish our voices, we make use of different fonts. *When Robyn writes, her words are in italics*; with Beverly, her words are in nonitalicized font. More important than font is the opportunity for the researched to engage in how she is represented by the researcher and for the researcher to engage the concerns of the researched.

Beverly's Reflections

The first time that I met Robyn "Niki" Lyons (the "Robinson" came along with her marriage), she was a senior English major at Ohio State University. Over the past nineteen or so years, we have become friends, fellow church members, and members of the same profession—and most recently, Robyn and members of her club, PWI, have become my research participants in an ethnography of literacy practices in PWI. For sixteen months, I was a participant-observer in this African American women's club, exploring the role of literacy in the club of which Robyn, her mother, aunt, now deceased grandmother, several of their extended family, coworkers, and friends were founding members. During the initial data collection and analysis process, I was drawn to what was to become an intriguing and valuable pattern within the club—how the club makes use of the talents and resources of individual members to enrich the club and help the club achieve its mission—"to provide women of diverse backgrounds the opportunity to enjoy social gatherings and community service activities that will enrich their lives, as well as the lives of others in the central Ohio area. We are women who hold shared values, interests, and goals." For several of these women, literacy was at the root of the talents and resources that they provided the club, most particularly for Robyn, who was the PWI president during my fieldwork. Often, Robyn's roles in the club and with various club members revolved around her experiences and expertise with literacy, especially academic literacy. From her role in the naming of the club, borrowed from the Maya Angelou poem "Phenomenal Woman" to her choice of the book—Obama's *Dreams from My Father*—that the club read and discussed as part of their 2009 Black history month celebration (see Moss, 2010), Robyn is often at the center of how the women in this club engage multiple literacy practices. From writing a report to helping someone else in the club learn how to do the minutes, whatever the task, if it was or is literacy related, Robyn seemingly has a hand in it.

My early attempts at characterizing Robyn's literacy relationship with, and literacy expertise in, Phenomenal Women Incorporated began with me using Brandt's concept of literacy sponsorship. Brandt, in *Literacy in American Lives,* defines *literacy sponsors* as:

> any agents, local or distant, concrete or abstract, who enable, support, teach, and model, as well as recruit, regulate, suppress, or withhold, literacy—and gain advantage by it in some way. . . . It is useful to think about who or what underwrites occasions of literacy learning and use. Although the interests of the sponsor and the sponsored do not have to converge (and in fact, may conflict), sponsors nevertheless set the terms for access to literacy and wield powerful incentives for compliance and loyalty. (2001, p. 19)

Parts of Brandt's definition fit Robyn's role quite well. She often enables, supports, teaches, and models literacy for her fellow PWI club members, thus seemingly placing her in the role of literacy sponsor. For example, in addition to composing the program and the mistress of ceremony's script for the club's annual Phenomenal Woman of the Year signature dinner, Robyn also prepares and distributes a guide/model script to use for soliciting donations from local businesses for the signature dinner. In the club's beginning years, she took a leadership role in preparing the agenda for meetings. She invited the club to participate in her school's local African American Read-In Chain and kept them informed about cultural and intellectual events in which they might be interested.[1] However, as we discuss later, when Robyn and I really began to examine her literacy relationship within the club, literacy sponsor did not account for the whole of this literacy relationship, a relationship that is tied to familial bonds, professional identities, and reciprocal relationships. We highlight moments where Robyn's interests and the club's converge and moments where they conflict. Whether their interests converge or conflict, we call into question the hierarchical relationship between the sponsor and the sponsored. Where Brandt's literacy sponsors "set the terms of access . . . and wield powerful incentives for compliance and loyalty" (2001, p. 19), we suggest that literacy sponsors may, in fact, in many contexts hold little of the power that is implied by Brandt's definition nor do they necessarily set the terms of access. Through Robyn's example, we complicate the concept.

Because of her academic background and the rights and affordances that it provides her, Robyn is in a unique position to support, teach, and model literacy. An English professor at the local community college, it is through her training in English studies—she has both a BA and MA in English and an MA in Women's Studies—and her profession that Robyn is provided with many of the resources that she can call on for PWI. The example that Robyn writes about in the next section makes very real how in many ways her literacy was the official literacy of the club. When she was not producing a record of the club's actions through their minutes, she was helping someone else, in this case her Aunt Charlene, produce them. The example also demonstrates how she positions and is positioned as literacy educator in the club.

Robyn Comments

During the period in which I served as vice president, I often found myself assisting the secretary with proper documentation of club meeting minutes and agenda items. It was during this time that my Aunt Charlene had the job of club secretary. Although she and her husband had recently purchased a home computer, she felt the least comfortable with such technology. But she was willing to learn, which motivated the educator in me. I often teased her about her left-handedness as she meticulously recorded minutes during our general meetings. She knew that no matter what she recorded during a meeting, she and I would get together to decipher her notes, correct grammar and mechanics, and fill any content gaps. During these post-meeting get-togethers, either at her dining table or over the phone, I would type her handwritten notes in preparation for the next club meeting. Over time, our post-meeting gatherings became shorter and less frequent, as Charlene became more comfortable with word processing, printing, and copying meeting minutes and agendas on her own (using her own home computer) and using templates I had introduced to her.

Oftentimes, I had to suppress the editor in me—a consequence of my English professor role—as Aunt Charlene's developing (digital) literacy produced errors in formatting (using all caps and unnecessary bolding), voice, grammar, and mechanics that would be revealed during her oral reading of minutes at the start of each general meeting. Fortunately, our familial relationship as aunt and niece allowed her the room to become more familiar with business writing conventions and me the liberty to support her efforts and her emerging literacy while modeling, for her, new literacy practices.

Beverly

The way that Robyn describes how she worked with her Aunt Charlene to teach her how to do the club minutes, use her computer, and essentially be the club secretary, a literacy-based job, highlights several things: first, the importance of Robyn's role as an English teacher; second, her role as the dutiful niece who is the family scribe (we come back to this later); and third, her desire to have club members be active agents of literacy. I look at how Robyn uses her own literacy skills to help the club, help her aunt meet immediate goals, and teach her aunt lifelong literacy skills that allow her to take charge of her own literate life. Robyn's literacy identity begins to take even clearer shape in my first interview with Mawarine, Robyn's mother and the founder of PWI. Mawarine describes how the club got its name: "My daughter [Robyn]. We all wrote down little phrases what we wanted it to be called. And leave it to my daughter, the professor, she thought of 'Phenomenal Women'"(personal interview, June 5, 2008). It is no surprise that Mawarine, even at the infancy stage of PWI, recognizes the link between Robyn's profession and the club. Mawarine, a proud mother, situates Robyn as "the professor," the literacy educator who, of course, because of her profession, is the person who has the "right stuff" to come up with the right name. Robyn, who has a background in African American literature, Women's Studies, and composition, relies on that background and her knowledge of Angelou's poem to suggest it as a name for the club. From the very beginning, Robyn was a literacy resource and facilitator for the club, and from the beginning, the resources, material and intellectual, to which she has access became resources for PWI. She made use of her resources to assist the club in creating its identity and eventually carrying out its mission. When Robyn was not writing reports or engaging in other literacy activities for the club, she was modeling literacy practices for or encouraging other members to take on new literacy activities, as with Charlene. We discussed her literacy roles in one of our first interviews:

> BEVERLY. Okay. So who did the actual [writing], putting it [words] on the page, the print version?
> ROBYN. Um, I did. I did and continue to do a lot of the paperwork. Marketing materials and that.
> BEVERLY. Why is that, do you think?
> ROBYN. A number of different reasons. A lot of our members don't feel comfortable with their writing skills. Another reason is I have access to computers more readily than they do. And because most of our members are retired, they're not even in an environment where they can produce these kinds of documents. So I end up doing it a lot. It's just easier for me to do it. Although I'm trying to get people to get more—take more responsibility for doing a lot of that.
> BEVERLY. . . . so is it the literacy skills that you bring to that, to the organization, that have people look to you to do that kind of work? Or do you volunteer because of the literacy skills, or do they just say, oh you know how to do that because you're the English [professor]?
> ROBYN. I think a little bit of both. I don't mind doing it. Although lately I would say in the last four to five years I've kind of said, you

can do this part! You know, like I used to like, one person would be
the secretary, but I would be typing the notes. [*Laughs*.] And now, I'm
like, you can type the notes now. You can type the treasury reports
now. Um. So it was a little bit of both initially, and um . . .

> BEVERLY. Is that because they didn't, whoever had those positions,
didn't have confidence? Or they just—? Or they didn't have access to
the technology?

> ROBYN. They didn't have access to the technology, and they wanted
it to look right, you know.

One can see that not only does Robyn voluntarily take on this literacy leadership role, to help club members make "it look right," but she is expected and
invited by club members to be the literacy expert because of her credentials
and experience. That experience includes her access to and expertise with
technology.

*Unlike most of the club members, technology was my ally due to professional
access and generational interest; that is, many more people in my generation
are more comfortable with a range of digital technologies. Where my fellow club
members were just beginning to feel comfortable with cell phones, I was using
computer technology regularly in my personal and professional life. Whenever
possible, I sought to share my knowledge and use of technology with club members. It was important to me that club members feel empowered by the ability
to communicate effectively as representatives of Phenomenal Women Inc.*

Robyn is very aware of the material resources to which she has access as
well as what her degrees mean to the club. And while Robyn's credentials
and experience position her to be a literacy sponsor, her literacy relationship
with the club complicates that role. As she suggests below, she is not comfortable with the label. Even when she refers to herself as a literacy sponsor,
as she does for the drafting of this essay, she is tentative as she tries on the
concept. Her negotiation of her literacy identity within the club is tied to
her literacy identity with her family and her academic pursuits. In fact, it
was the family ties that established her early literacy role in PWI.

*When Beverly first talked to me about my role as a literacy sponsor for
the women of Phenomenal Women Inc., I couldn't help but feel some reser-
vation about claiming this role. My perspective on the organization's literacy
practices and my role as a literacy sponsor in those practices are conflicted.
From the genesis of the group, I had a vested interest in its viability. As the
daughter of the group's founder, Mawarine, I was perhaps the first to learn
of her desire to have a social club that would be open to all, particularly
those who felt excluded from established clubs which my mother was often*

invited to join. My mother felt a need, a push, to do something that mattered in the lives of the women she knows, women who worked toward retirement at their government and healthcare jobs, women who had limited formal educations but who were "blessed" to have secured jobs that paid most of the bills. Perhaps as a literacy sponsor, I acted out of a need to protect not only my mother's vision of such a club but also her right to have it, despite the multiple literacy challenges that I knew lay ahead. [Beverly: Note Robyn's extending of the role of the literacy sponsor to "to protect" the vision of the sponsored, who actually set the agenda and terms of access.] *Having been involved in organizations as a college student, I was familiar with the legalities and documentation that were required.*

By the time the organization was founded, I felt comfortable using literacy to advance my own agenda, as well as that of others. As a graduate of an English master's program at the time the club started, I had developed literacy skills that enabled me to negotiate the increasingly narrow pathways of the Ivory Tower. In 1995, I secured a tenure-track teaching position at a large community college, affirming that I had "made it." But for the women in my family, I was already "the professor" (a title that I officially earned some thirteen years later) whom others could depend on when it came to negotiating the "ins and outs" of the dominant culture.

One aspect of the dominant culture that I was able to negotiate, and by doing so help my family and the club, was computer technology. I had access to the "Net," personal computers, printers, et cetera, and could produce professional-looking documents. But Phenomenal Women Inc. did not begin with these technologies. The organization was started on my mother's back porch with a legal pad (which I used), rough agenda, and the single vision of my mother.

In so many ways, literacy sponsorship within Phenomenal Women Inc. has been, and still is, a two-way street. For as much as I may have served to sponsor the literacy development of these extraordinary women, over the years each of them has shaped my own cultural and social literacy. I think what I struggle with most about seeing myself as a literacy sponsor is the idea of myself giving but not receiving, which is how I think of a sponsor. This may or may not be what Brandt is talking about. Sponsorship also suggests a lack of agency on the part of the recipient. That clearly is not what happens in our organization. I have learned so much about myself as a mother, wife, teacher, and woman thanks to these women. They have shared their "mother-wit" with me; I'm learning, more and more, how to appreciate that.

Robyn's use of words like *perhaps* and *may have* point to how guarded she is about describing her relationship with the club as one of sponsorship. Her literacy relationship with the club is a two-way street that is very much tied to her role as a daughter, granddaughter, and niece and her role as one of the youngest members of the club. These roles complicate her role as a sponsor because the first set of roles position her as working for and on behalf of others and at the service of others, sometimes in a subordinate position. Robyn also raises concern about the reciprocal relationships between her and the other clubwomen being overshadowed by the sponsor-sponsored relationship. Brandt (2001) suggests that "sponsors nevertheless enter a reciprocal relationship with those they underwrite. They lend their resources or credibility to the sponsored but also stand to gain benefits from their success" (p. 19). In explaining how she has benefitted from literacies of the women in the club, Robyn's notion of reciprocity differs from Brandt's in that what Robyn gains does not rely upon the success of her fellow clubwomen. Robyn's relationship with the club questions what sponsorship may bring—an implied power differential, a sense of the sponsor controlling access to literacy. For me, Robyn's roles and relationships complicate who has power, when power is shared, and how the reciprocal relationship of literacy within the club is enacted. As Robyn continues her narrative, she sheds more light on her role of making literacy work for the club and the complexities of sponsorship. She points to her literacy role in her family (which is central to her literacy role in PWI) not as a sponsor but more as a "literacy go-between" or as stated earlier, a family scribe.

Robyn: Literacy Sponsorship—a Family Affair

Since the start of my undergraduate education, my family has relied on me to communicate important family business and news in writing. I would be trusted to produce and write family reunion newsletters, eulogies, party announcements, et cetera, whatever needed to be communicated with an aura of formality, even if the formality was unnecessary. As the only daughter of the oldest daughter of the only daughter who cared for the family's oldest matriarch and patriarch, lineage directed my role in the family. My grandmother, aunt, and mother, the trio that did everything together and for each other, trusted the literacy skills they believed I was learning as the first-generation college student. "Oh, but you know how to say it better than us . . ." was the pressure they used to get me writing, often reluctantly, a letter to an out-of-town relative or a child-custody mediator. Looking back, these women clearly understood the power of my academic literacy, which, in turn, empowered them. A letter written by me could serve as an "ace in the hole" if needed.

In 1997, the year of the club's founding, I was a budding college English instructor at a local community college. I had recently completed a master's degree at the Ohio State University, which became my "pass" to academia.

My cheerleaders throughout the triumphs and trials of graduate school were my mother, grandmother, and aunt. Growing up, I was very conscious of the role I would play in their dreams for a better family future.

Having served as a "literacy sponsor" in the familial realm, the transition to a "literacy sponsor" for what would become Phenomenal Women Inc. was effortless on the surface. I can recall how during the weeks before the first planning meeting, my mother made personal phone calls to her girlfriends and coworkers while I wrote semi-formal letters of invitation to follow up the call. I also developed an agenda for the first meeting, having no idea what exactly needed to be covered. It was commonplace for me to do the writing while my mother did the talking. I distinctly recall initiating the written documents [application for 501C status] that would help to give the club its "official" status. I was determined to see my mother's vision as far as it would go using the skills, knowledge, and resources available to me at the time.

At the first meeting, as my mother shared her vision, I distributed an agenda I adapted from an African American investment club I had joined a year prior. It was one of many model agendas I had encountered during my undergraduate years serving on committees and participating in campus activities. Tentatively, I selected the investment club agenda as a model for PWI because its first agenda item was an "Opening Prayer." Beginning a formal meeting with prayer is commonplace within the African American community. It is a moment of self and group reflection on the purpose of a meeting and a reminder of who's really in charge, a higher power, in case anyone loses sight of the purpose, and most of these women were church-going women. At twenty-seven, I was the youngest woman present at the initial planning meeting, so I needed unofficial permission to "be seen AND heard." The last time most of the eleven women present had seen me was at my high school graduation. No matter how many degrees I had earned since then, I was still Mawarine's daughter, Niki. I knew I had to walk a fine line between serving as a resource to these women and showing respect to them as "Aunt or Miss So-and-So." Presenting each woman with a copy of the agenda was a start toward "earning my voice."

As I observed during data collection, Robyn emphasizes here her familial roles that continued in the club. Just as she had done for the women in her family, as she had been trusted by them to do, Robyn used her literacy expertise and experience to help her mother turn her vision into a reality. I might argue that Robyn was far more concerned with being a good daughter and fulfilling that "trusted" family role than being a literacy resource for this potential club. Although many first-generation college graduates experience similar literacy identities within their families as Robyn did in her family—being a family scribe—the extending of that role outside the family boundaries to the club adds a layer that Robyn must negotiate. What she refers to as family trust takes her literacy role out of the realm of an obligatory chore and into the realm of an honored position. Her family's pride in her accomplishments led them to trust and depend on her to represent them well. Her literacy is their literacy, a family accomplishment meant to be used for the family. As Robyn suggests, the family was empowered by her literacy.

During my time as a participant-observer, I saw Robyn's role as literacy expert and resource for both club and family often become one and the same. From the very beginning of the club, however, she was establishing a complex literacy relationship with the club that brought together her diverse worlds—home, family, school, church, and club, among others. Robyn's focus on modeling the first PWI agenda on one from her investment club that opens with a prayer indicates her understanding of the African American church as an influential institution in the lives of the potential club members. Robyn, as I suggested earlier, calls on her many resources, this time her membership in an investment club, her understanding of African American cultural (religious) traditions, and her family roles to act on behalf of and be an official representative of the club. She is demonstrating what many literacy scholars (Heath, 1983; Brandt, 2001; Moss, 2003) suggest is typical of African American literacy traditions, situating it within a spiritual context. Brandt reminds us that "for many historical reasons, the ideological context of African American–sponsored literacy retains a strongly spiritual component"(2001, p. 143). That is especially true of Phenomenal Women Incorporated, and Robyn honored that tradition from the club's very beginning.

It is also striking that Robyn saw herself as having to "earn her voice" within this club when she seemed to be so essential to how the club established its identity and to how the club continues to reach its mission. She was acutely aware at the age of twenty-seven—she is now forty-four—that she had to establish a new identity with the club to complement but not erase her previous one as Niki.[2] I go back to Veronica's statement at the beginning of this essay: "We've watched her grow." She was now an adult who contributed to the club; yet, many saw her as Mawarine's baby girl who had "gone over there to Ohio State." That girl—Niki—did not have the power to be in grown folks' business unless she could prove that she had something to offer as a grown-up herself. In other words, Niki needed to "earn her voice" as Robyn in this new club. She began to do so with the naming of the club, a literate act that along with providing an acceptable first agenda, helps the initial club women create a space for Robyn to enter and establish a new relationship with many of them while extending the literacy relationship she had with her family. Interestingly, showing herself as a grown-up means calling on her academic literacies and professional identity. Robyn writes below of her first steps toward earning her voice.

Whether it was at the start of the meeting or toward the end, I don't recall, but I do recall the moment the group decided on a name for the club. Many of the suggestions were ideas based on other women's clubs, and some reminded me of 1980s sit-coms and mini-series. My mother came up with "Intrigue" after the Oldsmobile she had just purchased. The first thought that ran through my mind was that people would think the club represented some type of after-hours lounge where grown-ups could drink and gamble in private. What I saw instead was a group of beautiful, full-figured, self-assured, strong, black women who were successful on their own terms whether single, married, widowed, divorced, employed, retired, laid-off, independent, dependent, disabled, abled, heterosexual, homosexual, asexual. They were the women I grew up referring to as "Aunt" and "Miss." "Intrigue" just didn't feel right as a club name for these women, so I blurted out, "What about Phenomenal Women?" without mentioning that I was plagiarizing Angelou's poem. Although I am not Angelou's greatest fan, her poem "Phenomenal Woman" had stuck with me throughout my college years, and it seemed to fit the women who had shaped my vision of black womanhood. Not surprising, many of the women present were familiar with the poem and agreed on the name. Without dissent, "Phenomenal Women" was voted as the name of the club. Legally incorporating the name and organization would be the next step, but that would have to wait for the next club meeting. My mother was ecstatic to say the least about the club's name and that I had earned a voice in the club she had founded.

Whether she recognized it or not, Robyn was also using her literacy expertise to protect the club—to create an image of black women that countered a stereotype. Does taking on the role of protector make one a sponsor? Can a person who has to "earn her voice" in spite of the literacy resources and credentials that she brings to this particular space still be a literacy sponsor? Clearly, Robyn was not "set[ting] the terms for access" nor was she "wield[ing] powerful incentives for compliance." She was looking out for her mother and the women she cared about. Elaine Richardson in *African American Literacies* points to "serving and protecting" others as a major value surrounding African American women's language and literacy practices (2003, p. 90). Robyn is clearly oriented toward using literacy practices to serve and protect her family and the women in PWI.

Though Robyn was earning her voice in the club, the role of protector and literacy expert also complicated the path to that voice and signals that she was constantly negotiating her literacy identity within the club. She was constantly reminded, most often in a gentle way (though not always, as we see later), that she did not know everything, that these women had much to teach her about multiple literacies. These reminders also emphasized that whatever cachet Robyn may have had as a literacy expert was temporary at best and simply irrelevant at times. Robyn's narrative, then, is not a seamless one that positions her as leading this group of black women to the literacy promised land because of her "sponsorship." Her role as sponsor is not a consistent role. There are disruptions to this role/identity. There seem to be times when the women refuse to be sponsored.

By its first general meeting in September 1998, Phenomenal Women had established its identity within the Columbus community and had begun to create a community service and activist profile with its connections with a local nursing home and a national black women's health organization. We needed funding to continue with these projects and begin new ones. Yet, we were a grassroots organization who knew very little about writing grants to fund projects. We raised money by buying, frying, and delivering (in person) chicken dinners to people at work who had purchased food tickets. By this time, my role had become more visible as someone who could create and send advertising e-mails and create and print food tickets. I gladly took on this role, as I could not be as trusted with knowing how to properly clean chicken legs and wings or prepare flavorful greens and baked beans. I knew my limits and strengths, and the club members knew mine as well. The club members also knew their strengths and weaknesses. While showing them the power of marketing, they revealed to me the importance of satisfying the customer's need by giving more than what is expected.

During one chicken-dinner preparation on a midweek morning at my aunt's house, I received one of many "reality checks." Since most of my work was upfront "soft" labor (fliers, e-mails, ticket printing), I was also able to help with packaging the dinner containers in preparation for delivery (I was not allowed near the ten-gallon, stainless-steel deep fryers that boiled over with hot chicken grease on my aunt's back porch). I couldn't help but be bothered by the number of meat pieces I was ordered to include in each dinner package. I could clearly see that selling a three-piece chicken dinner for five bucks wasn't going to return a profit. I complained that we were wasting our time and no one was considering the unmeasured labor costs we were incurring (imagine thirteen women in the same space cleaning, seasoning, flouring, frying, slicing, chopping, wrapping, and labeling from 7 A.M. to 11 A.M.). Where I only saw a loss of profit, these women envisioned a flurry of repeat customers who would generously give PWI their support after having enjoyed a hot, tasty midday meal of well-seasoned chicken legs and wings, greens, cornbread, and sweet potato pie. In this moment, I was developing an understanding of the need to build relationships that would serve as a foundation for future fund-raising. More specifically, these women were teaching me how to build a relationship with the community we wished to serve and to whom we would look for support of our future projects. It was one of many lessons I would learn from these women. Although I may have had a specific kind of literacy expertise, I learned that it was limited and that I needed to look to other women in the club for their knowledge and wisdom.

My own financial literacy began as a child watching my mother and grandmother balance their checkbooks on the edge of their beds on Saturday mornings. Although she was never elected president of PWI, my grandmother's strict attention to detail and record keeping (she was also an avid stamp and coin collector) as club treasurer helped to stabilize the organization's financial records for years to come. Yet, my term as club treasurer was my least effective. My academic training did not prepare me for creating income-and-expense reports. I was least confident about being club treasurer, so I would make it a point to have my mother help me prepare treasury reports the night before a general meeting. Even with her help, I dreaded the moment the agenda called for the treasury report. I knew my calculations would be questioned by each member, as these women were used to paying attention to detail when it came to their money and how it was spent; no penny went unnoticed. As I would fumble over my report, my mother would be sure to add in footnotes to clarify what I was reporting. I imagine the questions I would have gotten from members would have been more intense had my mother not intervened.

I can understand as I read Robyn's narrative why she feels uncomfortable with me trying to place the literacy sponsorship label on her literacy relationship with the club. She reminds me that not only did she rely on the financial literacy expertise of her grandmother and mother to help her acquire a particular kind of literacy to which she had little access but she also relied on their authority and status in the club to bolster that "voice" that she was still on her way to earning. Although she may have had access to material literacy resources that were valuable to the club, other members also had resources that were as valuable and on which Robyn had to rely to fulfill her obligations to the club. She emphasizes the reciprocal nature of her literacy relationship and role within the club. First and foremost, the roles and relationships are dynamic; they shift and change. Second, because of the reciprocity, Robyn and her fellow club members sponsor each other. These shifting roles and relationships suggest that Robyn's literacy identity is not static. It shifts based on the reciprocal nature of her relationship with the other women.

With her academic credentials and literacy expertise, Robyn was offering, as she suggests, a particular kind of literacy resource connected to academic training. But that was not the only literacy that was of value to the members of PWI. These women were literate in ways that Robyn had yet to master, such as financial literacy and community building. They also had a kind of authority that comes with age and life experience as well as the multiple literacies that they, too, engaged. Robyn reminds me that sponsorship and authority are intricately intertwined, that the authority that comes from an academic space is not necessarily always welcome in this black women's cultural space, and even when it is, the invitation—and it is an invitation—can be revoked. The "scholarship committee incidents" are interesting examples of when the academic space was rejected, and the invitation seemed a bit in jeopardy.

In 2006, Phenomenal Women Inc. decided to create a scholarship award for local high school graduates intending to pursue a college degree at a two-year or four-year college or university. It was important to club members that the scholarship be awarded to those students who "did not get all A's" and who "needed a little help." I recall the discussion about scholarship criteria was intense as club members voiced conflicting views about who should qualify for the two $500 awards and who was not worthy. Some club members had had negative experiences with financial-aid resources that had denied funding to their own college-bound children, grandchildren, nieces, and nephews. Others spoke from their own personal feelings of academic inadequacies as former high school students. It was very clear during the planning of scholarship criteria that there was no standard we all shared, and if there was, we intended to break the mold of what constituted a "qualified scholarship applicant."

One particular point of contention was the grade-point average for scholarship applicants. I was well aware of the standard 3.0 GPA requirement of most colleges and universities. As a literacy resource, I explained to club members how the numerical GPA translated to a letter grade on a 4.0 scale. After listening to my explanation, many club members expressed concern that such a high GPA would exclude applicants who had nonacademic accomplishments that mattered. Club members came to the agreement that community service, a central mission of Phenomenal Women, should be considered more valuable than GPA. What did these high school students do to assist others less fortunate than themselves? What about candidates who took on part-time jobs while attending school? Should they be "penalized" because they couldn't keep their grades up because they had to work?

After much debate about the GPA requirement (I explained the importance of using the GPA requirement as a filter for student commitment and potential), I attempted to translate the concerns club members raised into the scholarship award application that I was composing. Ultimately, the club determined that a 2.0 GPA would encourage those academically challenged students to apply for the Phenomenal Women Incorporated's Althea Jackson Educational Scholarship Award.[3] Applicants would also need to demonstrate community service involvement and activities, as well as financial need, as part of the application process. While the GPA debate suggests that my "sponsor" role is tenuous, the scholarship selection committee discussion proves that the sponsor-sponsee role can be flipped on its head.

I had served on the organization's scholarship award committee since its inception. This role has been consistently challenging as I have had to prepare, market, distribute, and process scholarship applications. Once applications are received, I prepare copies for the committee members to review and judge. In 2009, my second year as president, I took it upon myself to introduce "objective judging" to the process as a means of making the scholarship judging more "formal" and academic. I invited professional colleagues of mine to serve as "external" scholarship judges. The judging process would begin with internal review of applications by Phenomenal Women Inc. scholarship committee members. The internal judges would select three finalists whose applications would then be judged by "professional" external judges. The external judges included a Columbus State English professor and a former PWI Woman of the Year awardee who was a K–12 educator. Both external judges were African American and female. I knew they had experience with scholarship judging, and I believed they would add an academic and professional element to the scholarship award process. My decision to make these changes to the process without first consulting the scholarship committee members was a mistake I would soon regret.

Although club members had trusted me with handling the scholarship process until this point, their trust did not extend to my authority to select external judges and especially without the consent of scholarship committee members. This was revealed during my reporting of the scholarship committee status at a general meeting. I was interrupted by a club member who questioned why the judging process was changed to include judges who were not club members. I explained that using external judges was standard procedure used in the academy to ensure a certain level of objectivity in the judging. This response was not received well by any of the club members, including my mother and aunt. I recall immediately a feeling of suspicion seemed to fill the meeting room. I had underestimated the vested interest these club members had in the scholarship award. What I experienced as a cumbersome task that needed to get done efficiently with as much objectivity as possible, they experienced as an opportunity to utilize their own literacy skills, knowledge, and discernment. What I didn't know was how much time and effort they put into judging the applications. I was not privy to the phone conversations they had amongst each other regarding the applicants. I did not witness their moments of contemplation about each applicant. Serving as scholarship judges, a literacy in itself, empowered these women. I had no right to take that opportunity from them nor to assume that their literacy skills were inadequate.

I was present at meetings where the scholarship committee discussed criteria for the scholarship and Robyn's changes to the scholarship selection process. While the discussion of the external scholarship judges was filled with far more tension than the scholarship GPA criteria, I remember thinking about both of them that the women were pushing back against something. Implicit in their discussion about grade-point average was their belief that the average student was being ignored in the schools. They even said to Robyn, "The 3.0 student will always have help but not the 2.0" (Moss, field notes, February 8, 2008). In their rejection of the academy's narrative that the spoils go the best and brightest, the PWI women saw themselves as serving community members who needed the most help. They were recognizing and valuing the literacies not valued by this other space that Robyn occupied. I thought that it was ironic that Robyn's academic space—the community college—often caters to the underserved group that the PWI women wanted to serve and is, itself, a space that is often not valued as an important academic space. Although the discussion about the scholarship grade-point average ultimately ended in the women making a successful argument for their position, Robyn, from my perspective, was not really seen as trying to impose the rules of the academy onto PWI.

However, that was not the case about the "scholarship selection committee incident." As she suggests in her discussion above, everyone who spoke about this incident at this meeting disagreed with Robyn's change and questioned her authority to do so. What seemed to be at stake was why she had made this change without consultation of the committee—even her status as president did not give her the right to do so—and what could these "external" judges bring that the PWI committee members could not. The club women saw no value in the external judges' academic credentials when it came to deciding who received the scholarship. I, too, witnessed, how invested the women were in their ability to make decisions about who received the scholarships. They were offended that they were not trusted to make their own decisions and, ultimately, rejected the literacy skills of the external judges. In my field notes about the scholarship selection process, I wrote: "Daryl and Flora ask Robyn why there were external reviewers. Flora voices her objections to having people outside the club choosing the scholarship winner" (April 24, 2009). I noted the tension.

Having been witness to these meetings and then having conversations with Robyn about both incidents then and now, I reflect on the not-always-comfortable alliance between academic space and African American community space, spaces where Robyn lives daily. I think about how Robyn negotiates her expected literacy role and identity within the club (and her family). I think about how her literacy identities shift depending on what values are in control, whose authority reigns, and what and how the clubwomen's own literacy is positioned. Finally, I go back to Robyn's discussion of "earning her voice." These latter examples of which Robyn writes suggests that she does not necessarily consistently control access to literacy or set the agenda for how literacy is used, which places her sponsorship role in question.

Although she certainly has a literacy identity within the club, which we have both discussed throughout this essay, that identity shifts. Her literacy expertise is welcomed most times but not all times. Her academic credentials and experiences do not trump life experiences. While her fellow PWI sisters are proud of her literacy educator role and status, there are lines that she cannot cross, as the scholarship committee discussions suggest. And earning her voice is not a mountain that she climbs and is finished. It is a series of hills to be negotiated. The "scholarship committee selection incident" demonstrates that members of the club, while relying on Robyn's literacy expertise in some moments, choose to ignore that expertise when it does not suit their purposes and their desires and choose to call on their own literacy expertise. It is at this point that Robyn finds herself renegotiating her literacy identity within the club.

So how do we characterize Robyn's literacy identity with the club? When Beverly asked Robyn about being a literacy sponsor, Robyn stated, "It makes me feel like I'm doing something for them, something on my own agenda. Our relationship is more reciprocal than that." As we hope we have demonstrated above, these women exerted their authority over the agenda of the club when they felt the need to. They set the agenda; Robyn helped them reach their goals. In many ways, Robyn used her literacy to be the keeper and protector of the club's mission and the women themselves. However, she rarely did so from a position of power.

Ultimately, Robyn rejects the notion of herself as having some kind of power over someone else. This rejection occurs for many reasons: not wanting to have power over adult family members; still being among the youngest club members (though no longer the youngest); and grappling with the negative connotations and baggage of "sponsor," "sponsored," and "sponsorship." She accepts, instead, a view that she and the women in the club exchange literacies, talents, and information. We see her literacy identity as that of a resource that can be used in a variety of ways and at the pleasure of the group. However, we are reminded that as much as literacy domains and spaces can be shared, like academic, family, and community domains, those spaces can also create tensions and conflict. When one person privileges one domain over the other at the wrong time—Robyn privileging the academic domain in the scholarship discussion—conflict arises. So the concept of literacy sponsorship is a starting point but not an ending point.

Examining Robyn's literacy identity within this club teaches us that to understand the complexities of literacy sponsorship as a theoretical concept, we need to examine it from the perspective of the sponsor, recognize that "sponsor" is an unstable and shifting position, and more closely examine the reciprocal relationships that characterize literacy sponsors and sponsored. Finally, we suggest that literacy sponsorship needs to be evaluated within the context of the multiple identities that race, gender, class, and ethnicity, among other identity markers, require us to negotiate. These "phenomenal women" operate within a racialized and gendered space where they fight for and against the realities of literacy as both liberating and enslaving, inclusive and exclusive, worthy of praise and worthy of suspicion—requiring its members to make literacy work for the club through an exchange of literacy expertise, talents, and materials.

Notes

1. The National African American Read-In Chain is sponsored by the National Council of Teachers of English, and its goal is to promote the reading of African American literature across the country and across ages, races, and cultures. The event is usually held in February, Black History Month.

2. Robyn had discarded Niki, a childhood name, by the time that we met. However, to many of the women in the club, she will always be Niki.

3. Althea Jackson is Robyn's grandmother and a founding member of PWI.

References

Brandt, Deborah. 2001. *Literacy in American Lives.* New York: Cambridge University Press.
Heath, Shirley Brice. 1983. *Ways with Words: Language, Life, and Work in Communities and Classrooms.* New York: Cambridge University Press.

Moss, Beverly J. 2003. *A Community Text Arises: A Literate Text and a Literacy Tradition in African American Churches.* Cresskill, NJ: Hampton.

———. 2010. "Phenomenal Women," Collaborative Literacies, and Community Texts in Alternative "Sista Spaces." *Community Literacy Journal,* 5(1), 1–24.

Richardson, Elaine. 2003. *African American Literacies.* New York: Routledge.

10. Seeking Sponsors, Accumulating Literacies: Deborah Brandt and English Education

Michael W. Smith

The chapters in this volume make the influence of Deborah Brandt's ideas on composition studies abundantly clear. In this chapter I argue that Brandt's thinking can be equally generative for English education, basing my argument on what I see as the instructional implication of two key constructs, both generated through the in-depth interviews of eighty ordinary people that were the source of data for *Literacy in American Lives* (2001) and a number of articles: sponsors of literacy and accumulating literacy.

Sponsors of Literacy: In Teaching English

In her first formulation of the notion of sponsors of literacy, Brandt describes them as "any agents, local or distant, concrete or abstract, who enable, support, teach, model, as well as recruit, regulate, suppress, or withhold literacy—and gain advantage by it in some way" (1998, p. 166). Brandt's notion of sponsorship helped me see that the literate activity in my classroom is a function not just of what students know and are able to do but also of the institutions that authorize their knowledge and activity.

Perhaps the reason I did not recognize the importance of sponsorship was that the sponsor of my literate activity is a distant and abstract one: the discipline. Take, for example, one common kind of literate activity: the discussion of a particular literary text, especially a canonical text. I was an English major, and even if I hadn't studied the text we were discussing in college or graduate school, I had studied others like it. Like most teachers, I knew the technical terms used to describe literary effects, literary movements, and so on.

Moreover, like most teachers, I was teaching texts I had read many times to students who were reading them for the first time, a situation that, as Rabinowitz and Smith (1998) point out, has significant effects on the way literature is taught. In my classroom, as in most others, the reader who had the most disciplinary training also had the advantage of multiple readings. Teachers who do not notice technical nuances on a first reading are likely to recognize them on a second, third, or fourth. Teachers' training and their multiple readings make them comfortable reading and speaking and writing with the sponsorship of the discipline. Little wonder that students who lack that sponsorship are often reluctant to contribute, particularly when the focus is a technical one, a situation that is most clearly manifested in the wealth of studies that demonstrate the extent to which teachers control classroom discussion (see, for example, Marshall, Smagorinsky, and Smith, 1995).

The recognition of the importance of sponsorship and of the power of my distant and abstract sponsors has led me to think about how classrooms could be arranged to provide students with concrete and local sponsors who could serve to authorize students' literate activity as they were moving to being able to draw upon the sponsorship of the discipline. A study I did with Eli Goldblatt, one of the editors of and contributors to this volume, in a first-year reading and writing class that he taught has had a significant influence on my thinking. Our work together has convinced me of the importance of keeping the power of sponsorship firmly in mind in designing a course.

In his own scholarly work, Eli articulates the importance of sponsorship this way:

> We can't talk about authors unless we recognize the institutions which have authorized them to write. Since writers must create their texts within the context of institutions—sometimes within the context of multiple institutions—authors must always fulfill two roles: they act both as representers of a socially shared and institutionalized reality and also as representatives of sponsoring institutions. (1995, p. 25)

Eli was very much aware first-year students could not call upon a discipline to sponsor their work. Most of them had had no formal training in their declared majors, and many of them would be switching majors at least once before graduation. That is why Eli sought to tap the sponsorship power of the classroom itself, a local institution that all of his students had access to.

Eli made a variety of instructional moves designed to allow students to read and write with his classroom as sponsor. One was to divide students into groups of three, groups in which students would stay the whole semester. Eli arranged the desks in his class in a large circle. Students could sit anywhere as long as they sat next to their group mates. A regular occurrence in his class, especially when the class was discussing a particularly difficult interpretive issue, was for Eli simply to say "groups" and for the students to discuss in their triads before the whole-class discussion started again. Eli explained that these triads provided a home base for students. That is, when they spoke in class, they could do so as a representative of the group. The triads, then, acted as sponsoring institutions.

Eli also made instructional moves so that students could draw on larger classroom structures for their sponsorship. He incorporated book clubs into the course. Students divided themselves into interest groups to discuss a play and a series of poems that they selected. In introducing this activity, Eli spoke openly of his goal to encourage students to become adult readers in the mode of book-club members—readers who read for their own purposes and who talk about books in order to enjoy and understand them in personal ways.

Eli's emphasis on the adult book clubs was informed by research I had done (1996) on the patterns of discourse that characterized the talk of two adult book clubs. One of my most noteworthy findings was the social dimension of the clubs, a dimension manifested in how often the book-club members drew on their own life experience as a source of knowledge in their discussions. To the extent that Eli's book clubs operated in a similar fashion, in creating the clubs he not only allowed his students to draw on this larger classroom structure to sponsor their literate activity but he also created a context that would make it more likely that they would draw on their home institutions.

In addition, he created activities in which students could draw on their previous school histories. For example, discussion itself was a subject of discussion for the class. Students wrote about their conception of good discussion three times during the class, the class talked about transcripts of the adult book clubs that I provided, and the class regularly reflected upon the small and large group discussions the students had had in the course.

At the end of the course, we collected from each student a portfolio that included the three prompted journal entries on what makes a good discussion, two papers that students selected to represent their work in the class, two additional journal entries, and one written response that the student had made to a classmate's writing. A close examination of the work of one student indicates the impact of Eli's instruction.

Anthony was a white eighteen-year-old first-year student who wrote that he "grew up in a working class neighborhood" in the heart of the traditionally Italian section of the city. Anthony came to Eli's course without the kinds of institutional affiliations that could give him the expectation that his ideas would be attended to in a university classroom. This is reflected in his initial consideration of what makes a good discussion: "A good discussion is one that brings to light new ideas or perspectives another may have on a particular topic. It may be an idea that you never imagined, thereby broadening your horison. A good discussion can also bring out ideas you (I) (one) may have but need coaxing to bring out."

Anthony was uncertain of himself as a capable participant in discussions. His menu of pronoun referents—"you (I) (one)"—reflects both his hesitance to place himself in the discussion and his uncertainty about whether he was adopting an appropriately academic register in his writing. Anthony seemed intimidated by some of his classmates. He reported to Eli later that in his first year of college—where he was surrounded by students from wealthier and more suburban backgrounds than his own—he was hesitant to speak his mind in front of people he regarded as better educated and more socially privileged than he.

Anthony's feelings that he lacked appropriate institutional sponsorship are evident in his early writing about literature. He began a paper written during the first third of the course, an explication of a passage from Shakespeare's *All's Well That Ends Well*:

> I choose this passage for two reasons, the comedy aspect and the affect it had on the story. It is a very lively and intriguing passage that might seem tong in cheek at first, however on examining the passage one finds it has greater meaning. The passage affects Bertram in one of two possible ways. The two ways are quite different, however the ending of the play doesn't allow us to make a clear judgement as to the morality of Bertram. This ambiguity is how I can justify presenting two different possibilities on how the passage may have affected Bertram.

Anthony never takes a position on these two possibilities. He closes: "Which one of these two possible outcomes really happened to Bertram, is up to the reader to decide." Like the ideal discussion he describes, his writing serves to raise possibilities rather than to argue an already formulated position.

By the end of the class, Anthony had modified his approach. In his final inquiry, he sees good discussions as occasions "where most of the class is involved creating many different viewpoints on one particular topic. To have a good discussion, it also helps to have people with a variety of different backgrounds in order to get a well-rounded discussion. For example, a person from the country could talk about farming while you need a person in the city to talk about the subway." In his final inquiry, Anthony seems to see good discussions as exchanges in which experts would contribute discrete pieces of a puzzle. And according to Anthony, what makes people experts are the institutional affiliations they bring with them.

His reference to subways is an explicit attempt to draw on the sponsorship in a home institution in the way he might have in his book club. He described his background in the final inquiry.

> [T]he positive difference between where I live as opposed to the suburbs is that I remember (and still do) playing in the schoolyard or playground games some have never heard of like jailbreak, hide the belt, and more common games that we played everyday like handball, chink, and roller hockey. These and things like sneaking into the box seats at the [city's stadium] are the events that shape who I am today.

The fact that the classroom could accommodate his background as part of who he could be gave him the opportunity to see himself as a worthy participant in conversations that were more academic in nature.

Anthony's writing became more assertive as he accepted the sponsorship of the classroom. His final paper on Updike's "Ex–Basketball Player" has a far different tone than does his paper on *All's Well That Ends Well.*

> In the poem "Ex–Basketball Player" we enter the life of a man who goes from star athlete to gas-station attendant. He is exploited for his talents to play basketball by society, then cast aside when he can no longer serve their purposes. . . . My thesis is that society is at fault for not educating Flick, but Flick himself is also to blame for not educating himself. I will make a stanza by stanza analysis of the poem to support my thesis.

Anthony casts himself in the role of one of those experts who offer their opinions to the audience. The tentativeness of his early paper is gone. Of course, some of the difference in his writing may be a function of the accessibility of the material. However, Anthony could have explored his idea by asking, "Who is at fault, society or Flick?" and presented evidence for both sides of that question. Instead, he cast himself in the role of a speaker with a definite opinion on the character and his relation to society.

His thesis also represents a political position: Social forces may make the environment hostile for a child's growth, but it is up to the individual to stand up for himself or herself. During conversations well after the class, Anthony reported to Eli that this political position emerged out of a crucial conflict he was trying to resolve during his early college career. In his parents' world, an individual was held fully responsible for what he or she became. In college, however, he came to see historical and social forces as important or even dominating influences in individuals' lives. He needed to reconcile that newfound sociological perspective with a belief rooted in the lives of people he knew in the neighborhood: that despite adversity a determined person could succeed and prosper. He said in retrospect that the paper on Updike's poem forced him to confront that conflict directly.

A similar conflict surfaced, rather unexpectedly for us, in Anthony's final inquiry. After commenting on the homogeneity of his Italian and Catholic neighborhood, he included a long digression about race relations.

> Growing up in neighborhoods you had to stay in an area that you are familiar with otherwise could be roughed up in a black neighborhood for example. The whole race issue is two fold for me, I realize history and sympathise with the plight of blacks but at the same time most of my friends and even my brother has been jumped and beaten up by blacks because we had to walk through a black neighborhood to get to school. I guess you could say I'm at the front lines of the race issue. I have been fed racism from the streets for as long as I can remember and it's hard to free myself from these ideas, but I try.

Eli and I believe that this comment suggests that the class served as a sponsoring institution for writing that explored ideas in a way he could not approach either at home or in a discipline-dominated classroom. At home or among his neighborhood friends, he told Eli later, attitudes were strongly held and hard to speak against; he knew no one who would be willing to have a thoughtful conversation on race. In a disciplinary discussion of historical or sociological texts, however, he could not feel comfortable even mentioning the attitudes he heard on South Philly streets. Eli's course served as a safe haven from these two institutional extremes he had to reconcile; in the writing classroom, classmates could act as less-threatening surrogates for members of a learned discipline. As Anthony's final inquiry suggests, he felt that he had a unique perspective that he could offer his classmates, a perspective that was worthy of attention. The sponsorship of the classroom allowed him to weigh home and academic positions and to develop a position for himself out of all that he had heard. Thus, in writing sponsored by a classroom open to a variety of influences, he could come to judge the character of the ex–basketball player in terms influenced by home attitudes but not dominated by them.

Although I did not have the language for it at the time, I had understood, in James Gee's words, that classroom discourse about literature is a particular Discourse, that is, that it is a way of "behaving, interacting, valuing, believing," as well as "speaking, and often reading and writing" (2007, p. 4).

I had understood that Discourses are a way of being, again according to Gee, "people like us" (2007, p. 4) and believed that students are advantaged to the extent that they can take on that role. Brandt's notion of sponsorship has helped me see that my efforts to help students be able to act as "people like us" would be powerfully supported by first letting them act as people like them, that is, by allowing them to access sponsors they already have and then by creating a classroom structured so that students could also draw on it to sponsor their reading and writing as they work to develop new sponsors "to enable, support, teach, model" their literate activity (Brandt 1998, p. 166).

Sponsors of Literacy: In Teaching Teachers

My teaching has centered on teaching preservice teachers, but on occasion I have also taught inservice teachers, and here, too, Brandt's notion of sponsorship has been very important. Inspired in part by the work she was doing, I developed a course in which teachers read and watched a variety of stories of language learners, for example, Gloria E. Anzaldúa's *Borderlands/La Frontera*, wrote and shared their own literacy autobiographies, and conducted an interview modeled on those reported in *Literacy in American Lives* (2001) with someone different from themselves on some demographic detail. The culminating assignment for the course was to write a paper in which they considered what I think is a crucial question: Are there themes that cut across stories, or do attempts to generalize across stories (or some meaningful subset of stories) always hurt those who are generalized about by minimizing the unique experience of an individual? We read "Accumulating Literacy" (1995) and "Sponsors of Literacy" (1998) as models for the kind of thinking they could do.

The last year I taught the class included one of my most memorable teaching moments ever. After reading "Sponsors" and talking about what it meant for us as teachers, I asked this question: "We've been talking about sponsors of literacy. Now I want to discuss sponsors of literacy teaching. Think about your teaching. Who's sponsoring it? Who is 'gain[ing] advantage by it in some way?'"

The question proved to be a potent impetus for introspection. One teacher said something like the following: "I think of myself as a student-centered teacher, somebody who always has the best interests of her kids in mind. But I see now that in many ways I have been acting as an agent for interests that may not align with those of my kids: ETS [the Educational Testing Service], the Chamber of Commerce, and college admissions departments." What ensued was a lengthy and impassioned discussion both about who sponsored our teaching and whose sponsorship we should try to invoke.

One of my aims in working with teachers has always been for them to think hard about the politics of their teaching. But I have not always been successful in that goal. Brandt's careful and compelling argument on sponsorship provides a powerful analytic for fostering the kind of thinking I am aiming for.

Accumulating Literacy

The notion of accumulating literacy has also been a powerful influence on my thinking and teaching. Brandt's (1995) fundamental argument is deceptive in its simplicity. She argues that new forms of literacy are proliferating. But these new forms of literacy are not replacing the old ones. In the popular imagination, tweeting might have replaced texting, which might have replaced IMing, which might have replaced e-mailing, which might have replaced letter writing. But we still have occasion to write letters.

Brandt explains the consequences of this proliferation of literacies:

> Contemporary literacy learners—across positions of age, gender, race, class, and language heritage—find themselves having to piece together reading and writing experiences from more and more spheres, creating new and hybrid forms of literacy where once there might have been fewer and more circumscribed forms. What we calculate as a rising standard of basic literacy may be more usefully regarded as the effects of a rapid proliferation and diversification of literacy. And literate ability at the end of the twentieth century may be best measured as a person's capacity to amalgamate new reading and writing practices in response to rapid social change. (1995, p. 651)

Many of the preservice teachers whom I teach come to my classes with a profound belief in the value of some of the circumscribed forms of literacy to which Brandt refers. Little wonder: Their ability to perform those literacies has advantaged my students throughout their academic careers. Those students typically hold progressive pedagogical understandings, so they are amenable to investigating ways to invigorate the teaching of canonical literacies. But they often resist calls to introduce new literacies because they see time spent on those literacies coming at the expense of time spent on canonical ones.

The notion of accumulating literacies helps me make the call for reform more effectively to my more resistant students. That is, Brandt establishes that new literacies don't supplant established ones. Rather, they exist alongside and are often intermingled with each other. The construct of accumulating literacies, then, provides a springboard for me to argue that new literacies are worthy as objects of study and production in and of themselves even as I must recognize that canonical literacies are equally worthy.

The recognition of the proliferation of new literacies also helps me make an argument for the importance of transfer, an argument absolutely central to my understanding of what teaching ought to be. Perhaps because *transfer* is a psychological term in a sociocultural age, it doesn't seem to me to get the attention it deserves.

My colleague Jeff Wilhelm and I have argued elsewhere (Smith and Wilhelm, 2006, 2010) that transfer ought to be our single most important concern as teachers. When the nature of literacy changes as much and as rapidly as Brandt demonstrates, we need always to think about how the literacy teaching we do today prepares students for the literacy learning in which they will engage both in and out of our classrooms, literacy learning the nature of which we cannot predict.

It seems to me that teachers count on the fact that transfer occurs. D. N. Perkins and Gavriel Salomon (1988) concur in an article that has long influenced my thinking. They argue that teachers rely on what they call the Little Bo Peep view of transfer; that is, if we "leave them alone," they come to a new task and naturally transfer relevant knowledge and skills. They go on to argue that "leaving them alone" is ineffective, for "a great deal of the knowledge students acquire is 'inert,'" something that shows up on a multiple-choice test but not in "new problem-solving contexts where they have to think about new situations" (p. 23).

Haskell (2000) concurs: "Despite the importance of transfer of learning, research findings over the past nine decades clearly show that as individuals, and as educational institutions, we have failed to achieve transfer of learning on any significant level" (p. xiii).

Haskell, however, argues that we can teach to transfer. He presents eleven conditions that foster transfer that I think can usefully be reduced to four:

1. If students have command of the knowledge that is to be transferred
2. If students have a theoretical understanding of the principles to be transferred
3. If a classroom culture cultivates a spirit of transfer, and
4. If students get plenty of practice in applying meaning-making and problem-solving principles to new situations. (pp. 45–46)

Haskell's arguments resonate with what Perkins and Salomon (1988) call *high-road transfer*. High-road transfer, they explain, requires "mindful abstraction of skill or knowledge from one context to another" (p. 25). That is, to transfer knowledge from one context to a dissimilar context requires you to know just what it is you do. If literacies are multiple and malleable, as Brandt explains, as teachers we need to help students understand just what it is they do when they read and compose texts of various kinds in various contexts. We need to engage them in investigating the extent to which what they do is consistent across the wide range of literacies they employ.

My conversations with Deborah Brandt began in the late 1980s at the University of Wisconsin–Madison. Initially, they were conducted through our students. Deborah was teaching a course on composition for teachers, and I taught the same students in their secondary English methods class, so I would be sure to hear when something I said did not jibe with something that she said. It was not long before those mediated conversations were replaced by face-to-face ones in the reading group we established for the composition and English education faculty. I was new to the academy, so I did not realize until later that this kind of collegiality across departmental boundaries is all too rare.

I left the University of Wisconsin twenty years ago, but my conversations with Deborah have not ended, though they primarily occur now through her work. But they have the same character. She continues to push me to think about my job in new ways. Deborah Brandt is not an educational researcher, though she has a deep and abiding interest in education and is a wonderful teacher herself. However, her work has profound implications for those of us working in education.

I do not have many of the kind of interdisciplinary conversations that I have had with Deborah. I don't go to CCCC anymore; I do not feel at home there. It seems to me that English education and composition studies have moved away from each other. Writing this paper has reminded me that that need not be the case. So I leave it with the resolve to be open to a wider variety of conversational partners. Another lesson I learned from Deborah Brandt.

References

Anzaldúa, Gloria E. 1987. *Borderlands/La Frontera: The New Mestiza.* San Francisco: Aunt Lute Books.

Brandt, Deborah. 1995. "Accumulating Literacy: Writing and Learning to Write in the Twentieth Century." *College English,* 57(6), 649–68.

———. 1998. "Sponsors of Literacy." *College Composition and Communication,* 49(2), 165–85.

———. 2001. *Literacy in American Lives.* New York: Cambridge University Press.

Gee, James. 2007. *Social Linguistics and Literacies: Ideology in Discourses.* 3rd ed. London: Routledge.

Goldblatt, Eli. 1995. *'Round My Way: Authority and Double-Consciousness in Three Urban High School Writers.* Pittsburgh: University of Pittsburgh Press.

Haskell, Robert E. 2000. *Transfer of Learning: Cognition, Instruction, and Reasoning.* San Diego: Academic Press.

Marshall, James D., Peter Smagorinsky, and Michael W. Smith. 1995. *The Language of Interpretation: Patterns of Discourse in Discussions of Literature.* Urbana, IL: National Council of Teachers of English.

Perkins, D. N., and Gavriel Salomon. 1988. "Teaching for Transfer." *Educational Leadership, 46*(1), 22–32.

Rabinowitz, Peter J., and Michael W. Smith. 1998. *Authorizing Readers: Resistance and Respect in the Teaching of Literature.* New York: Teachers College Press.

Smith, Michael W. 1996. "Conversations about Literature outside Classrooms: How Adults Talk about Books in Their Book Clubs." *Journal of Adolescent and Adult Literacy, 40*(3), 180–86.

Smith, Michael W., and Jeffrey D. Wilhelm. 2006. *Going with the Flow: How to Engage Boys (and Girls) in Their Literacy Learning.* Portsmouth, NH: Heinemann.

———. 2010. *Fresh Takes on Teaching Literary Elements: How to Teach What Really Matters about Character, Setting, Point of View, and Theme.* New York: Scholastic.

11. Combining Phenomenological and Sociohistoric Frameworks for Studying Literate Practices: Some Implications of Deborah Brandt's Methodological Trajectory

Paul Prior

> One can take a pencil and trace lexical reiteration, pronoun reference, and other devices by which texts point back and forth and usually in at themselves. But tracing such structural patterns in language-on-its-own is like coming upon the scene of a party after it is over and everybody has gone home, being left to imagine from the remnants what the party must have been like. I have been arguing in this chapter for a view of texts that is based on how they are coming over the horizon for writer and reader.
> —Deborah Brandt, *Literacy as Involvement*

Over the last three decades, phenomenological and sociohistoric theories have shaped the way literate practices have been theorized and studied (Prior, 2005, Russell, 2010). However, while sociohistoric (or cultural-historic activity) theory has been actively discussed and debated, phenomenological theory has rarely been foregrounded and is often not well understood or even recognized. The way phenomenology was central to Deborah Brandt's early work but then seemed to disappear illustrates this tendency. Teasing out the place of phenomenology in Brandt's scholarship may offer some insight into her important body of work (which has occasioned this volume), but I pursue this issue here primarily because I believe it can help clarify the significant, but often unrecognized, ways phenomenology has animated literacy studies, that it can prompt a clearer mapping of theory in this area, and, finally, that it will clarify how combining phenomenological and sociohistoric frameworks can inform literacy research. The epigraph of this chapter, on parties and texts coming over the horizon, epitomizes Brandt's (1990) phenomenological argument against the great orality-literacy divide (e.g., Ong, 1982), a divide driven by an artifact-centered, decontextualized, asocial image of text on its own.[1] Arguing that literate practice is grounded in intersubjective knowledge of what readers do as they interpret texts and writers do in composing texts, the epigraph emphasizes the dynamics of literate activity—the way people navigate texts as they emerge moment by moment over the horizon. From that perspective, Brandt (1990, 1992) argues, literacy actually involves an intensification of, not a separation from, social contexts.

Explicitly arguing for a phenomenological/ethnomethodological approach to the study of writing processes, Brandt (1992) analyzes a think-aloud protocol, not to construct flow-chart boxes of cognitive processes in writing (compare Flower and Hayes, 1981) but as evidence of the deeply social, intersubjective, reflexive, and indexical character of literate work. To get at this still in-flux work, researchers and theorists, the epigraph's analogy suggests, need to attend to the live action of the party, not sift through the aftermath and imagine the party as though its sediments contain its purest sense. Evoking the promise of ethnomethodology in relation to a canonical scene of literacy research, the classroom, Brandt notes the way ethnomethodology decenters taken-for-granted social categories (teacher, student, class, assignment), seeing them as accomplishments (not givens), thus requiring "inquiry into how any instance of classroom life actually gets accomplished on a day-to-day, minute-to-minute basis by the participants at the scene" (1992, p. 346). Brandt acknowledges limitations of this kind of local, one-event approach and discusses Heap's (1991) call for a "cultural phenomenology" more focused on the antecedent cultural forms that populate any local event (while still recognizing that such forms are reshaped in reflexive, contingent uptake). However, Brandt concludes that her interest was in the situated moment-by-moment contingency of uptake (the live scene of the party).

Brandt's research after 1992 shifted to systematic, life-history interviews of individuals (ten to ninety-eight years old) and explored how individuals' literate experiences related to social, economic, and technological histories. Aiming to trace the contours and channels of literacy over decades, this research culminated in *Literacy in American Lives* (2001a) and a series of related essays. In the process, Brandt seemed to leave ethnomethodology behind: We find no references in *Literacy in American Lives* to the ethnomethodologists, conversation analysts, and phenomenological sociologists of 1992 or, for that matter, to Brandt's own work in the early 1990s. Brandt (2001a) is decidedly offering not situated studies of live parties but accounts of parties long past. In what might be read as the most direct break with her earlier call for attention to live action, Brandt and Katie Clinton (2002) critique social-practice accounts for being overly focused on the local and on participants' perspectives.

Considering Brandt's shift from arguing for direct evidence of parties (literate practices) as they happen to arguing for life-history studies (using interviews and other indirect evidence) of parties long past, a reasonable interpretation might be that Brandt's party analogy (and her attention to ethnomethodology) was just a phase in her scholarship, that once the strong-text and cognitive paradigms dominant in the 1980s had receded, she turned to a larger social canvas, examining the social and economic forces that channel, afford, and sponsor literacy practices, that attach value to literate acts, artifacts, and actors. Certainly, Brandt did not hew to conversation analytic or typical ethnomethodological methods in her subsequent research. Perhaps she rejected phenomenological theory more thoroughly. However, I argue for a different read,[2] one in which a sustained resonance with phenomenological sociology spans Brandt's career, in which situated study of live action and historical inquiry can be understood as complementary phenomenological methods and in which phenomenological and sociohistoric approaches share considerable common ground (see also Prior, 2005, Russell, 2010).

Three Phenomenologies

To assess Brandt's engagement with phenomenological sociology, we first need to untangle three lines of thought in phenomenology that are often confused (sometimes one line being equated with the whole tradition). Historically, Conversation Analysis (CA) grew out of ethnomethodology, which in turn grew out of phenomenological sociology.[3] In the last three decades, CA has achieved a prominence that masks other phenomenological perspectives. CA focuses on talk (or face-to-face interaction) as the primary site for the achievement of social order (see Atkinson and Heritage, 1984). Its methodological principle of relevance (Schegloff, 1991) argues that participants in an interaction must display to one another the accountable sense of their acts, statements, roles, and contexts; analysts are, therefore, enjoined to strictly limit themselves to the data that participants themselves must rely on, meaning behaviors publically displayed by participants to one another in the interaction. CA takes the faithful representation of people's sequential talk in a transcript as objective evidence of the achievement of the social. It rejects any suggestion that CA analysis of a transcript represents an interpretation and rejects interviews, other accounts, history, and theory as tools for understanding people's practices. Interested in mundane social interaction, CA typically focuses on everyday conversation rather than institutional talk (e.g., in school, workplace, government). It is critical to recognize that CA takes a strictly agnostic position on cognition (LeBaron and Koschmann,

2003), seeing representations of thoughts and feelings as public accounting practices, not as evidence of inner psychological states of mind. In short, CA is radically behaviorist, localist, and ahistorical; interested in mundane, everyday settings; and focused almost exclusively on talk.

Drawing on phenomenology, Harold Garfinkel coined the term *ethnomethodology*, and his *Studies in Ethnomethodology* (1967) was a key announcement of this program. However, after 1967, Garfinkel fully embraced and helped define CA (while continuing to style his work as ethnomethodological). Ethnomethodologists (e.g., Cicourel, 1992; Suchman, 2000) aim, as conversation analysts do, to understand the methods cultural actors use to construct the social order. Ethnomethodologists do not, however, follow CA's views on relevance and thus use diverse methods, as Garfinkel (1967) did. In addition to sequential analysis of (video- or audiotaped) interactional records, they may also draw on interviews, local documents, other (including historical) accounts of social actors, and theories. Ethnomethodology is generally not cognitively agnostic: Many researchers evince a keen interest in the knowledge of cultural actors and how that knowledge comes to be established. In comparison to CA, ethnomethodology is more interested in institutional sites (workplaces, schools, laboratories) and in writing and other semiotics (e.g., Heath and Luff, 2000). (Further complicating matters, some researchers have begun to refer to ethnomethodological approaches as "Applied CA.") Ethnomethodology then focuses on the local but employs a full range of situated and ethnographic methods to understand interaction, is more oriented to institutions, often expresses a clear interest in cognition, and typically values theory as relevant.

Finally, phenomenological sociology refers to extensions of phenomenology's investigation of how perceptual phenomena and cognitive categories are achieved and ordered in embodied moments of action to questions of how the social order is likewise achieved. A phenomenological orientation to how social actors construct social categories and orders in activity has been widely, if diffusely, expressed in many well-known practice approaches, including those of Pierre Bourdieu (1990), Bruno Latour (2005), and Dorothy Smith (1990). Alfred Schutz, a key figure in this tradition, influenced various interactional approaches, including those of Erving Goffman (1974) and Garfinkel (1967). Not at all cognitively agnostic, Schutz was interested in knowledge, experience, and decisions and how different realities (or provinces of meaning) related to psychological states of consciousness (waking, dreaming, fantasizing, planning). He had a keen interest in action in the everyday world within the reach and direct perception of the individual, but he did not study situated behavior and did not equate the social to the local. Schutz (1962) states that "the world of everyday life is a universe of significance to us, that is, a texture of meaning which we have to interpret in order to find our bearings within it and come to terms with it," a texture of meaning that "originates in and has been instituted by human actions"—actions of our own, of those we interact directly with, and of more distant contemporaries and predecessors (p. 10). Beyond the within-reach social world of interaction, Schutz (1970) defined eight regions of social "contemporaries," concentric circles ranging from individuals I know (not currently present) and types of people I know of (e.g., "the postal employee who will process my letter") to collective entities (like organizations and states); "objective configurations of meaning" (like laws or the standard grammar of English); and material artifacts/tools (pp. 221–22).

Not cognitively agnostic and compatible with various methods of inquiry, phenomenological sociology is focused on the lifeworld of the individual but sees that world as historical and sees the social as radiating into and out from the world within reach. Russell (2010) offers a point-by-point comparison of Schutz and Lev Vygotsky, identifying many close correspondences in their theories, and concludes that Schutz's work, like that of sociohistoric activity theories, integrates a focus on the situated, tool-using subject with an interest in making "meso-level (institutional) and macro-level (ideological) generalizations" (pp. 362–63).

On Brandt and Phenomenological Sociology

If phenomenological/ethnomethodological approaches were equated with a strict CA focus on sequential analysis of moment-to-moment behavior, then Brandt's relationship to those approaches would be quite troubled because her work was never compatible with CA. Brandt's (1992) analysis of a think-aloud protocol to understand the social character of literate cognition-in-action clearly violated both CA's methodological principle of relevance and its cognitive agnosticism. However, that analysis and her earlier interest in the intersubjective character of literacy (Brandt, 1990) do fit with key tenets of ethnomethodology and especially of phenomenological sociology. In fact, in relation to phenomenological work in general and other contemporary uptakes of phenomenology in literacy studies, Brandt's focus in the early 1990s on the emergent, moment-to-moment character of literate practice, even if more trope than method, was innovative and continues to be relevant. Although Brandt (1992) noted early efforts (e.g., Heap, 1991) to develop ethnomethodological approaches to reading and writing, her attention to literacy contrasts with the situation Latour (2005) succinctly captures: "Strangely enough, for all his attention to practice Garfinkel never points out the practice of writing" (p. 122). Moreover, unlike other literacy work in that era, Brandt did not focus on Schutz's notion of typification, which became a cornerstone of genre theory (Miller, 1984; Bazerman, 1988). Even today, writing theory and research continue to be bedeviled by dominant cultural tropes that depict writing as artifacts or individual abilities rather than situated action, tropes that have, for example, almost completely obscured attention to the fact that people routinely engage in face-to-face writing and reading (Prior, 2009). Brandt's party analogy vividly countered such tropes, evoking a picture of writing and reading as fundamentally live, situated activity in a social scene.

Although off the map for CA and not typical of ethnomethodology (which continues to focus on analysis of recorded interactions), Brandt's shift after 1992 to collecting "life history accounts as a means to theorize the history of literacy" (2001b, p. 43) resonates with phenomenological sociology and sociohistoric theory as she focuses on the biographical, embodied, local, and mediated character of literacy. Although she aimed to depersonalize the cases she built out of the interviews, she wrote history in a very biographical idiom, seeking "to understand the vicissitudes of individual literacy development in relationship to the large-scale economic forces that set the routes and determine the worldly worth of that literacy" and attending to how economic forces are "systematically related to the local conditions and embodied moments of literacy learning that occupy so many of us on a daily basis" (2001a, pp. 18–19). Schutz and Thomas Luckmann (1973) also focused on how large social (and natural) forces appeared from the perspective of a person's embodied action:

> We must find our way about in the life-world and while acting and being acted upon must come to terms with the data imposed on us by nature and society. Now, however, it is through my somatic and somatically mediated activity that I seek to modify what is impressed upon me.... The life-world is above all the province of practice, of action. (p. 18)

Reflecting on her life-history interviews, Brandt noted that interviews depicted busy scenes of reading and writing, teeming

> with references to people and things who seemed ever present and involved: parents, teachers, religious figures, military officers, older relatives or friends, authors, prison personnel, supervisors,

physicians, therapists, librarians, product companies, government agencies, unions, school clubs, civil rights organizations, businesses and corporations, radio and television programs of all kinds, as well as an array of materials from ballpoint pens to newspapers, photographs to appointment calendars, toys to computers, that were sold, given, or issued to the people I talked with. (2009b, p. xiii)

Her list resonates strongly with Schutz's (1970) eight regions of contemporaries, even to inclusion of collective entities and material artifacts.

Brandt's life histories attend to the embodied, biographically centered activity and worlds of participants as indexes of sociohistoric conditions that have mediated literate practice. Consider the vignette that opens *Literacy and Learning: Reflections on Writing, Reading, and Society* (2009b). Describing the work of Calvin Lockett, a railroad dispatcher who operated a telegraph to coordinate route and schedule information at the turn of the twentieth century, Brandt evokes Lockett's situated activity in getting messages to trains:

After writing out the train order (an original and two carbon copies), Lockett would attach a copy to a spring-held hoop and, as the train slowed into the depot, he would hoist the hoop to the open window of the engine car. The engineer would reach out of the window, grab the hoop, remove the paper message, and throw the hoop back out the window of the moving train. In the meantime, Lockett would run along the tracks, sometimes as far as two hundred yards, pick up the hoop, dash back to the station, and insert a second copy of the train order into the hoop in time for the conductor at the back of the train to grab his copy as the caboose was passing by. (pp. ix–x)

Brandt's larger point—that Lockett became unemployed as his skills (including fine penmanship) could not keep up with the fast pace of changing technologies—was anchored in a close description of the embodied and mediated literate practices of the dispatcher.

Brandt and Clinton (2002) embraced actor-network theory (ANT), particularly for Bruno Latour's (1996) attention to following objects (nonhumans, tools, artifacts) that bring elements of far-flung networks (other times, places, and people) into local events:

Literacy is not, as Goody (1986) or Ong (1982) suggest, so much an abstraction of language and communication from human lifeworlds. Rather, it is an abstraction or redistribution of elements of the human lifeworld into the lives of things. What is folded in, how, and with what consequences become important analytical questions in the study of literate practices. (2002, p. 353)

Beyond lexical allusions to phenomenology ("lifeworlds"), there are three ways this turn to ANT can be linked to phenomenological frameworks. First, although Latour (2005) expressly rejects phenomenology as too human-centered, he quips at another point that ANT could reasonably be thought of as "half Garfinkel and half Greimas" (p. 54). Any theory that is half Garfinkel's ethnomethodology is deeply imbricated with Schutz and phenomenology. Second, interest in things and cultural forms was a long-standing feature of Schutz's phenomenology:

All cultural objects—tools, symbols, language systems, works of art, social institutions, etc.—point back by their very origin and meaning to the activities of human subjects. For this reason, we are always conscious of the historicity of culture, which we encounter in its traditions and customs. (1962, p. 10)

Schutz and Luckmann (1973) likewise highlighted the importance of *objectivations*—"the embodiment of subjective processes in the objects and events of the life-world" (p. 264)—to socialization into the lifeworld. Third, Latour also tropes on emergence, on situated over-the-horizonness. Analyzing scientific work, Latour (1987) repeatedly stressed the sharp differences between *science made* and *science-in-the-making*, much as Brandt evoked the scene of the party to stress *text-in-the-making*, those uncertain, over-the-horizon, in-flux moments before a text seems to become fixed.

Over her career then, Brandt's methods have never been grounded in CA principles but have continued to resonate with broader traditions of phenomenological sociology as well as sociohistoric theory. Brandt's (1990) party analogy pushed the field to go beyond artifacts, to theorize and investigate writing as situated, live action. It implied methods that would provide rich observation of ongoing parties. Over time, however, Brandt seems to have concluded that parties can be productively studied by multiple methods: attending to their artifacts and traces, studying their situated (live) practices, interviewing participants to obtain reflexive accounts, and locating the party in broad streams of sociohistoric practices and artifacts. With this shift in methods, Brandt's research could tune in to how people navigate *whatever* is coming at them over the horizon, not just texts but also technologies, national and global economic developments, changing modes of social organization, and historical events (World War II, the Depression, neoliberal deregulation).

Research with an Art and Design Group:
Things Learned at and after the Party

To illustrate some ways phenomenological and sociohistoric approaches to literacy research can blend, I turn now to research I have done on an art and design group engaged in remaking a web-based art object called *IO* (Prior, 2007, 2010). During the period of my research, Joseph Squier, an art and design professor who had designed and produced the original *IO*, worked with Nan Goggin, a graphic design professor whom Joseph had collaborated with regularly; Christian Cherry, a dance professor who specialized in sound (but worked on *IO* only the first three months before leaving for another university); and two graduate student research assistants: Tony, who programmed and managed the database, and Eunah, who worked on redesigning the interface. Drawing on data (videotapes of interactions in the studio, interviews, screen captures, print documents) collected over an eleven-month period, my analyses have attended closely to situated activity (based on video clips and transcripts) as the group worked to enhance *IO* using new programs and particularly to the nature of *semiotic remediation* (Prior and Hengst, 2010, Prior, 2010) in the design process. Research on *IO* illustrates the way phenomenological and sociohistoric approaches work together, encouraging close attention to the fine-grained, embodied, situatedness of activity but also to the historical trajectories of material-semiotic objects, people, and environments that are folded into, and radiate out from, any situated event.

Figures 11.1–11.4 display four moments in the redesign of *IO*. Figure 11.1 is a screen capture (altered to grayscale) from my online interaction with the original *IO*. On the right of the screen are layered and changing images, which seem to respond to pointing, clicking, and other actions. On the far left is a text-input box. When I typed in a word the program recognized, text appeared in the black space below. The text was animated, fed letter by letter (a typewriter effect) at an irregular rate controlled by an artificial-intelligence program. With line breaks and alignment shifts, it resembled poetry. For example, after typing in the letters "I O," the response captured in figure 11.1 begins,

here

is where I live,

In an interview, Joseph explained how he designed, produced, and compiled *IO* during a one-month Rockefeller fellowship at an Italian retreat, how he decided to revise *IO* (the first art piece he had revised) in part in response to critical review of the lack of integration between words and images and in part because the release of Flash 5 made such integration technically feasible—as long as he could gather a team to assist in the reprogramming and redesign.

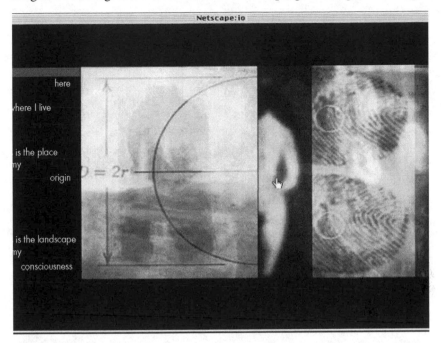

Fig. 11.1. Original *IO* screen (without color), showing a word-entry box on the left of images and *IO* word responses below it . Screen capture from IO at the place, an evolving repository of artwork created for distribution on the Web by Joseph Squier (http://theplace.walkerart.org/place.html)

Figure 11.2 shows work at the whiteboard at an early meeting of the group in February 2001. Joseph, Nan, Christian, and Tony were planning the digital infrastructure for the revised *IO*, assessing the options for *IO* with a set of new programs (PHP, an open-source database program; MySQL, an open-source inquiry language program; and Flash 5, a proprietary multimedia application that would be the front end of *IO*). They needed to assure one another that this suite of programs could achieve their goals and to make critical decisions about how to structure the database, access it, and present it. Tony was taking the lead in the programming. A videotape of the meeting in the studio displayed an important sequence of interactions at the whiteboard as Tony and Nan talked through how to store and call up the images. The drawing/text on the whiteboard represents a Flash template for a revised *IO* screen interface. It was drawn, written, talked, and gestured into existence in less than three minutes of somewhat muddled interaction. The representation involved at least twenty-nine separate actions that touched the surface of the whiteboard, movements made by Nan and Tony, who used two different colored markers to sketch the boxes (Nan), revise the boxes (Nan), add letters (Tony), and then add arrows from letters into the diagram (Nan). The drawing and discussion of this template were being coordinated with references to a PHP data entry screen on a laptop on the table, with another drawing on the whiteboard (representing a database architecture) and with many gestures in the air and over the diagram. Inscription at the whiteboard then emerged in sequential, temporal, co-present interactive acts, inscription as activity rather than artifact (although inscriptions became artifacts-in-interaction and might have longer duration).

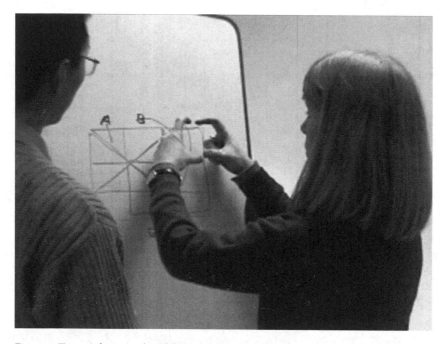

Fig. 11.2. Tony and Nan at the whiteboard in February, Nan gesturing over their jointly written and drawn diagram of the *IO* interface

Figure 11.3 shows an annotated pencil-on-paper drawing of the Flash template that Nan pulled out to guide discussions of the database in September (seven months after the whiteboard interaction), in the first studio meeting with Tony after summer break. Unlike the whiteboard version, which consisted of nine more-or-less equal squares, this version was subdivided with a narrow column running down the middle. It had also been annotated by hand with measurements of the lines in inches and points/

picas and with different intersections marked by their x-y coordinates in points (0/0 is the upper-left corner; 432/720 is the bottom-right corner). The annotations suggest variously sized rectangular or square images (such as a 6-inch by 4-inch space that is drawn and annotated in the lower left of the grid). As Nan and Tony talked about how images in the database would be categorized and called up, they used deictic language and gestures to elaborate an understanding of the paper. Nan, for example, described one image as "this size," tracing with her index finger a space on the paper template, then pointing to two areas it could go. Tony then confirmed that "type 1" (in the PHP database) would be "this," tracing with his index finger from the upper-left corner (0/0) to a middle line and down the page as he also looked at a PHP table displayed on his computer screen. It was only in an interview with Nan in December that I learned that this Flash template, which I had been seeing and analyzing for months in various forms, was actually designed to approximate mystical Pythagorean notions of mathematical harmony. Specifically, its point measurements, which were in turn encoded in PHP/Flash programs and in pixels on screens, were aligned with the golden section proportion that has been so widely used in Western art and architecture since ancient Greece. That proportion, approximately 1:1.618, was echoed in the 432 by 720 grid (1:1.66666) of the Flash template.

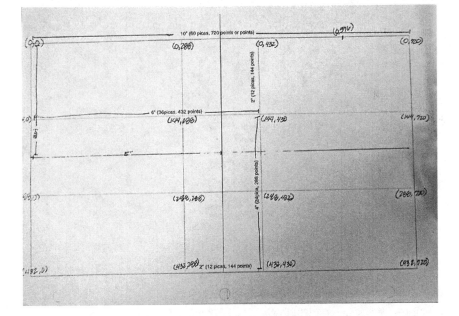

Fig. 11.3. Paper representation of the screen interface used at a meeting in September

Figure 11.4 comes from a videotape of a meeting in November, when the team had a working, if still buggy, version of the revised *IO*. Eunah has been showing Nan some of the navigational screens and interfaces (introductory page; log-in and quit windows). They have not yet settled on the default background image for these screens. Two are being considered. Eunah pulls up the second background image and says she likes it. Nan agrees and then elaborates on some of its advantages (warm colors, the way text is displayed in irregular brighter areas). Eunah notes that it also works best with the grid. She types in a command, and a digital grid based on Nan's pencil drawing overlays the image. The grid has a narrow column in the middle. Nan says, "That's good," in a quiet, uninflected way and then repeats it emphatically. Reaching out with a thumb–index-finger measuring gesture, she touches the screen near the top of the middle column. Eunah, who had just canceled the grid overlay, immediately keys it back in place, so fast that as Nan moves her thumb and index finger down the screen, the grid reappears before her fingers are halfway through this tracing. Nan notes that the central column matches where the text will be fed (good because its relatively uniform darkness will make the reversed, white, typeface quite visible).

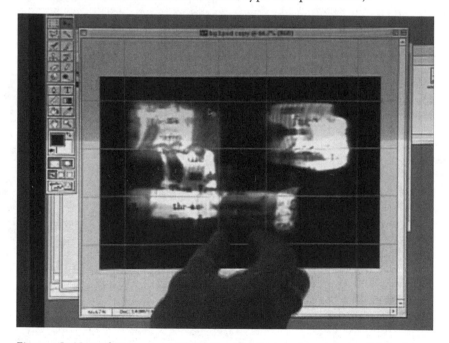

Fig. 11.4. In November, a screen with gridlines for the interface and a possible background image for the splash page, Nan's gesture highlighting the central area for display of words

In this research on *IO*, phenomenological attention to how things came over the horizon, moment by moment, helped capture detailed, nuanced practices (representational hand gestures, the use of paper drawings, whiteboard inscription, coordination of digital and paper representations), key practices that would have been lost without such attention. At the same time, the analysis highlighted the heterogeneous mediational means this high-tech, new-media art group used in production, not only cutting-edge computers, programs, and networks but also paper and pencil, gesture, whiteboard drawings, and talk. Much of analytic interest became visible only when a series of sessions were analyzed. If I had seen only the paper diagram in September (and the gestures around it), without reference to the interactions at the whiteboard in February, I would not have been able to infer that history any more than I could have predicted Eunah and Nan's interactions around the screen interface in November. Interviews and other accounts helped explicate the group's practices. Across the videotaped records for this group (fourteen meetings, usually lasting at least an hour, over eleven months) and several recordings of individuals working, there was never any mention of Joseph's production of *IO* at a funded retreat in Italy or of the alignment of the interface with Pythagorean golden section proportions. That kind of historicity seems to either fall at the edge of immediate practical concern or is so shared it becomes assumed common ground. In short, combining phenomenology's attention to the situated, emergent, embodied dimensions of practice with sociohistoric attention to mediated activity helped to capture the situated, emergent, and sociohistorically mediated practices of this group as well as to refine theoretical frameworks for such semiotic work (see Prior, 2010).

Bringing Phenomenological and Sociohistoric Frameworks to the Party

CA, ethnomethodology, and phenomenological sociology all circulate— generally in partial, blended, somewhat fuzzy fashion—through writing research and theory. I have argued that the early ethnomethodological phase of Brandt's work has greater resonance with her later research than is at first apparent, that her work displays a consistent orientation to understanding the intersubjective and social character of literacy, the emergent over-the-horizonness of lifeworlds, and the centrality of embodied and object-mediated action. Beyond explicating a facet of Brandt's work and identifying a phenomenological Ariadne's thread throughout her career, I hope this chapter sheds light on the three distinct phenomenological frameworks and suggests the value of phenomenological stances, not only for their orientation to situated activity but also to the way far-flung histories become enfolded in, and radiate out of, situated events. Attending a party may reveal much about the events of the party, but it will only offer the barest clues about how the food, drinks, smokes, music, electricity, language, and the people themselves came to exist, got to that event, and headed off after it. Phenomenological attention to the ways social order is achieved through actions in varying social zones and sociohistoric attention to the ways people act with mediational means align in striking ways (Prior, 2005, Russell, 2010). Together they offer richer opportunities for understanding the laminated worlds of humans and nonhumans that produce our literate parties and that our literate parties in turn participate in producing.

Notes

1. The epigraph of this essay has been cited before. Canagarajah (2000) quoted the first two sentences as the epigraph for his chapter examining how materially and culturally different literate scenes relate to conflicts over textual conventions. As I unpack how this analogy relates to literacy studies, the reason this passage has attracted attention may become clearer.

2. In this regard, it is worth noting that Brandt (2009a) cites her earlier work (1990) in support of the claim that intersubjectivity is "so central to literacy" (p. 61).

3. CA refers to a particular theoretical school, not to all types of analysis of conversational data.

References

Atkinson, J. Maxwell, and John Heritage, eds. 1984. *Structures of Social Action: Studies in Conversation Analysis.* Cambridge: Cambridge University Press.

Bazerman, Charles. 1988. *Shaping Written Knowledge: The Genre and Activity of the Experimental Article in Science.* Madison: University of Wisconsin Press.

Bourdieu, Pierre. 1990. *The Logic of Practice.* Translated by Richard Nice. Stanford: Stanford University Press.

Brandt, Deborah. 1990. *Literacy as Involvement: The Acts of Writers, Readers, and Texts.* Carbondale: Southern Illinois University Press.

———. 1992. "The Cognitive as the Social: An Ethnomethodological Approach to Writing Process Research." *Written Communication,* 9(3), 315–55.

———. 2001a. *Literacy in American Lives.* Cambridge: Cambridge University Press.

———. 2001b. "Protecting the Personal " In Deborah Brandt, Ellen Cushman, Anne Gere, Anne Herrington, Richard Miller, Victor Villanueva, Min-Zhan Lu, and Gesa Kirsch (contributors), "The Politics of the Personal: Storying Our Lives against the Grain. A Symposium." *College English,* 64(1), 42–44.

———. 2009a. "Writing over Reading: New Directions in Mass Literacy." In *The Future of Literacy Studies,* edited by Mike Baynham and Mastin Prinsloo, 54–74. Houndmills, England: Palgrave Macmillan.

———. 2009b. *Literacy and Learning: Reflections on Writing, Reading, and Society.* San Francisco: Jossey-Bass.

Brandt, Deborah, and Katie Clinton. 2002. "Limits of the Local: Expanding Perspectives on Literacy as Social Practice." *Journal of Literacy Research, 34*(3), 337–56.

Canagarajah, Suresh. 2000. *A Geopolitics of Academic Writing*. Pittsburgh: University of Pittsburgh Press.

Cicourel, Aaron. 1992. "The Interpenetration of Communicative Contexts: Examples from Medical Encounters." In *Rethinking Context: Language as an Interactive Phenomenon*, edited by Alessandro Duranti and Charles Goodwin, 291–310. Cambridge: Cambridge University Press.

Flower, Linda, and John Hayes. 1981. "A Cognitive Process Theory of Writing." *College Composition and Communication, 32*(4), 365–87.

Garfinkel, Harold. 1967. *Studies in Ethnomethodology*. Englewood Cliffs, NJ: Prentice Hall.

Goffman, Erving. 1974. *Frame Analysis: An Essay on the Organization of Experience*. Cambridge: Harvard University Press.

Heap, James. 1991. "Ethnomethodology, Cultural Phenomenology, and Literacy Activities." *Curriculum Inquiry, 21*(1), 109–17.

Heath, Christian, and Paul Luff. 2000. *Technology in Action*. Cambridge: Cambridge University Press.

Latour, Bruno. 1987. *Science in Action*. Cambridge: Harvard University Press.

———. 1996. "On Interobjectivity." *Mind, Culture, and Activity, 3*(4), 228–45.

———. 2005. *Reassembling the Social: An Introduction to Actor-Network Theory*. Oxford: Oxford University Press.

LeBaron, Curtis, and Timothy Koschmann. 2003. "Gesture and the Transparency of Understanding." In *Studies in Language and Social Interaction: In Honor of Robert Hopper*, edited by Phillip Glenn, Curtis LeBaron, and Jenny Mandelbaum, 119–32. Mahwah, NJ: Lawrence Erlbaum.

Miller, Carolyn. 1984. "Genre as Social Action." *Quarterly Journal of Speech, 70*(2), 151–67.

Ong, Walter. 1982. *Orality and Literacy: The Technologizing of the Word*. New York: Methuen.

Prior, Paul. 2005. "A Sociocultural Theory of Writing." In *The Handbook of Writing Research*, edited by Charles MacArthur, Steve Graham, and Jill Fitzgerald, 54–66. New York: Guilford Press.

———. 2007. "Remaking *IO*, Remaking Rhetoric: Semiotic Remediation as Situated Rhetorical Practice." In Prior, Janine Solberg, Patrick Berry, Hannah Bellowar, Bill Chewning, Karen Lunsford, Liz Rohan, Kevin Roozen, Mary Sheridan-Rabideau, Jody Shipka, Derek Van Ittersum, and Joyce Walker (contributors), "Re-Situating and Re-Mediating the Canons: A Cultural-Historical Remapping of Rhetorical Activity." *Kairos, 11*(3). Retrieved May 14, 2013, from http://kairos.technorhetoric.net/11.3/index.html

———. 2009. "From Speech Genres to Mediated Multimodal Genre Systems: Bakhtin, Voloshinov, and the Question of Writing." In *Genre in a Changing World*, edited by Charles Bazerman, Adair Bonini, and Debora Figueiredo, 17–34. Fort Collins, CO: WAC Clearinghouse. Retrieved May 14, 2013, from http://wac.colostate.edu/books/genre/

———. 2010. "Remaking IO: Semiotic Remediation in the Design Process." In *Exploring Semiotic Remediation as Discourse Practice*, edited by Prior and Julie Hengst, 206–34. Houndmills, England: Palgrave Macmillan.

Prior, Paul, and Julie Hengst. 2010. "Introduction: Exploring Semiotic Remediation." In *Exploring Semiotic Remediation as Discourse Practice*, edited by Prior and Hengst, 1–23. Houndmills, England: Palgrave Macmillan.

Russell, David. 2010. "Writing in Multiple Contexts: Vygotskian CHAT Meets the Phenomenology of Genre." In *Traditions of Writing Research*, edited by Charles Bazerman, Robert Krut, Karen Lunsford, Susan McLeod, Suzie Null, Paul Rogers, and Amanda Stansell, 353–64. New York: Routledge.

Schegloff, Emanuel. 1991. "Reflections on Talk and Social Structure." In *Talk and Social Structure: Studies in Ethnomethodology and Conversation Analysis*, edited by Deirdre Boden and Don Zimmerman, 44–70. Berkeley: University of California Press.

Schutz, Alfred. 1962. *Collected Papers I: The Problem of Social Reality*. Edited by Maurice Natanson. The Hague: Martinus Nijhoff.

———. 1970. *On Phenomenology and Social Relations: Selected Writings*. Edited by Helmut Wagner. Chicago: University of Chicago Press.

Schutz, Alfred, and Thomas Luckmann. 1973. *The Structures of the Life-World*. Edited by Richard Zaner and J. Tristam Engelhardt Jr. Evanston: Northwestern University Press.

Smith, Dorothy. 1990. *Texts, Facts, and Femininity: Exploring the Relations of Ruling*. London: Routledge.

Suchman, Lucy. 2000. "Making a Case: 'Knowledge' and 'Routine' in Document Production." In *Workplace Studies: Recovering Work Practice and Informing System Design*, edited by Paul Luff, Jon Hindmarsh, and Christian Heath, 29–45. Cambridge: Cambridge University Press.

PART THREE

Looking Forward at Literacy: The Global and Multimodal Future

12. Beyond *Literate Lives*: Collaboration, Literacy Narratives, Transnational Connections, and Digital Media

Cynthia L. Selfe and Gail E. Hawisher

> Learning to read and write has taken place amid convulsive changes in economic and social life, educational expectations, and communication technologies. This has been a time when the meaning of what it is to be literate has seemed to shift with nearly every new generation. Inevitably, pursuing literacy in the twentieth century entailed learning to respond to an unprecedented pace of change in the uses, forms, and standards of literacies.
> —Deborah Brandt, *Literacy in American Lives*

This chapter describes an ongoing study of globalized digital literacies inspired by Deborah Brandt's outstanding historical study of twentieth-century reading and writing in *Literacy in American Lives* (2001) from which the epigraph is excerpted. Our research has tried to extend the groundbreaking methodology Brandt describes in that volume in new directions and into different arenas while doing justice to her work on alphabetic literacies. A tall order to be sure. For this particular chapter, we describe our use of digital tools and environments as contexts for our study, the use of feminist and collaborative approaches for gathering and reporting on individuals' literacy stories, the ways in which we have extended our ongoing study into global and transnational contexts, our methodological and interpretive work with literacy narratives and narrative theory, and the ways in which we have deployed digital media, particularly video, both as a method of data gathering and as a method of reporting on our research to others in and out of the profession. Our goal, in part, is to demonstrate how digital tools of reportage along with a feminist emphasis and study of transnational contexts can begin to yield insights that help take us in different directions from those in *Literacy in American Lives* (Brandt, 2001) and beyond those in our own earlier print-bound *Literate Lives in the Information Age* (Selfe and Hawisher, 2004).

Beginnings

In 1998, after attending a talk Deborah Brandt gave at the University of Louisville's Thomas R. Watson Conference on her oral-history literacy project,
which was eventually published in 2001 as *Literacy in American Lives*, we
began interviewing individuals about their digital literacy practices and
values. Although we had been immersed for some fifteen years in studying
writing and the new information technologies, Brandt's approach to her
remarkable research prompted us to attend to a whole new way of thinking
about literacy and digital media as we moved irrevocably into the twenty-first century. In this effort, we were influenced, too, by Shoshana Zuboff's
(1988) *In the Age of the Smart Machine: The Future of Work and Power*. As
far back as 1988, Zuboff had this to say of new information technologies:

> The choices for the future cannot be deduced from economic data
> or from abstract measures of organizational functioning. They are
> embedded in the living detail of daily life at work as ordinary people
> confront the dilemmas raised by the transformational qualities of
> new information technology. For this reason [Zuboff focuses her
> research] upon the texture of human experience—what people say,
> feel, and do—in dealing with technological changes that imbue
> their immediate environment. (p. 12)

Taking both Brandt's and Zuboff's research insights to heart, we began to
develop an ongoing interest in characterizing how and why different people
from different cultural and experiential backgrounds, occupying various
subject positions, and faced with different situations acquired and developed
(or, for various reasons, failed to acquire and develop) digital literacies at a
time in history when the United States and many other parts of the globe
were becoming increasingly dependent on networked systems of digital
communication technologies.

The project at hand, which became *Literate Lives in the Information Age:
Narratives of Literacy from the United States* (2004), like Deborah Brandt's
(2001) scholarship, was grounded in oral-history and life-history research
(Bertaux, 1981; Bertaux and Thompson, 1993; Thompson, 1988, 1990; Lummis, 1987). But our project, which continues today, differs from Brandt's in
that it was intended to focus exclusively on literacy practices and values in
digital environments. What we have found over the years, however, is that it
is increasingly difficult to separate digital literacies from any consideration
of literate practices in general. As Brandt (2001) notes in the above epigraph
of the twentieth century, literacy trends appear to be holding fast for the

twenty-first century: "[W]hat it means to be literate has seemed to shift with nearly every new generation" (p. 12), and today this continuing shift tends to embrace a wide variety of digital media from desktop computers to laptops to handheld mobile devices to social-media sites and more.

We began our study with attempts to investigate digital literacy experiences of those in the United States by interviewing them in face-to-face settings using a standard list of interview questions that asked for demographic data and for information about family history, stories about literacy practices and values, memories of schooling environments and workplace experiences, and descriptions of technology use and avoidance. Our goal was to collect what we called at the time "literacies of technology"—stories or narratives from a wide range of people of differing ages, genders, ethnic and racial groups, and geographical backgrounds.

We continued this approach for the first year, working primarily with undergraduates and graduate students at our respective institutions. These early interviews, we have agreed, were useful—even if they did begin simply as relatively structured question-and-answer sessions using audiotape recorders (Burgess, 1982; Ritchie and Lewis, 2003). Before long, we began to make increasing use of digital environments for collecting information from participants, discovering the benefits of online interviews, online data gathering, and follow-up exchanges (Kivits, 2005; Shepherd, 2003). Thus, we were not only exploring digital literacies through interviews but also were deploying digital media in order to do so.

As we became more comfortable with the process of interviewing and clearer about our roles within such settings, we also came to appreciate the importance of making these exchanges more like conversations that involved participants in a joint project of inquiry. In particular, as scholars steeped in feminist theory and research (e.g., Britzman, 2000; Belenky et al., 1997; Lather, 2000; Reinharz, 1992), we realized, in these early sessions, just how much of our study was collaboratively composed by the research participants themselves and the importance of preserving as much of their own personal voices as we could when reporting on this project (Brettell, 1993; Visweswaran, 1994).

This awareness of the importance of participants' voices in our ongoing project also led us, increasingly, to encourage participants to tell us more stories about their digital literacy practices and values, small and large stories, stories that reinterpreted their pasts, constructed their present circumstances, and predicted their futures (Gergen and Gergen, 1983; Brodkey, 1986, 1987; Krauss, 2006; Lieblich, Tuval-Mashiach, and Zilber, 1998). It was through the representation of such complex literacy narratives (Eldred and Mortensen, 1992, 2006) we realized that these individuals were engaging with us in making sense of their own literacy technological communication practices, even as we, too, were trying to do so.

In subsequent years of our project, we expanded the scope of the research in two more important ways. First, we came to the understanding that we could not really record and make sense of the literate lives of those from the United States without also understanding something about the lives of individuals who came to this country from other places and who worked, studied, and lived in the United States at the same time that they inhabited transnational globalized contexts to stay in touch with families, friends, and loved ones (Appadurai, 1996; Jarratt, Losh, and Puente, 2006; Hesford, 2006; Panagakos and Horst, 2006). Second, as we gathered more literacy narratives, we also became increasingly dissatisfied with limiting either our research methods or our research reports solely to the modality of print. We experimented with various recording modes and settled on video because it allowed us to pass along the fullest possible range of semiotic information about the participants we met and the stories they told. Video also, as Roy Pea and Jay Lemke (2007) note, allowed us often to report on findings in much more richly textured ways than did print alone. We also asked participants to make use of video cameras to capture their literate practices and writing processes. Thus, we began to employ digital media as research tools for collecting and exhibiting life-history interviews while, at other times, we asked participants themselves to represent their literate practices by videoing their writing processes. In the sections that follow, we talk about how each of these changes to our original methodological approach added important dimensions to our ongoing investigations of globalized digital literacy practices (Hawisher and Selfe, 2000).

Focusing on the Digital

Despite the changes we have made over the years in our study of digital literacies—based on the work of scholars such as Brian Street (1995), James Paul Gee (1996), Harvey J. Graff (1987), and Deborah Brandt (2001)—we have always begun with the understanding that we could not hope to understand any literacy or language use—print or digital—until we understood the complex social and cultural ecology, both local and global, within which literacy practices and values are situated. To us, it was clear that the ways in which people acquired and developed digital literacies—or were prevented from doing so—depended on a constellation of factors including income, education, access and the specific conditions of access, geographical location, proficiency in English, and support systems (see, e.g., Hawisher and Selfe, with Guo and Liu, 2006).

Because our investigation focused on digital literacies and how they shaped and were shaped by individuals' literate lives, it also made increasing sense to work with individuals in online contexts that escaped the boundaries of both face-to-face exchanges and single-session interviews. Globalized computer networks during the late 1990s and early 2000s, along with more readily accessible digital tools (mobile phone technologies, instant messaging, texting, e-mail, listservs, emerging websites), enabled our interviewing and allowed us to resist the boundaries of single-session conversations and geopolitical locations. Using digital environments for communicating, we began interviews, for example, with colleagues Safia El-Wakil and Kate Coffield, who taught at the American University of Cairo in Egypt. With these colleagues, we met face-to-face in Cairo, for example, but we continued to exchange life-history narratives through online conversations via e-mail, strengthened our relationships during annual meetings of the Computers and Writing conference, and learned still more information about the lives of these extraordinary women in Houghton, Michigan, at a computers and writing workshop (Hawisher and Selfe, with Coffield and El-Wakil, 2007).

We also followed with increasing fascination the literacy narratives of graduate students we met at our home institutions and in other rhetoric and composition programs and kept in contact with—using digital environments for communication—in the years that followed. Two such students with whom we worked in the early 2000s, for example, were Lu Liu, from the People's Republic of China and a graduate student at Purdue University, and Yi-Huey Guo, from Taiwan and a graduate student at the University of Illinois, Urbana-Champaign. Each interviewed with us when she was thirty-one years old and continues to correspond with us online whether here or abroad. This use of computer-based communication allowed us to collaborate, collect, and tell the stories of these two women who have acquired English and digital literacies over the course of their thirty-some years and who deploy these literacies to communicate within and between cultures as they advance their educations and careers. As we worked with Lu and Yi-Huey—sometimes in person, sometimes online—we came to realize the intimate relationship between their learning of English and their acquisition of digital literacies. English enabled them initially to work with the US computer interfaces while their growing digital proficiency gave them more opportunities for learning English. In their first years of learning software programs, English was implicated in all aspects of their digital learning and communication environments, and that close relationship has continued today. Their everyday work as professors—in the case of Lu at China's Peking University and Yi-Huey at Taiwan's Tunghai University—has been intimately connected to their fluency in English and their expertise in rhetoric and composition and digital writing studies.

Focusing on Feminist Theory

Indeed, it was our regard for women like Kate, Safia, Lu, Yi-Huey, and the many others whom we met as we continued our multifaceted and now multimodal project that convinced us to begin the practice of coauthoring with the participants with whom we worked, most of whom contributed at least as insightfully and fully to our research projects as we ourselves, and many of whom continue to share cogent interview information with us long after our initial exchanges. By the time we had launched *Literate Lives in the Information Age* (2004), we were already experimenting with ways to demonstrate the active and continuing involvement of participants and to acknowledge more materially and visibly the full range of their contributions in our research projects. Most recently, we have been influenced in this effort by scholars in our own field, such as Gesa Kirsch and Jacqueline Jones Royster (2010), who remind us of the need to seek more richly rendered understanding—listening to and learning from the women themselves, going repeatedly, not to our assumptions and expectations but to the women—to their writing, their work, and their worlds, seeking to ground our inquiries in the evidence of the women's lives, taking as a given that the women have much to teach us if we develop the patience to pay attention in a more paradigmatic way. By incorporating Kirsch and Royster's insightful advice, we endeavor to keep the women and men with whom we collaborate at the forefront of the feminist methodology we have attempted to craft and deploy across multiple settings.

Caroline B. Brettell's feminist collection, *When They Read What We Write* (1993), also continues to exert a tremendous influence on our research. In her edited collection, Brettell offers a series of perspectives on studies like ours—interview-based ethnographies and life histories—and talks about the ways in which modernist approaches to reporting on such research has often suffered from the limited perspectives of some academics and professional scholars. As Alexandra Jaffe (1993) argues in Brettell's collection, such research approaches claim a "distance between observer and observed" that is, to a great extent, an "ethnographic fiction," one that scholars have employed to maintain "control and authority over . . . 'subjects'" (p. 51). As a corrective to this modernist approach, Brettell and others in this collection suggest an alternative method of having subjects "talk back" (p. 9), comment on, modify, change, correct scholars' interpretations of what they said. Talking back, as Jaffe goes on to say, helps to "undermine" professional ethnographers' "ability to construct an unproblematic Other, and hence, an unproblematic self" (p. 52) from interviews and observation encounters. In our experience, the reflexivity established by this dialogue is not only a positive and productive characteristic of more recent anthropological research but, as Jaffe points out, a realistic and "essential condition of interaction with the people we study" (p. 51).

Other feminist researchers who questioned their own abilities to represent accurately the narratives of interview participants also shaped our thinking. From Deborah P. Britzman (2000), for example, we learned that although, like her, we desired to tell

> good stories filled with the stuff of rising and falling action ... that there is a contradictory point of no return, of having to abandon the impossible desire to portray the study's subjects as they would portray themselves. (p. 32)

We recognized this dilemma and decided that coauthorship, as a refinement in feminist method, would give the participants more say in the politics of interpretation. We looked, too, to experimental sociologist Laurel Richardson (1997), whose work encouraged us to ask how the "theoretical concepts of feminist poststructuralism—reflexivity, authority, authorship, subjectivity, power, language, ethics, representation" (p. 2)—played out in our study. And we turned to Patti Lather (2000) and her decision to situate her research on women living with HIV/AIDS in a "feminist post structural problematic of accountability to stories that belong to others" all the while attending to "the crisis of representation" (p. 285). How, in other words, we asked, could we change our actual ways of writing and interpreting the results of our interview-based project to learn more from and with the participants we studied rather than just about them (Reinharz, 1992)?

To our minds, coauthorship seemed a viable, practical, and ethical resolution. In thinking through our decision, we also realized that the project we had undertaken was no longer our own. It belonged, as well, to the people we interviewed and surveyed—their words and their stories were continual reminders that they had claimed the intellectual ground of the project as their own. When we turned to the participants featured in the *Literate Lives* project, finally, and asked if they would be willing to coauthor their chapters with us, the great majority of those whom we approached accepted.

Focusing on Transnational Contexts

As we continued to work on our project during the first decade of the twenty-first century, the globalized contexts inhabited by the many participants in our studies became increasingly important to us. We began to meet and talk to individuals on various research trips abroad and to talk to them about the digital literacy practices they had taken up since the 1980s. Most of them inhabited the globalized educscape (Luke, 2006), a term Carmen Luke adopts to call forth an image of international education that corresponds with Appadurai's (1996) use of *scapes* in his *Modernity at Large* to mark transnational flows of cultural ideas across the global landscape.

By 2006, we were well into a new series of research reports based on the lives of people who were brought up or lived in multiple countries for extended periods of time: Australia, Bangladesh, Bosnia, China, Great Britain, Indonesia, Mexico, Nigeria, Norway, Peru, South Korea, and the United States, among them. Some of the participants in this phase of our research—not unlike others inhabiting transnational contexts during the late twentieth and early twenty-first centuries—moved frequently from one area to another because of wars, the quest for education, or because global capitalism and the shifting of available jobs and careers presented the promise of opportunity. Several of the participants grew up in relatively rural areas, several in good-sized towns, and others came of age and attended schools in large cities, such as Beijing, Belgrade, Lagos, Lima, London, Oslo, Sarajevo, and Sydney. Of the group, the majority of participants represented in our emerging transnational study are women, but men, too, are central to the research. The participants all have earned high school diplomas, most have completed college, and several are graduate students enrolled in programs to earn master's degrees or doctorates in the United States, and several are now faculty members in universities around the world.

The stories of these individuals, we believe, provide an interesting set of cultural tracings of how individuals inhabiting transnational contexts learn, take up, and use digital communication technologies to extend their communicative reach, to maintain their social and cultural identities, and to construct their worlds. As Carmen Luke (2001) points out, our understanding of globalized culture is intelligible only from a local perspective: "Globalization is as much about difference and ambivalence as it is about the sameness and similarities at the level of local uptakes, appropriations, identities, and engagements with global processes, structures, and ideologies" (p. 95). Because the participants also grew up under markedly different local circumstances, we believe their narratives help us further appreciate the importance of situating an understanding of digital literacies in specific cultural, material, educational, and familial contexts. For these individuals, information and communication technologies represent a fundamental feature of a globalized world undergoing a period of major social, educational, and technological change, one in which peoples' lives and literacies have been altered in fundamental and specific ways.

We believe such stories will assume increasing importance in the coming years as scholars attempt to identify and describe the globalized environments many individuals inhabit. A number of scholars in the field of rhetoric and composition and in this collection have indeed made the "global turn" to which Hesford (2006) refers and, in doing so, have turned specifically to literacy acquisition and development among those with transnational connections. We are thinking here, for example, of John Duffy (2007) and his study of a Hmong American community; Kate Vieira (2010) and her article on a Portuguese-speaking immigrant community in Fall River, Massachusetts; Bruce Horner, Min-Zhan Lu, and Paul Matsuda (2010) and their collection on *Cross-Language Relations in Composition*; and Morris Young (2004) and his award-winning book on Asian American literacies. All these colleagues continue to make important contributions to our own thinking and scholarship on what Paul Prior calls literate activity, in which acts of literacy are not only "situated, mediated, and dispersed" (1998, p. 287) but also may include ongoing interactions, sometimes face-to-face, in the actual production of various types of texts (Prior, 2010).

Focusing on Literacy Narratives

Although our work has always been informed by Deborah Brandt's (2001) scholarship and, thus, grounded in oral-history and life-history research, it has also at times focused on shorter digital literacy narratives and literacy narratives as they are revealed through writing-process videos. Literacy narratives, as we use the term, take into their field of vision reading and/ or composing, language acquisition, literacy practices, and literacy values. These narratives are structured by "learned" and "internalized" understandings about literacy, which are culturally constituted. Literacy narratives often include "explicit images of schooling and teaching" (Eldred and Mortensen, 1992, p. 513) within formal and official sites of literacy, but they just as frequently focus on literacy as it is taught, learned, and practiced in informal settings, such as home, churches, online, and other nonacademic environments (Selfe and Hawisher, 2004; Brandt, 1995, 1998, 1999, 2001; Street, 1995). Literacy narratives have social, cultural, ideological, and tropical dimensions for us, as well (Eldred and Mortensen, 2006). Literacy accounts, as Linda Brodkey's (1986) work has established, are structured by a series of cultural "tropes," and, thus, serve as "cultural Rorschachs" (p. 47) that provide a historically situated snapshot of what specific cultures and subcultures mean by literacy. Such narratives are rich in meaning because they "twice encode culture" as simultaneously "practices and artifacts" (Brodkey, 1987, p. 46). Because our cultural understandings of literacy are the material of which literacy narratives are woven, even though some narratives affirm and some resist "culturally scripted ideas" about literacy (Eldred and Mortensen, 1992, p. 513), literacy narratives cannot avoid reflecting, in some way—either directly or indirectly—what it means to read and compose in a particular culture or time and place. We have found the writing-process videos that participants themselves have constructed to be especially revealing in this regard with their often culturally grounded representations of writing with music and images from their homelands.

Storytellers use these personal accounts—written, oral, video—to position themselves within the contexts of their own lives at home, within the family, with peers, in school, in the community, and in the workplace. Through literacy narratives, individuals connect these contexts to their understanding and practice of literacy. Because literacy narratives, as we define them here, are autobiographical, they always involve a degree of self-representation and performance. Thus, we understand such stories to be sites of "self-translation" (Soliday, 1994, p. 511). As people tell and perform literacy stories, they also formulate their own sense of self; with each performance, this self changes slightly according to a constellation of social and cultural factors, personal aspirations and understandings, the audiences being addressed, and the rhetorical circumstances of the telling itself, among many other factors.

The value of eliciting such stories has been well documented by scholars from cognitive theory, social theory, and narrative theory, among many other disciplines. As Jerome Bruner (2001) maintains, in autobiographical narratives, individuals have the opportunity to "set forth a view of [the] . . . Self and its doings" (p. 26) and, in telling stories, to create the "texts" of their lives (p. 27). So, against the ground of their narratives and videos about digital literacy values and practices—at home, in school, and in community settings—we understood participants not only to be helping us understand how they used digital technologies but also to be composing themselves into the fabric of an increasingly technological world through their utterances and actions.

In this important sense, we came to understand participants to be using the interview settings and the narratives they told within these settings as their own personal form of social action, a narrative strategy available to all humans (Brockmeier and Carbaugh, 2001). Revealed in these stories were not only glimpses of the challenges with which participants struggled when they sought access to technology or assistance in learning to use technology but also tacit and often unconscious acts of world making, of discursive and rhetorical codings that helped them both to articulate the cultural conventions of the technological world in which they lived and to shape that world to their needs. This grounding in narrative—combined with our increased attempts to fold the digital into our research—frames much of the research in which we currently engage.

Moving Images with Video

Video cameras play increasingly prominent roles as research tools in helping us collect and portray representations of literacy narratives as we have moved into transnational contexts. Working with contributors in the United States, as well as in Oslo, Norway, and Sydney, Australia, we began the practice of video-recording our interview conversations and also asking participants to video their encounters with digital literacies. Over the last decade and more, scholars in a number of humanistic disciplines—among them, social sciences (Rosenstein, 2002), linguistics and disabilities studies (Neidle, 2001), folklore (Schüller, 2008), musicology (Stock, 2004), history (Frisch, 2006; Sipe, 2006), education (Hitchcock, Prater, and Dowrick, 2004; Erickson, 2006), psychology (Goodwin and Goodwin, 1999), international policy and development (Braden, 1999), and anthropology (Pink, Kürti, and Afonso, 2004)—have advocated using both digital video and audio to record interviews and other kinds of research observation. These researchers note, for example, that video recordings provide the potential for recording a fuller range of information about human interaction, language, and behavior than conventional observation and note-taking approaches alone. With the use of digital video, for example, researchers can record more of what is said, and to whom, and how social exchanges of information happen among researchers and participants through speech, facial expressions, gestures, and glances, among other paralinguistic data (Erickson, 2006).

Along with refining our methods for collecting literacy narratives through the use of digital video cameras, we have also encouraged participants to make use of video cameras in tracing their own writing processes and digital literacies. Participants capture a representation of their writing processes on camera to try to demonstrate some of the thinking they experience as they approach and carry out a writing task. In studying these videos, we have found that the use of digital media seems to open up new opportunities for making meaning, reflecting upon that meaning, and trying to communicate what we do as we engage literate practices. As we work to represent—in words, images, and sound—processes of inquiry, the actual doing tends to reshape the way we experience and situate literate activity in our lives. Digital video also has the potential to afford us richer means of reflecting on such dispersed activity and what it means to our literate lives (Hawisher and Selfe, with Kisa and Ahmed, 2010; Hawisher, Prior, et al., 2009). Although video and audio have been used for a number of years to collect and report on data in disciplines, such as anthropology, biology, and political science, such methods have not seen widespread use in other humanities disciplines, like rhetoric and composition studies, in part due to the limitations of publication venues. With the advent of digital-media publications, however, it is now possible for researchers to expand their reports beyond the range of the alphabetic.

In our recent interviews with those who inhabit transnational contexts, for example, we used digital video and audio to both record and report on interviews in which students shared narratives about their use of various digital technologies to maintain their relationships with family, friends, and coworkers (Hawisher and Selfe, with Kisa and Ahmed, 2010). Rendered in a more conventional form—that is, through transcripts and quotations— such narratives would not only be monodimensional but also would tend to be much less complete, accurate, and informative. Transcribed accounts of these interviews, for example, would contain the students' words, but they would fail to convey other important information: the English dialects of speakers from various regions and parts of the world; the rhythm and pace of their voices as they talk about particular incidents involving their parents, their friends, or their siblings; the vocal emphasis they place on some words and phrases as they tell their stories about emigration, the violence of war, and the challenges of adapting to a new culture; the revealing gestures and facial expressions they use to accompany a specific narrative about a mother, a father, a sister; and the bodily presence they invested in conversations about school, travel, technology, and belonging to multiple cultures and locations.

We argue that these media clips not only can add additional semiotic information to alphabetic representations of research but also have the added benefit of supporting readers in validating the information and interpretations we collaboratively provide, thus, offering some triangulated perspectives on our own explanations of literate behavior. Indeed, Roy Pea and Jay Lemke (2007) suggest that digital-media representations of research data—the use of digital video clips to represent instances of communicative exchanges—should be used in tandem with written descriptions of specific phenomena to support a closer and more detailed reading of collaborative peer-to-peer interpretations that, ultimately, allow for clearer explanations:

> [A] sample of original video allows scholarly peers to assess the
> results of [alphabetic] transcription and to place analyses in the
> wider context of features of the video-recorded event that may not
> have appeared relevant to the original researchers. . . . The purposes
> are to enable researchers to more clearly convey the evidentiary
> basis of their arguments and to permit a closer assessment of the
> work reported. (p. 41)

Influenced by the thinking of these researchers, we published with Patrick Berry in 2012 *Transnational Literate Lives in Digital Times*, the first
born-digital text we have authored. By the term *born digital*, we mean that
the content of the project, because it incorporates video and audio, cannot
be fully, or even adequately, rendered by only print on a page. This project,
in fact, has taken us several years to produce, in part, because there were no
real models for similar scholarly texts, and we were unaware of any press
actively recruiting born-digital, peer-reviewed scholarly works with the
same specific gravity of a book, albeit in very different formats.

On the way to publishing *Transnational Literate Lives in Digital Times*
(2012), we have also established Computers and Composition Digital Press
(CCDP), a peer-reviewed imprint of Utah State University Press to accommodate new forms of digital scholarship. The press has now published several
outstanding projects, including *Technologies of Wonder: Rhetorical Practice
in a Digital World* (Delagrange, 2011), which won the 2012 outstanding book
award from the Coalition of Women Scholars on the History of Rhetoric and
Composition and the 2013 outstanding book award from the Conference on
College Composition and Communication (CCCC). We hope that *Transnational Literate Lives in Digital Times*, which also received in 2013 both the
Advancement of Knowledge Award and the Research Impact Award from
CCCC, will join *Technologies of Wonder* and the other texts as testimony to
the power of video as a research and reporting tool for literacy scholarship.

Final Comments

As we recount the many different paths our research has taken since 1998
when we first heard a chapter from Brandt's research on *Literacy in American
Lives* (2001), we are reminded all over again of the tremendous influence that
her project has exerted on approaches that we bring to our scholarly work.
We also hope that our own turn to digital media, feminist perspectives,
and transnational contexts works to shape a powerful research methodology that adds to Brandt's groundbreaking studies. *Transnational Literate
Lives in Digital Times* (Berry, Hawisher, and Selfe, 2012) through sound,

video, and digital images—through different tools of reportage—begins to yield insights not always available in *Literacy in American Lives* (Brandt, 2001) or in our own earlier print-bound *Literate Lives in the Information Age* (Selfe and Hawisher, 2004). The participants in *Transnational Digital Lives in Digital Times* sometimes chose an array of tools (e.g., handwriting, print, still images, video, and voice) through which to convey their literacy narratives and that we then render on the screen. Each of these representations, furthermore, tends to reveal slightly different takes on the research findings. Presenting a video image, for example, of combing one's hair while viewers listen to a voice-over of grandparents' speculations on the proper deportment of women was a strategy that Shafinaz Ahmed of Bangladesh used in a self-authored digital poem and tends to cast a slightly different interpretation on literate activity than the printed word alone. And the language or languages that the participants bring to their transnational perspectives for the telling of the narratives also came into play. Although the study's participants primarily chose English, other languages emerged: Ismael of Mexico plays with English, Spanish, and increasingly Spanglish in representing his practices on social-network sites; Hannah of the United States ties to her literacy narrative and photos Korean cultural understandings bound by the language her relatives speak; and Gorjana of Australia relates, in part, through gestures captured on video the different communication styles she adopts in telephone conversations with different family members in the former Yugoslavia. In other words, digital analytical tools have helped us delve more deeply into the literate activity that the study's participants display in their everyday lives in the United States and abroad.

We also believe that the literacy narratives that we and others continue to collect will assume increasing importance in the coming decade as scholars attempt to probe the globalized literacy environments that many today inhabit. Although Brandt's study is not usually associated with digital media, she herself is no stranger to the changing challenges each generation takes up as people struggle, often within technological contexts, to build meaningful literate lives. It is this attention to broadly conceived literate lives—and the theory that emerges from studying the historical and contemporary settings in which literacy makes its home—that persists in making Brandt's research so important to us. She succeeds admirably in her goal of trying "to put descriptions of events and thoughts into historical currents of literacy and from that [building] a theory of literacy worthy of the public interest" (Brandt et al., 2001, p. 43). Without Brandt's ongoing research into the theory and practice of literacy, our own research would have suffered immeasurably. In no uncertain terms, it is the richer because of her scholarship, and, for this, we thank her.

Note

Portions of this chapter were previously published in Berry, Hawisher, and Selfe 2012.

References

Appadurai, Arjun. 1996. *Modernity at Large: Cultural Dimensions of Globalization.* Minneapolis: University of Minnesota Press.

Belenky, Mary F., Blythe M. Clinchy, Nancy R. Goldberger, and Jill M. Tarule. 1997. *Women's Ways of Knowing.* New York: Basic Books.

Berry, Patrick W., Gail E. Hawisher, and Cynthia L. Selfe. 2012. *Transnational Literate Lives in Digital Times.* Logan: Computers and Composition Digital Press/Utah State University Press. Retrieved from http://ccdigitalpress.org/transnational/

Bertaux, Daniel. 1981. *Biography and Society: The Life History Approach.* Beverly Hills: Sage.

Bertaux, Daniel, and Paul Thompson. 1993. *Between Generations: The Life History Approach.* Beverly Hills: Sage.

Braden, Su. 1999. "Using Video for Research and Representation: Basic Human Needs and Critical Pedagogy." *Learning, Media, and Technology, 24*(2), 117–30.

Brandt, Deborah. 1995. "Accumulating Literacy: Writing and Learning to Write in the Twentieth Century." *College English, 57*(6), 649–68.

———. 1998. "Sponsors of Literacy." *College Composition and Communication, 49*(2), 165–85.

———. 1999. "Literacy Learning and Economic Change." *Harvard Educational Review, 69*(4), 373–94.

———. 2001. *Literacy in American Lives.* Cambridge: Cambridge University Press.

Brandt, Deborah, Ellen Cushman, Anne Ruggles Gere, Anne Herrington, Richard E. Miller, Victor Villanueva, Min-Zhan Lu, and Gesa Kirsch. 2001. "The Politics of the Personal: Storying Our Lives against the Grain." *College English, 64*(1), 41–62.

Brettell, Caroline B., ed. 1993. *When They Read What We Write: The Politics of Ethnography.* Westport, CT: Bergin and Garvey.

Britzman, Deborah P. 2000. "'The Question of Belief': Writing Poststructural Ethnography." In *Working the Ruins: Feminist Poststructural Theory and Methods in Education,* edited by Elizabeth St. Pierre and Wanda Pillow, 27–40. New York: Routledge.

Brockmeier, Jens, and Donal Carbaugh. 2001. Introduction. In *Narrative and Identity: Studies in Autobiography, Self, and Culture,* edited by Brockmeier and Carbaugh, 1–22. Amsterdam: John Benjamins.

Brodkey, Linda. 1986. "Tropics of Literacy." *Journal of Education, 168,* 47–54.

———. 1987. "Writing Ethnographic Narratives." *Written Communication, 4*(1), 25–50.

Bruner, Jerome. 2001. "Self-Making and World-Making." *Journal of Aesthetic Education, 25*(1), 67–78.

Burgess, Robert G. 1982. "The Unstructured Interview as a Conversation." In *Field Research: A Sourcebook and Field Manual,* edited by Burgess, 164–69. London: Allen and Unwin.

Delagrange, Susan H. 2011. *Technologies of Wonder: Rhetorical Practice in a Digital World.* Utah State University Press/Computers and Composition Digital Press. http://ccdigitalpress.org/wonder/

Duffy, John. 2007. *Writing from These Roots: Literacy in a Hmong-American Community.* Oahu: University of Hawaii Press.

Eldred, Janet Carey, and Peter Mortensen. 1992. "Reading Literacy Narratives." *College English,* 54(5), 512–39.

———. 2006, October 5–7. "Revisiting Literacy Narratives." Paper presented at the Watson Conference on Rhetoric and Composition, Louisville, Kentucky.

Erickson, Frederick. 2006. "Definition and Analysis of Data from Videotape: Some Research Procedures and their Rationales." In *Handbook of Complementary Methods in Educational Research,* edited by Judith L. Green, Gregory Camilli, Patricia B. Elmore, Audra Skukauskaite, and Elizabeth Grace, 177–93. London: Routledge.

Frisch, Michael. 2006. "Oral History and the Digital Revolution." In *The Oral History Reader,* edited by Robert Perks and Alstair Thomson, 2nd ed., 102–14. London: Routledge.

Gee, James Paul. 1996. *Social Linguistics and Literacies: Ideology in Discourses.* 2nd ed. London: Taylor and Francis.

Gergen, Kenneth, and Mary Gergen. 1983. "Narratives of the Self." In *Studies in Social Identity,* edited by Theodore R. Sarbin and Karl E. Scheibe, 166–85. New York: Praeger.

Goodwin, Marjorie Harness, and Charles Goodwin. 1999. "Emotion within Situated Activity." In *Communication: An Arena of Development,* edited by Nancy Budwig, Ina C. Užgiris, and James V. Wertsch, 33–54. Westport, CT: Greenwood.

Graff, Harvey J. 1987. *The Legacies of Literacy: Continuities and Contradictions in Western Culture and Society.* Bloomington: Indiana University Press.

Hawisher, Gail E., and Cynthia L. Selfe, eds. 2000. *Global Literacies and the World Wide Web.* New York: Routledge.

Hawisher, Gail E., and Cynthia L. Selfe, with Gorjana Kisa and Shafinaz Ahmed. 2010. "Globalism and Multimodality in a Digitized World: Computers and Composition Studies." *Pedagogy,* 10(1), 55–68.

Hawisher, Gail E., and Cynthia L. Selfe, with Kate Coffield, and Safia El-Wakil. 2007. "Women and the Global Ecology of Digital Literacies." In *Women and Literacy: Local and Global Inquiries for a New Century,* edited by Beth Daniell and Peter Mortensen, 207–28. New York: Routledge.

Hawisher, Gail E., and Cynthia L. Selfe, with Yi-Huey Guo and Lu Liu. 2006. "Globalization and Agency: Designing and Redesigning the Literacies of Cyberspace." *College English,* 68(6), 619–36.

Hawisher, Gail E., Paul Prior, Patrick W. Berry, Amber Buck, Steven E. Gump, Cory Holding, Hannah Lee, Christa Olson, and Janine Solberg. 2009. "Ubiquitous Writing and Learning: Digital Media as Tools for Reflection and Research on Literate Activity." In *Ubiquitous Learning,* edited by Bill Cope and Mary Kalantzis, 254 64. Urbana: University of Illinois Press.

Hesford, Wendy S. 2006. "Global Turns and Cautions in Rhetoric and Composition Studies." *PMLA,* 121(3), 787–801.

Hitchcock, Caryl H., Mary Anne Prater, and Peter W. Dowrick. 2004. "Comprehension and Fluency: Examining the Effects of Tutoring and Video Self-Modeling on First-Grade Students with Reading Difficulties." *Learning Disability Quarterly,* 27(2), 89–104.

Horner, Bruce, Min Zhan Lu, and Paul Matsuda, eds. 2010. *Cross-Language Relations in Composition*. Carbondale: Southern Illinois University Press.

Jaffe, Alexandra. 1993. "Involvement, Detachment, and Representation on Corsica." In *When They Read What We Write: The Politics of Ethnography*, edited by Caroline B. Brettell, 51–66. Westport: Bergin and Garvey.

Jarratt, Susan, Elizabeth Losh, and David Puente. 2006. "Transnational Identifications: Biliterate Writers in a First-Year Humanities Course." *Journal of Second Language Writing*, 15(1), 24–48.

Kirsch, Gesa, and Jacqueline Jones Royster. 2010. "Feminist Rhetorical Practices: In Search of Excellence." *College Composition and Communication*, 61(4), 640–72.

Kivits, Joëlle. 2005. "Online Interviewing and the Research Relationship." In *Virtual Methods: Issues in Social Research on the Internet*, edited by Christine Hine, 35–50. Oxford, England: Berg.

Krauss, Wolfgang. 2006. "The Narrative Negotiation of Identity and Belonging." *Narrative Inquiry*, 16(1), 103–11.

Lather, Patti. 2000. "Drawing the Line at Angels: Working the Ruins of Feminist Ethnography." In *Working the Ruins: Feminist Poststructural Theory and Methods in Education*, edited by Elizabeth St. Pierre and Wanda Pillow, 284–311. New York: Routledge.

Lieblich, Amia, Rivka Tuval-Mashiach, and Tamar Zilber. 1998. *Narrative Research: Reading, Analysis, and Interpretation*. Thousand Oaks, CA: Sage.

Luke, Carmen. 2001. *Globalization and Women in Academia: North-West/South-East*. Mahwah, NJ: Erlbaum.

———. 2006. "Eduscapes: Knowledge, Capital and Cultures." *Studies in Language and Capitalism*, 1, 97–120.

Lummis, Trevor. 1987. *Listening to History: The Authenticity of Oral Evidence*. London: Hutchinson.

Neidle, Carol. 2001. "SignStream: A Database Tool for Research on Visual-Gestural Language." *Sign Language and Linguistics*, 4(1–2), 203–14.

Panagakos, Anastasia N., and Heather A. Horst. 2006. "Return to Cyberia: Technology and the Social Worlds of Transnational Migrants." *Global Networks*, 6(2), 109–24.

Pea, Roy, and Jay Lemke. 2007. Sharing and Reporting Video Work." In *Guidelines for Video Research in Education: Recommendations from an Expert Panel*, edited by Sharon J. Derry. Chicago: Data Research and Development Center. http://drdc.uchicago.edu/what/video-research-guidelines.pdf

Pink, Sarah, László Kürti, and Ana Isabel Afonso. 2004. *Working Images: Visual Research and Representation in Ethnography*. London: Routledge.

Prior, Paul. 1998. *Writing/Disciplinarity: A Sociohistoric Account of Literate Activity in the Academy*. Mahwah, NJ: Erlbaum.

———. 2010. "Remaking *IO*: Semiotic Remediation in the Design Process." In *Exploring Remediation as Discourse Practice*, edited by Paul A. Prior and Julie A. Hengst, 206–34. London: Palgrave Macmillan.

Reinharz, Shulamit. 1992. *Feminist Methods in Social Research*. New York: Oxford University Press.

Richardson, Laurel. 1997. *Fields of Play: Constructing an Academic Life*. New Brunswick, NJ: Rutgers University Press.

Ritchie, Jane, and Jane Lewis, eds. 2003. *Qualitative Research Practices: A Guide for Social Science Students and Researchers.* London: Sage.

Rosenstein, Barbara. 2002. "Video Use in Social Science Research and Program Evaluation." *International Journal of Qualitative Methods, 1*(3), 22–43.

Schüller, Dietrich. 2008. *Audiovisual Research Collections and Preservation.* TAPE: Training for Audiovisual Preservation in Europe. http://www.tape-online.net /docs/audiovisual_research_collections.pdf

Selfe, Cynthia L., and Gail E. Hawisher. 2004. *Literate Lives in the Information Age: Stories from the United States.* Mahwah, NJ: Erlbaum.

Shepherd, Nicole. 2003, July 17–19. "Interviewing Online: Qualitative Research in the Network(ed) Society." Paper presented at the Association of Qualitative Research Conference, Sydney, Australia. Retrieved from http://espace.library.uq.edu.au /view/UQ:10232

Sipe, Dan. 2006. "The Future of Oral History and Moving Images." In *The Oral History Reader,* edited by Robert Perks and Alistair Thomson, 2nd ed., 406–15. London: Routledge.

Soliday, Mary. 1994. "Translating Self and Difference through Literacy Narratives." *College English, 56*(5), 511–26.

Stock, Jonathan P. J. 2004. "Documenting the Musical Event: Observation, Participation, Representation." In *Empirical Musicology: Aims, Methods, Prospects,* edited by Eric Clark and Nicholas Cook, 15–35. Oxford: Oxford University Press.

Street, Brian V. 1995. *Social Literacies: Critical Approaches to Literacy in Development, Ethnography, and Education.* London: Longman.

Thompson, Paul. R. 1988. *The Voice of the Past: Oral History.* Oxford: Oxford University Press.

———. 1990. *I Don't Feel Old: The Experience of Later Life.* Oxford: Oxford University Press.

Vieira, Kate. 2010. "'American by Paper': Assimilation and Documentation in a Biliterate Bi-Ethnic Immigrant Community." *College English, 73*(1), 50–72.

Visweswaran, Kamala. 1994. *Fictions of Feminist Ethnography.* Minneapolis: University of Minnesota Press.

Young, Morris. 2004. *Minor Re/Visions: Asian American Literacy Narratives as a Rhetoric of Citizenship.* Carbondale: Southern Illinois University Press.

Zuboff, Shoshana. 1988. *In the Age of the Smart Machine: The Future of Work and Power.* New York: Basic Books.

Epilogue: Literacy Studies and Interdisciplinary Studies with Notes on the Place of Deborah Brandt

Harvey J. Graff

Claims about literacies, and their lack, surround us, multiplying like meta-phorical insects.* Different observers see either an abundance of literacies forming foundations for flowing multimodalities or a crisis rooted in the presumed absence or inadequacy of appropriate literacies threatening the foundations of our civilization and polity (Graff and Duffy, 2008; Graff, 1995a).[1]

In typical formulations, literacy studies embraces two more-or-less op-posing positions: that of "many literacies" *and* that of dangerously low levels of literacy, their causes, and their consequences. When conceptualized com-plexly—not the most common practice—their contradictory relationships form part of our subject of inquiry and part of the challenge for explication and explanation.[2] And the demand for interdisciplinarity.[3]

The difficulties and the potentialities attendant with literacy gave rise to a field of literacy studies during the last one-third to one-quarter of the twentieth century. Sociolinguist David Barton relates,

---

* **Literacy Studies and Interdisciplinary Studies: Reflections**

My own definition of *literacy* emphasizes literacy as the ability to read—make and take meaning—and the ability to write—express understanding and make other com-munications—and their metaphors and analogies across distinct media and modes of communication.

For me, *interdisciplinarity* is defined by questions and problems and the means developed to answer them in new and different ways that are constructed or built on or from elements from different disciplines. This might involve approaches, methods, theories, orientations, comparisons, understandings, or interpretations. I emphasize the former—questions and problems, not the disciplines. Or to put it another way, interdisciplinary defined or realized comes from fashioning interdisciplinarity via method, theory, and conceptualization to form a new and distinct approach or under-standing derived from or based on aspects of different disciplines. This will differ by discipline and disciplinary clusters. Interdisciplinarity is not a matter of the number of disciplines. Therefore, there is no need to "master" two or more disciplines, as more than a few pundits have asserted.

This essay is drawn from a longer piece, Graff, 2011b.

The meaning of the word literacy is to be found not just by examining dictionary entries. It has become a unifying term across a range of disciplines for changing views of reading and writing; there has been such a growth of study in the area that is now referred to as Literacy Studies or the New Literacy Studies. (2007, p. 23)[4]

This is the realm of theory and practice that Deborah Brandt joined and was influenced by in the 1980s and 1990s. By the late 1990s and 2000s, English professor and compositionist Brandt herself became a shaping force (1990, 2001, 2009; Brandt and Clinton, 2002).

Literacy Studies

Literacy studies developed as an *interdisciplinary* field of study and knowledge, the theme of this exploratory essay. Barton further notes,

In many ways Literacy Studies grew out of a dissatisfaction with conceptions of reading and writing which were prevalent in education in all areas, from early childhood reading to adult literacy programmes: these were conceptions of reading and writing which were based on over-simplistic psychological models. The critique has been made from a range of disciplinary vantage points and in a range of ways. (2001, p. 93)[5]

From "dissatisfaction" and "over-simplistic models" to criticism from multiple disciplinary "vantage points" and "ways": This is one of the principal paths to the development of areas of interdisciplinary study and interdisciplines. In fact, that path also gives rise to the unique set of programs, rooted in part in history, that constitute LiteracyStudies@OSU, for example, which I direct at the Ohio State University and introduce later.

Not surprising, tensions between the principal disciplines and their contributions to an interdiscipline mark the dynamics of change and development. The most common and perhaps most notorious is the clash between the cognitive/psychological in psychology (and sometimes also in literature, history, linguistics, or philosophy) *and* social/contextual approaches in anthropology, sociology, linguistics, and history. These differences often parallel the conflicts between "strong" or "great divide" theories *and* practice/contextual understandings. More practical but no less important is the long struggle between departments of English and colleges of education over institutional "ownership" of literacy. These recognitions remind us that efforts at interdisciplinarity are inseparably part of the processes of disciplinary formation, maintenance, and shifts themselves, not a later or separate movement.[6] As she moved from *Literacy as Involvement* to *Literacy in American Lives*, Brandt reflects those dynamics.

The perspective outlined here also highlights key factors among the critical elements that contributed to the decline of an earlier consensus. That understanding––indeed, faith—was rooted in an integrative and "over-simplistic psychological" narrative that promulgated the universal unmediated and transformative, epoch-making power of writing and/or reading—literacy—(what Brian V. Street calls "the autonomous model" of literacy), and stimulated the search for alternatives. Brockmeier, Wang, and Olson summarize evocatively,

> a theory of literacy was outlined that made strong claims for the cultural and cognitive implications of writing. It was argued that alphabetic literacy is an unique technology of representation and communication which has been of fundamental importance for the development of Western culture. According to this theory, oral language and written language are intellectual technologies which are causally responsible of two different types of culture, cultures of orality and of literacy. Some critics of the "literacy hypothesis" thus spoke of a "great-divide theory" (Finnegan). The watershed, to stick to the metaphor, between speech and writing, oral and literate culture was the invention (or, once it was invented, the introduction) of the alphabet. (2002, pp. 6–7)

According to this version of the "received wisdom," the consequences were epochal and without limits: "Patently, the domain of culture upon which literacy was expected to have its impact was exceedingly broad."

> Literacy was claimed to impinge upon the entire gamut of cultural phenomena from the intellectual to the aesthetic and political, including the production of science, philosophy, history, literature, art, and religion, as well as the institutions of education, documented law, and democratic forms of social organization. Further, literacy was seen as having an impact on the individualism of modern Western thought along with forms of mentality (rational and logical), cognition (conceptual and analytical), memory (objective and accumulative), as well as forms of communication (decontextualized and emotionally distanced) and grammar (reflective and prescriptive). Here, the vision of culture that unfolded with literacy, printing, and the alphabet, merged with the idea of civilization in general.[7] (2002, pp. 6–7)

Alternatives that arose to counter this understanding include Barton's Literacy Studies or New Literacy Studies, or Brian Street's "ideological model" of literacy, claiming authority in part by the act of naming. How often do incipient interdisciplines proclaim or identify themselves as "new"? It is no coincidence that the earlier dominance of "strong theories," "great divides," or dichotomous understandings of literacy had no need for a nominal cover like "literacy studies." Literacy was unreflectingly incorporated into the principal narratives of the rise of the West and the triumph of democracy, modernization, and progress. Indeed, literacy was equated with those qualities, each seemingly the cause of the other in confused causal order. Regardless of confusion, the qualities presumed for modern civilization and for literacy became interchangeable.[8] An image of literacy's presumptive or expected history substituted inadequately for its study.

No less coincidental is that the search for confirmation of grand theories of literacy and their "consequences," in Goody and Watt's original formula, ironically, did more to fuel skepticism and the search for more specific and documented contextual interpretations. (This was revised to "implications," by Goody in response to criticism.) That shift, in turn, led to new and different findings and orientations that contributed to bringing literacy studies explicitly to the realm of interdisciplinarity research.[9]

Interdisciplinary literacy studies thus developed from different methods and sources and different presuppositions and expectations. As suggested by Brockmeier, Wang, and Olson (2002), "over-simplistic psychological" notions were often rooted in reductive great leaps across relatively rarified cognitive and philosophical artifacts. Radical dichotomies substituted for dynamics of social and cultural change. Generalizations without qualification were applied without hesitation to large numbers of persons. And the dynamics of literacy itself were reduced to cartoonish images of literacy versus orality and print versus manuscript.

In contrast, across the sweep of the twentieth century, empirical and critical studies in oral literature, folklore, psychology, anthropology and archaeology, linguistics, philosophy, sociology, classics, and history began to tell different and more variegated stories. They turned to more direct evidence of literacy's development, distribution, and uses via case studies, ethnographies, and histories that gave more attention to matters of practice and social context. Sources and subjects were approached and read more carefully and critically. Ironically, "New Literacy Studies" scholars over the past three or four decades only slowly rediscovered the truly groundbreaking work earlier in the century of oral literature researchers who climbed mountains in Eastern Europe from the 1920s to record performances, constructing

"Singers of Tales," as Milman Parry and Albert Lord famously dubbed them, and comparing oral narratives (Lord, 1960/2000; Parry, 1971). No less momentous but often neglected is the dynamic activism of the cultural-historical psychology of Lev Vygotsky, Alexander Luria, and their colleagues from the 1930s.[10] So much richer than the modernization studies of American sociologists and political scientists after World War II, this work seems destined for repeated rediscovery. That phenomenon may also be a stop on paths to interdisciplinarity, constituting a step forward accompanied by a constraining half-step backward.[11]

By and large, these approaches and their appropriation for literacy studies derived from several distinct disciplines, in particular, anthropology, linguistics, and cognitive psychology. Through these origins or sources, literacy studies represents a search for a different but common or shared place amid the disciplines and often outside the walls of colleges and departments of education and/or psychology. More implicit, that place ideally should be outside the blinders of Western civilization. Literacy studies turned toward anthropology, linguistics, and cognitive (psychology) studies, with strong assistance from history, classics, and, most recently, cultural studies.

Street articulates a credo and point of origin for the New Literacy Studies:

> The field of literacy studies has expanded considerably in recent years and new, more anthropological and cross-cultural frameworks have been developed to replace those of a previous era, in which psychologistic and culturally narrow approaches predominated (as they arguably still do in much educational and developmental literature). Where, for instance, educationalists and psychologists have focused on discrete elements of reading and writing skills, anthropologists and sociolinguists concentrate on literacies—the social practices and conceptions of reading and writing. The rich cultural variation in these practices and conceptions leads us to rethink what we mean by them and to be very wary of assuming a single literacy where we may simply be imposing assumptions derived from our own cultural practice onto other people's literacies. Research in cultures that have newly acquired reading and writing draws our attention to the creative and original ways in which people transform literacy to their own cultural concerns and interests. (1993, p. 1)[12]

Barton speaks more specifically to certain central threads of interdisciplinary literacy studies and the making of an interdiscipline of literacy studies:

> A key to new views of literacy is situating reading and writing in
> its social context. . . . [P]eople in different disciplines have been
> moving in the same direction. . . . [T]he work of Sylvia Scribner
> and Michael Cole, Brian Street, and Shirley Brice Heath . . . [i]n
> their different ways . . . provide[s] three threads to weave together
> to represent the beginnings of literacy studies and they have become
> classics in the field. (2007, p. 24)

Psychologists Scribner and Cole wrote *The Psychology of Literacy* (1981),
anthropologist Street, *Literacy in Theory and Practice* (1984), and sociolinguist Heath, *Ways with Words: Language, Life and Work in Communities
and Classrooms* (1983). As classics, they became powerful signposts and
markers. Barton elaborates,

> They are part of different research traditions but they actually
> have a great deal in common. All three academic studies looked at
> particular societies in detail, examining different groups within
> a society and how they use literacy. They start from everyday life
> and what people read and write. They observe closely and they are
> willing to make use of a wide range of evidence. . . . Part of what
> comes with these studies is a recognition of the complexity of the
> idea of literacy and the fact that much of our understanding of it is
> not obvious. This leads to new definitions of literacy. (2007, p. 24)

History, represented by my book *The Literacy Myth: Literacy and Social
Structure in the Nineteenth-Century City* (1979/1991, 2010), is one missing
link. In these charter statements, there is no recognition of precedents or
longer-term perspectives.

Nevertheless, these are important observations. Implicit in Barton's
words are both the possibilities and the complications for literacy studies'
turn (necessarily incompletely) toward interdisciplinary studies. The impact of both similarities and differences in "research traditions" demands
more attention, especially with respect to the institutions and traditions of
disciplinarity and changing sociocultural currents regarding literacy and its
imperatives. Brandt (2001), for example, builds upon both literacy studies
and criticisms of what she considers its exaggerations (Brandt and Clinton,
2002). (Comparing the two would be instructive.)

However ironic, literacy studies lacks a memory and a sense of its own
history or genealogy. Neither Barton nor Street casts his gaze much before the
recent past, not even to the middle decades of the twentieth century, let alone
earlier. Neither Street nor Barton is much concerned with the institutional,

intellectual, or cultural context of either older or more recent literacy studies. Interdisciplinary studies of literacy would benefit from knowledge of, at least, the history of specific fields, disciplines, and interdisciplines.[13]

Regardless, literacy studies simultaneously seeks to distinguish and differentiate itself in an effort to integrate, synthesize within clearer limits, and bind major components of the "new" field. Along with other interdisciplines, literacy studies developed and grew both within disciplines and across them, sometimes building toward interdisciplinarity, sometimes developing separately.[14] Both efforts influenced interdisciplinary movements, together constituting contradictory influences on the field's integration and differentiation. This mode of inter/disciplinary development can risk a linear, progressive, or almost teleological epistemology and explanation for the rise and effects of literacy itself as well as interdisciplinary literacy studies. For example, the more one looks, the more literacy, or literacy practices, one finds, often in complex cultural and communicative contexts. This may be accompanied by a tendency to see "more" literacy leading to more and greater effects, in part by blurring distinctions between individual, collective, and societal impacts, shifting ideologies, causes and effects, and expectations. Developments within several disciplines at once only exacerbate these complications.[15]

Theories of modernity and postmodernity create anticipations of soaring needs for literacy/literacies that sometimes exceed those that can be estimated or measured empirically or attained popularly. At times the opposite—the limits of literacy—seems at least as compelling. Modernization models do this in part by projecting incomplete or erroneous narratives (and images) of the past onto the future.[16] Ironically, constructing a separate, recognized field of literacy studies runs the risk of reifying Street's "autonomous model" of transformative, unmediated literacy. Yet, when literacy studies initially sought confirmation of "strong theories" and "great divides," more was learned about the specific contexts of literacy's uses and influences. There is also a danger of exaggerating the import of a new field of study striving for and promoting its case for recognition and institutional place. This, too, is a common component of paths to interdisciplinarity.

Interdisciplinary Studies

My approach to, and strong presumptions about, the social history of interdisciplinarity in my current research project, *Undisciplining Knowledge: Pursuing the Dream of Interdisciplinarity*, contrasts with most writing in this area. It begins with the argument that interdisciplinarity is a central part of the historical process of the making and ongoing reshaping of modern disciplines since at least the mid- to late nineteenth century. Contrary to many notions, interdisciplinarity is inseparable from the disciplines, neither a rejection nor opposition or circumvention, neither an end run nor an end point or endgame. Nor is it primarily a post–World War II or more recent development as implied by Barton, Street, or many others. *Undisciplining Knowledge* seeks to demonstrate historically that the organization, structures, production, and dissemination of knowledge around universities, disciplinary departments, and research institutes, especially in the United States and the modern West more generally, give rise to interdisciplinary efforts and movements across the expanse of fields over time. Interdisciplinarity is a (historical) construct that varies by field and also by time, place, relationships, and circumstances. As educational and research institutions have changed over time and space, so, too, have interdisciplines and disciplines in various ways that demand to be charted comparatively. Literacy studies' relatively recent rise and race for recognition is a case in point. But so, too, are the important historical developments that are often obscured. Among the many contributions from recent studies in the history of literacy are important lessons for the present and future (Graff, 1995a, 1995b).

Literacy studies, and interdisciplinary studies, can be better understood with more attention to a longer chronological span of intellectual and sociocultural development and a broader, more dynamic focus on its place and play among a wide array of disciplines and institutional locations (subfields in disciplines or interdisciplines that deal with literacy include reading, writing, child and human development, cognitive studies, comparative and development studies, communication or media studies). "External" factors and developments—social, cultural, political, economic—that is, external to the normal workings of a discipline or field, such as wartime needs, consequences of global cross-cultural contacts and colonialism, "discovery" of new social problems—combine, often contradictorily, with shifting currents within and across disciplines. They may then stimulate changing views that, in the context of universities and their organization of knowledge, lead to criticism, different assertions, and sometimes institutional articulations both within and outside the "boundaries" of departments or divisions that take the name of interdisciplinarity.[17]

A more complete and useful approach to literacy studies, one that also deepens our understanding of interdisciplinarity, begins no later than the 1920 and 1930s (as above). It looks back carefully to the period spanning the mid-eighteenth century through the early twentieth century. Ideally, it embraces a longer (if briefer) glance back to the Renaissance and also classical antiquity. There it locates in historical context the dynamic building blocks for our expectations, understandings (including theories and policies), and institutions that culminate in modern literacy(ies) and their travails, and literacy studies.

Modern arrangements and judgments grew from the foundational (if sometimes contradictory) currents of Enlightenment emphases on human malleability, perfectionism, learning capabilities, environmentalism, and institutionalism. They were partly reinterpreted by Romanticism's deeply divided recognition of the power and significance of the "other," the alien or primitive within ourselves and in "strangers," both within the modernizing West and in "newly discovered" regions. Questions about language and order lay at the core of both. The beginnings and foundations of literacy studies also lay in "civilization's" confronting many "Wild Child[ren]" (*enfants savage*), noble or savage; South Sea islanders who confronted explorers; missionaries (whose work in creating alphabets and written languages initially to "translate" the Bible in aid of their proselytizing is fundamentally a part of literacy studies and linguistics); colonizers and colonists. They all deployed early (and later) modern notions of Western literacy and its expected influences in their efforts at expansion, "conquest," and domesticating and elevating the primitive and different.

Charles Dickens and Henry Mayhew taught that the "other" was also close at home especially in the swelling cities of the "modernizing West," sharing the difference, deviance, and deficiency of those much farther away. Those nearby could be more threatening than those farther afield. In anthropology and the arts, the primitive and the oral were grounds for celebration at times, compromising wholly positive associations of literacy and negative associations of illiteracy. Strong currents from the Enlightenment and Romanticism intertwined, sometimes contradicting but sometimes supporting expectations about progress and modern development.[18]

From earlier eras, including the Renaissance and classical antiquity, came haltingly at first the conviction that writing, and reading it, were, at least in some circumstances, superior to other means of communication, especially the oral. On one hand, this was a functional development, but, on the other hand, personal and eventually collective cognitive change might follow, some persons of influence thought. So commenced *early* literacy studies. The first general uses derived from the needs of religion, government, and commerce. That was followed slowly by a faith in the powers of formal instruction in places called schools, initially first for the relatively few, primarily boys. Some agendas stressed socialization for citizenship and its correlates; others emphasized literacy as useful or necessary practices or abilities. Over time, places for instruction expanded to include many more and to focus especially on the young. In these formulations, literacy stood at the center of training that embraced social attitudes and control and civic morality, along with at least rudimentary intellectual practice, and training in skills for productive contributions to economy, polity, and society. The tools began with simplified alphabets that helped to link signs and sounds to words and sentences and expanded to include paper, pens, and various means of reproducing and circulating texts that were first handwritten and later printed. The superiority of technology and the inferiority of the "unlettered" stood as certainties, framing constructions of literacy. Literacy's story, right or wrong, came to occupy the center (though often implicitly) of the rise of civilization and progress in the West.

These elements became inseparable as they joined capitalism's relentless efforts to remake the world—and the word, written or printed—in the image of the marketplace and its institutions (with other images), and to remake the young, in particular, for the strange new world. They mark and also serve as representations of literacy in the traditions that emerged to study and understand literacy from the Renaissance (or earlier) forward. Not surprising, the development and institutionalization of disciplines in the nineteenth- and twentieth-century Western university incorporated the understandings of literacy to which they were the heirs, especially but not only in the social sciences—anthropology, linguistics, psychology—and the humanities—classics, history, literature, philosophy, politics. Early relationships resist efforts at change. The resulting disciplinary fragmentation, as discussed in this essay, not only contributes to efforts to build interdisciplinary literacy studies but also limits them. They also underwrote the many contradictions—what I call "the literacy myth," for one—in the place of literacy in Western cultures and the lives of many persons yesterday and today (Graff, 2010).

Interdisciplinary possibilities and limits on opportunities stem from the interplay within and across what I call "disciplinary clusters." (The humanities, arts, social sciences, and basic sciences constitute major disciplinary clusters.) No less important is the sometimes very dynamic interplay—critical and complementary—between disciplines. Of this, the key disciplines of anthropology, linguistics, and psychology provide powerful examples. Among them, orality and oral literature, everyday and privileged writing practices, the ubiquity of "reading" across multiple media, and the search for cognitive and noncognitive "implications" of literacy are telling. So, too, is literacy's active presence as values, ideology, and both cultural and political capital. Destabilizing times can become opportunities to advance or to fall from favor for disciplinary approaches and moments for interdisciplinary movements.[19]

For literacy studies across the last two centuries at least, one of the most powerful forces has been the fear, and often the certainty, that literacy is declining (or not rising), and with it, families, morality, social order, progress, and socioeconomic development are also declining. This accompanied one of the most momentous transformations in the history of literacy and its study: from a "premodern" order in which literacy was feared and (partly) restricted to a more modern order in which illiteracy (or literacy gained outside of formal institutional controls) is feared. When taken comparatively, and further heightened by international conflict or competition (most famously perhaps in France's defeat by Prussia in the 1870 Franco-Prussian War), social disorder and division, international migration of "aliens," declining fertility and rising mortality, failure for "human capital" to grow, and similar circumstances, literacy levels become flashpoints for study and action to reverse the dreaded tide. Schools and popular culture attract attention, which has, in turn, the potential to propel disciplinary action and conflict and, sometimes, interdisciplinary efforts. The apparently endless "crisis" of literacy in the mid- to late twentieth century is inseparable from Cold War anxieties, global economic restructuring and collateral social and cultural change, communicative and media transformation, and both new and persisting inequalities. Seemingly unprecedented "social problems" become calls for and stimulants of interdisciplinary "solutions." Literacy's role as either or both cause or consequence is very tricky to unravel, a complication in literacy studies' development.

For literacy studies, these complications often impinge on one or another of the "great divides" prominent among approaches that see literacy—almost by its very "nature"—as universal, unmediated, and transformative in its impact. Often cited are reading or writing as "technology of the intellect," the power of the Greek alphabet, the impact of print, cognitive shifts from writing or reading, and the like. Constructing this tradition of study and understanding was relatively uncomplicated.[20] In recent decades, however, others have emphasized increasingly the sociocultural influences and contextual effects from literacy. Among the elements stressed are psychological theories, schools and other environments, families and communities, cultures of practice, and the practice and use of reading and writing.

In the second half of the twentieth century, in conjunction with other disciplines and interdisciplines, literacy studies has taken social, contextual, cognitive, linguistic, and historical, among other "turns." With the turns came the adoption of signifying French theorist "godfathers" from Levi-Bruhl and Levi-Strauss to Pierre Bourdieu and Bruno Latour. These developments at times interact with and deepen conflicts among disciplines and promote interest in interdisciplinary resolution.[21] Implicitly and explicitly, they also illustrate the dangers of failing to grasp this history.

Literacy studies' paths are revealing. Recent years witness an emphasis on the everyday and the practical, including the concept of practice itself. This led to an effort at overturning the dominance of grand theories that stressed the universal importance of the written over the oral, the printed over the written, the literate over the unlettered and untutored. Practice and context, explored in a variety of contexts and traditions, replaced presumptions of the unmediated powers and advantages of literacy. In part, literacy studies' emerging interdisciplinarity stemmed from perceptions of the inadequacy of earlier conceptualizations and presumptions, the search for new methods and sources on which to base a major revision, and reactions to it.

Successful construction of recognized interdisciplines is *not* the most common consequence of developments and changes in the disciplinary process. Although success or failure can be hard to determine, literacy studies is no exception. Some observers refuse the interdisciplinary mantle to literacy studies because of a general absence of Departments of Literacy Studies, despite many centers and programs.[22] Adding to the complexity and grounds for confusion is the fact, on the one hand, that interdisciplinarity can be strikingly different, say, in the sciences or technology fields than in the humanities or social sciences.[23] On the other hand, disciplines and interdisciplines are not synonymous forms of organization or production. They differ considerably from each other, both within and across disciplinary clusters, from history to physics or the arts. Consequently, while most programs and the occasional department of literacy studies are often in colleges of education, there are also programs, concentrations, or definite interests in the social sciences and humanities, with either or both institutional location or intellectual foundation. LiteracyStudies@OSU differs at least in part. A university-wide initiative, it is housed in the Department of English within the College of the Arts and Sciences. A few programs reach for the mantle of science.[24] In other words, understanding literacy studies calls for a critical perspective derived from interdisciplinary studies along with a comparative and historical view. At the same time, literacy studies provides a valuable case study that tests our understanding of interdisciplinarity.

For interdisciplinary studies in general, the biological or physical sciences *or* the behavioral sciences or cognitive science stand on top, slighting the humanities, historical and social sciences, and many professional programs.[25] For literacy studies, emphasis and a struggle for dominance come from anthropology, psychology, and linguistics, amid confusion over the proper disciplinary (or interdisciplinary) place for the critical (re)consideration of reading and writing to occupy. The search for understanding and applications to the contemporary literacy scene within the domain of Education has mixed results and raises other issues regarding location and disciplinary status or power.

The lines between disciplines and across them are less clear than we are trained to expect. Perceived overlap leads to competition as well as collaboration. There are linguists, for example, in anthropology, psychology, English, and education departments. English has long claimed (if somewhat incompletely and inconsistently) a special relationship with reading and writing via tutelage and practice but more formally through subdisciplines like Rhetoric and Composition. During the last five to ten years, RC (or CR) programs, as they are called, began to rename and sometimes reframe themselves as RCL—"L" for literacy. This act represents what I call "the lure of literacy" for currency and relevance and enrollments and funding. English and literature departments are also (at least sometimes) home to other elements of interdisciplinary literacy studies, including oral literature, folklore, popular culture, disability studies, graphic literature, film, and linguistics, as well as variations along the lines of writing and reading. Seldom do they work closely together or build interdisciplinarity within their space.

Literacy Studies and Interdisciplinary Studies

Interdisciplinary literacy studies continues to struggle with foundational dichotomies—the making of myths—between oral and literate, writing and print, print and electronic, and literacy as transformative—that continue to guide and divide opinion and orient studies. Consequently, the long-standing neglect of rich research on orality and oral literature is almost as much a mark of the limits of many interdisciplinary endeavors as of the power of disciplines. The proponents of the New Literacy Studies have not reclaimed Lord or Parry or Vygotsky. The persistence and importance of orality is regularly rediscovered across disciplines, as is, for example, the sociality of much reading and writing. The heterogeneity of constructions of the cognitive domain also plagues literacy studies, another instructive matter of connections.

Striving for recognition, literacy studies occupies ambiguous ground both disciplinarily and interdisciplinarily. In part, this is a question of location. But it is also a question of status. The "rise" of literacy studies, part of its generally successful emergence and development (within limits), contributes to its presence in a number of academic departments and disciplines. This holds for education, the social sciences, and the humanities and usually to a lesser extent in the sciences, medicine, public health, the law, and business.[26] This pattern is problematic in some critical respects. In the pantheon of disciplines, centers of interest in literacy studies do not usually rank highly.[27] That literacy, for good reasons, is often seen as basic or elementary does not boost its standing. By reputation, it is often viewed as inseparable from Education.[28] When not overtly problematic, the diversity among locations of interest in literacy is certainly challenging. LiteracyStudies@OSU confronts eighteen separate colleges with real but incomplete success.

Both "literacy" and "interdisciplinary" at times become promotional labels: new, relevant, sexy—in academic terms—and appealing for applied and practical reasons to citizens, governments, corporations. A sometimes unstable mix of currency, practicality, and applied "science" paves certain paths to interdisciplinarity, with ambivalent (or negative) responses by others within universities.

Of course, literacy studies is often an active presence in departments that are home to the disciplines most often identified as contributors to the New Literacy Studies or literacy studies more generally: anthropology, linguistics, and psychology. At one time or another, each of these social science disciplines has claimed the status of a science, applied if not always "pure" or "basic." Psychology, followed by linguistics, exhibits the greatest ambitions, with strong interests in reading, writing, development, and cognition. All three stress contemporary and sometimes comparative relevance. But so, too, do areas within the humanities.

My argument, oversimplified, is that literacy studies requires a greater awareness of the critical but contradictory influences of disciplinarity *and* interdisciplinarity, theory *and* history, social *and* intellectual locations, advances *and* limits, and self- *and* other-criticism in the making of the fields that claim its mantle. This is no easy task. It comes with many dangers. Not the least of them is the press we feel from contemporary circumstances. Our sense of the contemporary significance of the subject—our fears of the decline and inadequacy of literacy individually and collectively—can propel us into haste and ever more contradictions. We ignore that at our peril.

Today and Tomorrow?

English studies, especially the subdisciplines of Rhetoric and Composition, are another important location for literacy studies. Deborah Brandt's distinctive research, especially her landmark *Literacy in American Lives*, reflects well the development of literacy studies as a field of (potentially applied) research as traced in this essay, its advances, and its contradictions. Read in this way, it serves as a guide to the past and present, *and* the future of literacy studies, disciplinary and interdisciplinary, empirically and theoretically, limits and advances.

In nominating Brandt for the Grawemeyer Award in Education for 2002, I underscored the development of literacy studies as a field and her achievement within it:

> In *Literacy in American Lives*, Deborah Brandt raises the bar for the sound understanding of literacy . . . by embedding her understanding in an impressive blend of interdisciplinary approach and perspective; historical and cultural contextualization; and humane passion for the individual lives whose narratives undergird and mediate her interpretation.

The result is a rich blend of qualitative, ethnographic, and historical research approaches and analytic modes that together make an innovative contribution.

Brandt wades in dangerous waters where ideological and interpretive sharks swim. But her grasp of the complexities and contradictions of literacy within American economy, society, and culture—including the place of gender—across the twentieth century is paralleled by her recognition of the importance of the imperative to concretize and contextualize literacy, including individuals and institutions as "sponsors," one of her key concepts, as well as historical moments, and their transformations over time.

Brandt's attention to the critical conceptualization of literacy as a variable "resource" and site/source of contention shifting over time and between sponsors uniquely marks the book. *Literacy in American Lives* recapitulates the maturation of the field and simultaneously represents one of its major achievements.

At the same time, partly owing to its strengths and the development of the field, *Literacy in American Lives* attests to the limits of literacy studies and suggests, at least implicitly, possible alternative paths.[29] Among the critical tensions, strikingly, is the imbalance between the embrace of complexity and contradiction, and great hope that in the end, the achievement of a more equal distribution of a productive mass literacy will trump social, economic, and political inequality, in other words, an abiding faith in the literacy myth. For Brandt and others, the cards of race, ethnicity, and sometimes gender play here, although it is by no means clear which factors are causes and which are consequences. They, in turn, may lead to the assumption of or claim for "human rights to literacy and education" (with a nod to the United Nations Charter).

Now, there is nothing per se wrong with this, other than failing to embrace a consistent critical stance on the ideologies, rhetoric and discourse, cultures, and especially the political economics of literacy as conceptualized in different contexts, distributed, and experienced. To parse Brandt's title, both "literacy" and "American lives" cry out for deconstruction and contextualization. Literacy, we know well today, is a very slippery matter. More baldly, being literate does not guarantee a job, shelter, or food to eat. Of this Paulo Freire firmly reminds us in "The Adult Literacy Process as Cultural Action for Freedom" (1985, pp. 46–47).

In part these complications follow from the pervasive power of the literacy myth in American and western culture and politics. Persuasive presumptions also limit the power of interdisciplinary concepts, methods, and understanding consistently employed (for example, in equating interviews or oral histories with ethnography or confusing political and economic ideology with the contradictory realities of structural inequalities) and their role in critical approaches. As a result, we lack adequate critical treatments of the contradictory place literacy holds in popular, school, familial, and public cultures. Similarly, and, to my mind, more seriously, we lack an adequate political economy of literacy. Thus, the non- or extraproduction/consumption values and uses of literacy are less appreciated (except in studies of subgroups like adolescents or hip hop, itself a problematic circumstance).[30] Unlike its presumed value in a "knowledge economy," many everyday needs and uses of literacy are undervalued, not even measured metaphorically. The literacy needs of a "knowledge economy," we easily forget, do not bring likely employment and rewards to most in search of fair work and pay, *regardless* of their ability to read and write across different media and different languages. Baldly again, in the United States today, we may suffer simultaneously and incommensurably from literacy deficits and literacy surpluses.

Among the other consequences is the sometimes surprising reification of dichotomies. Brandt's conviction that "mass writing" has been neglected in literacy studies despite its rising value, compared to "mass reading," in a knowledge economy uncouples the two where their relationships may be more important. At this point, multiple or multimodal literacies call for attention but not in dichotomous relationship with "traditional" or "alphabetic" literacy. Writing revolutions apparently take their place in a line that looks back to reading, print, manuscript, and alphabetic revolutions.

The notion of a knowledge economy itself begs its dichotomized other, as do production and consumption of literacy and issues of multiple media and multiple languages of communication. After several decades of sharp and often telling criticism of the autonomous, independent powers of literacy, both familiar and new hierarchies have returned. Questions of the contextualization of literacy are reopening. The roster of literacy studies' (or New Literacy Studies') commissions and omissions is lengthy, we saw earlier. We cannot forget, moreover, that many of the issues on which this cluster of approaches can run aground are the most important and most difficult questions demanding our attention. Baldly put, "literacy(acies) *in* American lives."[31]

Notes

1. The subject of this essay, it should be clear, is literacy studies, not literacy itself. Although they are inseparable, they are not the same.

2. See the literature on New Literacy Studies, including Bartlett, 2003; Barton, 2001, 2007; Collins and Blot, 2003; Gee, 2007; Graff, 1995a, 1995b; Lankshear, 1999; Street, 1984, 1993, 1998; Street and Besnier, 2004; Stephens, 2000.

3. Frickel: "Interdisciplines are hybridized knowledge fields situated between and within existing disciplines (Klein, 1996). Like disciplines, interdisciplines are sites of institutional conflict. Their formation involves disputes over access to organizational, technical, financial, and symbolic resources, and their stabilization reflects a reordering of theoretical loyalties, epistemic assumptions, research practices, standards of evidence, and professional credibility and identity. But unlike disciplines, whose 'maturity,' coherence, or status within the broader academic field is often judged in terms of the strength or hardness of professional boundaries, interdisciplines maintain themselves through interactions with other fields and thus require boundaries that are *intentionally permeable*." 2004, p. 269. See also Abbott, 2001; Messer-Davidow, Shumway, and Sylvan, 1993; Klein, 1990, 1996, 2005.

4. Barton (2007) himself examines dictionary definitions of literacy. See also Barton, 2001; Brockmeier, Wang, and Olson, 2002; Collins and Blot, 2003; Olson, 1988, 1994; Street, 1984, 1993, 1998.

5. Compare with Street, 1984; Collins and Blot, 2003; see also Graff, 1995a, 1995b; Olson, 1988, 1994; Lankshear, 1999.

6. This occurs in a variety of forms and locations. In general, see Klein, 1990, 1996, 2005; Messer-Davidow, Shumway, and Sylvan, 1993. For literacy studies, compare the work cited in notes below of Goody and Olson with Street, Graff, and Barton.

7. See also Goody, 1968, 1979, 1986, 1987; Goody and Watt, 1968; Havelock, 1963/1976a, 1976b, 1982; Brockmeier et al., 2002; Greenfield, 1972; McLuhan, 1962; Olson, 1988, 1994; Ong, 1982; Tannen, 1981; Cole, 1996; Scribner and Cole, 1981; Halverson, 1991, 1992; Heath, 1983; Lord, 1960/2000; Parry, 1971.

8. See the works of Goody and Havelock in References; compare with Harris, 1989; Clanchy, 1979/1993. See now Clark, 2007. Post–World War II studies include Lerner, 1965; Inkeles and Smith, 1974. See also Olson, 1994; compare with Brandt and Clinton, 2002.

9. See Goody and Watt in Goody, 1968, pp. 27–68. That article was first published in 1963. Goody's introduction to that volume was titled purposefully imprecisely, "The Implications of Literacy." For tensions in the field, see Goody, 1968; Halverson, 1991, 1992; New Literacy Studies, in general; Graff, 1979/1991, 1987, 1995a, 1995b. On dangers in the shift, see Brandt and Clinton, 2002.

10. See Cole, 1996; Wertsch, 1985. Steve Witte also worked for their rediscovery.

11. Lerner, 1965; Inkeles and Smith, 1974. Among others, see Scribner and Cole, 1981; Heath, 1983; Street, 1984. See also McLuhan, 1962; Ong, 1982.

12. See Street and his critics, Bartlett, 2003; Brandt and Clinton, 2002; Collins and Blot, 2003; Collins, 1995; Maddox, 2007; Reder and Davila, 2005; Stephens, 2000. Neither Barton nor Street employs historical perspective on the relevant fields; their focus can be very narrow—a sign of striving for distinction as interdisciplinary. At times, they seem to presume the dominance of linguistics or anthropology that is implied.

13. See, for example, ENG 750 Introduction to Graduate Studies in Literacy syllabus. This is a required core course in the Graduate Interdisciplinary Specialization at the Ohio State University. See http://literacystudies.osu.edu/. For studies of disciplines, see Klein, 1990, 1996, 2005; Messer-Davidow, Shumway, and Sylvan, 1993; Abbott, 2001; Allen, 1975; Cole, 1996; Frank, 1988; Frickel, 2004; Kaestle et al., 1991; Lankshear, 1999; Lenoir, 1997; Smith, 2006; Weingart and Stehr, 2000.

14. See Graff, 1995b. There are excellent examples in history, economics, education, and rhetoric and composition.

15. See, for example, Clanchy, 1979/1993; Heath, 1983; Barton et al., 2007; Barton and Hamilton, 1998; Brandt, 2001.

16. See Pattison, 1982; also Graff, 1979/1991, and some of the responses to it.

17. Not discussed here but important are issues of interdisciplinary activity and establishment *before* interdisciplinarity is recognized and at least struggles to be institutionalized within universities. The accepted narrative of origins takes a supposedly early use of the word *interdisciplinary* at a meeting at the Social Science Research Council in New York in the late 1920s as the initiation of its arrival on the academic scene. See Frank, 1988.

While being aware of the dangers of anachronism, we need not wait so long to look for and find recognizable interdisciplinarity at play. Important examples include the fields of biology, genetics, and biochemistry and efforts, say, in sociology in the nineteenth century and the mid-twentieth. We must beware of romanticizing premodern university organization of knowledge as interdisciplinary or "before the fall." Nondisciplinary does not equal interdisciplinary.

18. On nonliterate and preliterate, see Duffy, 2007.

19. Good examples are the field of education and the long-standing and persisting conflicts among those who endorse reading's and writing's special affinities to cognitive development and "cultures" of reading and/or writing, as opposed to those who emphasize social context and practice. For recent efforts to go beyond a dichotomy, see Brandt and Clinton, 2002; Collins and Blot, 2003.

20. For more complications, see Brockmeier et al., 2002; Olson, 1988, 1994; Goody after the 1970s; Halverson, 1991, 1992; Kaestle et al., 1991; Graff, 1995a, 1995b; Graff and Duffy, 2008; New Literacy Studies more generally.

21. See and compare, for example, the work of Goody and Olson with that of Cole and Street. See also Brandt and Clinton, 2002.

22. Alternative locations for literacy studies include departments—disciplinary and interdisciplinary—centers, programs, committees, degrees, subgroups in departments or colleges, and the like. PhD programs include Language, Literacy and Culture at the University of California–Berkeley in the Graduate School of Education; Language and Literacy Studies in Education at UC–Santa Cruz; PhD in Literacy Studies in the Department of Literacy Studies, Education, Hofstra University; PhD in Language, Literacy,

and Culture, Education, University of Iowa; PhD, Department of Counseling, Leadership, Literacy, and Special Education, Lehman College, City University of New York (with a link to disabilities); Language and Literacy Education Concentration, Rutgers Graduate School of Education; PhD in Culture, Literacy, and Language, Division of Bicultural-Bilingual Studies, College of Education and Human Development, University of Texas–San Antonio; Graduate Program Area of Study, Literacy Studies, Department of Curriculum and Instruction, School of Education, University of Wisconsin–Madison.

23. In the humanities and social sciences, there is nothing like the hybridity or conjoint compounding of biochemistry and other compounds linking biology, chemistry, physics, for example, or the development of technical fields across or between science and engineering.

24. Middle Tennessee State University's doctoral movement is based on shifting from dyslexia to Literacy Studies, with the claim to science both implicit and explicit.

25. This is complicated and well worth study in its own right.

26. Science seems to have its own path(s) to interdisciplinarity. See Smith, 2006; Weingart and Stehr, 2000, among others. As suggested by the statements in support of or in opposition to interdisciplinarity quoted earlier, some see science as allied closely, even fundamentally connected, with at least some forms of interdisciplinarity. Others find it firmly opposed or resistant. The contradictions evoke the antimonies of interdisciplinarity as they relate to disciplinary clusters. Natural science is also home to such conjointly constructed or compounded interdisciplines as biochemistry and other compounds linking biology, chemistry, physics, and, recently, technology fields. The social or human sciences lack that kind of compound.

Interdisciplinarity in biology, for example, looks and proceeds and has contributed historically, very differently than interdisciplinarity in history or anthropology or geography. Historian of biology Garland Allen (1975) suggestively calls twentieth-century biology itself "a convergence of disciplines." On disciplines in science, see Lenoir, 1997. Similarly, when social scientists and natural scientists talk about laboratories and experiments, what they have in mind and what they expect to happen there are likely to differ greatly. Replication in the social sciences shares more metaphorically than materially with replication in natural science. This is part of common confusion with respect to interdisciplinary and perhaps disciplinary practice, meaning, discourse, location, and evaluation across clusters.

27. The sense of an implicit contradiction here is very real.

In addition, the accurate measurement of literacy levels with "hard" data is a perennial quest but probably an impossible dream. That, of course, doesn't limit generalizations or judgments. Research in different dimensions of literacy studies proceeds very differently. Psychologists including "cognitive scientists" and economists, in particular, seek the status of science within the domains of reading and writing as cognition for the former and "human capital" for the latter. They design their research to construct numerical data, often conducting experiments. Disability researchers increasingly join them. Discourse studies, ethnographies, case studies of literacy practices, written or recorded testimonies including life histories, and other studies of the acquisition, uses and value, impact, or ideologies of reading and writing, quantitative or qualitative, occupy other researchers across the human and social sciences, including education and professional studies. Each of the two divisions constructs its vision of interdisciplinarity in accord with these distinctions.

The imprecision of literacy's definitions and measures adds a certain vagueness that may facilitate its general appropriation for many incommensurate ends (for example, as one of a number of factors in a statistical manipulation, say, to explain economic growth or fertility levels). At the same time, it counters efforts to gain higher marks for the field when compared to other research of a more scientific or prestigious bent. Literacy studies has seen limited development in neuroscience and the more experimental domains of cognitive science, despite proclamations of their great value. Studies of disabilities and deficits are more common.

Another sign of literacy studies' emergence with limits on its status follows from the ubiquity of literacy as a factor—a "variable," independent or dependent—commonly employed in a wide range of studies across disciplines. Imprecision combines with a general but typically vague sense of its actual importance to simultaneously encourage the use of literacy data inconsistently, sometimes as indicators of schooling, training, or skills but also with respect to attitudes, values, morality, or experience symbolically or materially. Sometimes deemed "human capital," the answer to the basic question, "What does it mean to be literate?" is seldom satisfying. Yet, the simple fact that both notions and theories of civilization, progress, development, modernization, and so on include literacy among their ingredients enhances its appeal despite the limitations. See Graff, 1979/1991, 1995a, 1995b; Graff and Duffy, 2008.

28. The order of the terms *literacy, language*, and *culture* and the abbreviations vary from program to program, regarding the place, for example, of anthropology, linguistics, or psychology.

29. Writing with Katie Clinton, Brandt offers her own critique of the New Literacy Studies in "Limits of the Local."

30. See also Collins and Blot, 2003.

31. In conclusion, I point to another path through and beyond literacy studies. Since 2004, my work at the Ohio State University focuses on constructing what I call the LiteracyStudies@OSU initiative, an experiment in campus-wide interdisciplinary program development in theory and practice. The program's multilevel and multicentered hallmarks are historical, comparative, and critical. These building blocks integrate a series of public programs, faculty and graduate student seminars in literacy and the history of the book, and a Graduate Interdisciplinary Specialization or minor open to all Ohio State University graduate students and other student, faculty, and staff activities. Our cross-university breadth with primarily horizontal connections is unprecedented and path-breaking. Faculty, staff, and students across OSU's eighteen colleges (with more than ninety graduate programs) have participated in one or more programs. Informal and formal linkages dot the huge campus. Worthy of attention in its own right, both the successes and the constraints on interdisciplinary development are provocative.

For LiteracyStudies@OSU, see http://literacystudies.osu.edu/. See also my essay, Graff, 2011a, "LiteracyStudies@OSU in Theory and Practice."

That LiteracyStudies@OSU resides in the English department (within the College of Humanities and also in the Institute for Collaborative Research and Public Humanities) is partly a matter of chance and partly one of strategic thinking. It is not an outgrowth of disciplinary attributes or affinities. (No more, that is, than that our only major public conflicts are with the College of Education and Human Development, who claimed "ownership" of literacy.) Appropriately, the Office of Academic Affairs declared that literacy is a university-wide matter. The lessons for interdisciplinary literacy studies are ambiguous. A stable base with sufficient resources, wide-ranging goals, good advisers, interested and varied audiences and potential participants, and lots of energy may be more important than which disciplines lead and which ones follow. That Literacy-Studies@OSU is led by a social historian is probably more important.

References

Abbott, Andrew. 2001. *Chaos of Disciplines*. Chicago: University of Chicago Press.

Allen, Garland. 1975. *Life Science in the Twentieth Century*. New York: John Wiley.

Bartlett, Lesley. 2003. "Social Studies of Literacy and Comparative Education: Intersections." *Current Issues in Comparative Education*, 5(2), 67–76.

Barton, David. 2001. "Directions for Literacy Research: Analysing Language and Social Practices in a Textually Mediated World." *Language and Education*, 15(2–3), 92–104.

———. 2007. *Literacy: An Introduction to the Ecology of Written Language*. 2nd ed. Oxford, England: Blackwell.

Barton, David, and Mary Hamilton. 1998. *Local Literacies: Reading and Writing in One Community*. London: Routledge.

Barton, David, Roz Ivanic, Yvon Appleby, Rachel Hodge, and Karin Tusting. 2007. *Literacy, Lives and Learning*. London: Routledge.

Brandt, Deborah. 1990. *Literacy as Involvement: The Acts of Writers, Readers, and Texts*. Carbondale: Southern Illinois University Press.

———. 2001. *Literacy in American Lives*. New York: Cambridge University Press.

———. 2009. *Literacy and Learning: Reflections on Writing, Reading, and Society*. San Francisco: Jossey-Bass.

Brandt, Deborah, and Katie Clinton. 2002. "Limits of the Local: Expanding Perspectives on Literacy as a Social Practice." *Journal of Literacy Research*, 34, 337–56.

Brockmeier, Jens, Min Wang, and David R. Olson, eds. 2002. *Literacy, Narrative and Culture*. Richmond, England: Curzon Press.

Clanchy, Michael. 1979/1993. *From Memory to Written Record: England, 1066–1307*. Oxford, England: Blackwell.

Clark, Gregory. 2007. *A Farewell to Alms: A Brief Economic History of the World*. Princeton: Princeton University Press.

Cole, Michael. 1996. *Cultural Psychology: A Once and Future Discipline*. Cambridge: Harvard University Press.

Collins, James. 1995. "Literacy and Literacies." *Annual Review of Anthropology*, 24, 75–93.

Collins, James, and Richard K. Blot. 2003. *Literacy and Literacies: Texts, Power, and Identity*. Cambridge: Cambridge University Press.

Duffy, John. 2007. *Writing from These Roots: Literacy in a Hmong-American Community*. Honolulu: University of Hawaii Press.

Frank, Roberta. 1988. "'Interdisciplinarity': The First Half-Century." In *Words for Robert Burchfield's Sixty-Fifth Birthday*, edited by E. G. Stanley and T. F. Hoad, 91–101. London: D. S. Brewer.

Freire, Paulo. 1985. "The Adult Literacy Process as Cultural Action for Freedom." In *The Politics of Education: Culture, Power, and Liberation*, 43–65. New York: Bergin and Garvey.

Frickel, Scott. 2004. "Building an Interdiscipline: Collective Action Framing and the Rise of Genetic Toxicology." *Social Problems*, 51(2), 269–87.

Gee, James. 2007. "The New Literacy Studies and the 'Social Turn.'" ED442118 http://
      www.schools.ash.org.au/litweb/page300.html
Goody, Jack, ed. 1968. *Literacy in Traditional Societies*. Cambridge: Cambridge Uni-
      versity Press.
———. 1979. *The Domestication of the Savage Mind*. Cambridge: Cambridge University
      Press.
———. 1986. *The Logic of Writing and the Organization of Society*. Cambridge: Cam-
      bridge University Press.
———. 1987. *The Interface between the Written and the Oral*. Cambridge: Cambridge
      University Press.
Goody, Jack, and Ian Watt. 1968. "The Consequences of Literacy." In *Literacy in Traditional
      Societies*, edited by Goody, 27–68. Cambridge: Cambridge University Press.
Graff, Harvey J. 1979/1991. *The Literacy Myth: Literacy and Social Structure in the
      Nineteenth-Century City*. New York: Academic Press/New Brunswick, NJ:
      Transaction.
———. 1987. *The Legacies of Literacy: Continuities and Contradictions in Western Society
      and Culture*. Bloomington: Indiana University Press.
———. 1995a. "Literacy, Myths, and Legacies: Lessons from the History of Literacy." In
      The Labyrinths of Literacy, 318–49. Pittsburgh: University of Pittsburgh Press.
———. 1995b. "Assessing the History of Literacy in the 1990s: Themes and Questions."
      In *Escribir y leer en Occidente*, edited by Armando Petrucci and M. Gimeno
      Blay, 5–46. Valencia, Spain: Universitat de Valencia.
———. 2010. "*The Literacy Myth* at 30." *Journal of Social History*, 43(Spring), 634–61.
———. 2011a. "LiteracyStudies@OSU as Theory and Practice." In *Literacy Myths, Legacies,
      and Lessons: New Studies*, by Graff, 141–78. New Brunswick, NJ: Transaction.
———. 2011b. "Literacy Studies and Interdisciplinary Studies: Reflections on History
      and Theory." In *The Scope of Interdisciplinarity: Theory, Practice, Pedagogy*,
      edited by Raphael Foshay, 273–307. Athabasca, Alberta, Canada: Athabasca
      University Press.
Graff, Harvey J., and John Duffy. 2008. "Literacy Myths." In *Encyclopedia of Language
      and Education*, Vol. 2, *Literacy*, edited by Brian V. Street and Nancy Horn-
      berger, 41–52. Berlin: Springer.
Greenfield, Patricia. 1972. "Oral or Written Language: The Consequences for Cogni-
      tive Development in Africa, the United States, and England." *Language and
      Speech*, 15, 169–78.
Halverson, John. 1991. "Olson on Literacy." *Language and Society*, 20, 619–40.
———. 1992. "Goody and the Implosion of the Literacy Thesis." *Man*, 27, 301–17.
Harris, William V. 1989. *Ancient Literacy*. Cambridge, MA: Harvard University Press.
Havelock, Eric. 1963/1976a. *Preface to Plato*. Cambridge, MA: Harvard University Press.
———. 1976b. *The Origins of Western Literacy*. Toronto: Ontario Institute for Studies
      in Education.
———. 1982. *The Literate Revolution in Greece and Its Consequences*. Princeton: Prince-
      eton University Press.
Heath, Shirley Brice. 1983. *Ways with Words: Language, Life and Work in Communities
      and Classrooms*. Cambridge: Cambridge University Press.
Inkeles, Alex, and David Horton Smith. 1974. *Becoming Modern: Individual Change in
      Six Developing Countries*. Cambridge, MA: Harvard University Press.

Kaestle, Carl F., Helen Damon-Moore, Lawrence C. Stedman, Katherine Tinsley, and William Vance Trollinger Jr. 1991. *Literacy in the United States: Readers and Reading since 1880*. New Haven: Yale University Press.

Klein, Julie Thompson. 1990. *Interdisciplinarity: History, Theory, & Practice*. Detroit: Wayne State University Press.

———. 1996. *Crossing Boundaries: Knowledge, Disciplinarities, and Interdisciplinarities*. Charlottesville: University Press of Virginia.

———. 2005. *Humanities, Culture, and Interdisciplinarity: The Changing American Academy*. Albany: State University of New York Press.

Lankshear, Colin. 1999. "Literacy Studies in Education: Disciplined Developments in a Post-Disciplinary Age." In *After the Disciplines: The Emergence of Cultural Studies*, edited by Michael Peters, 199–228. Amherst, MA: Bergin and Garvey.

Lenoir, Timothy. 1997. *Instituting Science: The Cultural Production of Scientific Disciplines*. Stanford: Stanford University Press.

Lerner, Daniel. 1965. *The Passing of Traditional Society: Modernizing the Middle East*. New York: Free Press.

Lord, Albert B. 1960/2000. *The Singer of Tales*, 2nd ed. Cambridge, MA: Harvard University Press.

Maddox, Bryan. 2007. "What Can Ethnographic Studies Tell Us about the Consequences of Literacy?" *Comparative Education*, 43, 253–71.

McLuhan, Marshall. 1962. *The Gutenberg Galaxy: The Making of Typographic Man*. Toronto: University of Toronto Press.

Messer-Davidow, Ellen, David R. Shumway, and David J. Sylvan, eds. 1993. *Knowledges: Historical and Critical Studies in Disciplinarity*. Charlottesville: University Press of Virginia.

Olson, David R. 1988. "Mind and Media: The Epistemic Functions of Literacy." *Journal of Communication*, 38, 27–36.

———. 1994. *The World on Paper: The Conceptual and Cognitive Implications of Reading and Writing*. Cambridge: Cambridge University Press.

Ong, Walter. 1982. *Orality and Literacy*. London: Methuen.

Parry, Adam, ed. 1971. *The Making of Homeric Verse: The Collected Papers of Milman Parry*. New York: Oxford University Press.

Pattison, Robert. 1982. *On Literacy: The Politics of the Word from Homer to the Age of Rock*. New York: Oxford University Press.

Reder, Stephen, and Erica Davila. 2005. "Context and Literacy Practices." *Annual Review of Applied Linguistics*, 25, 170–87.

Scribner, Sylvia, and Michael Cole. 1981. *The Psychology of Literacy*. Cambridge: Harvard University Press.

Smith, Barbara Herrnstein. 2006. *Scandalous Knowledge: Science, Truth and the Human*. Durham, NC: Duke University Press.

Stephens, Kate. 2000. "A Critical Discussion of the 'New Literacy Studies.'" *British Journal of Educational Studies*, 48, 10–23.

Street, Brian V. 1984. *Literacy in Theory and Practice*. Cambridge: Cambridge University Press.

———. 1993. "Introduction: The New Literacy Studies." In *Cross-Cultural Approaches to Literacy*, edited by Street, 1–21. Cambridge: Cambridge University Press.

————. 1998. October 19. "New Literacies in Theory and Practice: What Are the Implications for Language in Education." Inaugural Professorial Lecture, King's College, London.

Street, Brian V., and Niko Besnier. 2004. "Aspects of Literacy." In *Companion Encyclopedia of Anthropology*, edited by Tim Ingold, 527–62. London: Routledge.

Tannen, Deborah. 1981. "The Myth of Orality and Literacy." In *Linguistics and Literacy*, edited by William Frawley, 37–50. New York: Plenum.

Weingart, Peter, and Nico Stehr, eds. 2000. *Practicing Interdisciplinarity*. Toronto: University of Toronto Press.

Wertsch, James V. 1985. *Vygotsky and the Social Formation of Mind*. Cambridge: Harvard University Press.

Afterword

Anne Ruggles Gere

In 2002 I wrote a review of *Literacy in American Lives* in which I explained that reading Deborah Brandt's book helped me understand my own family history better; it illuminated the many things that contributed to the fact that my mother, the youngest child, graduated from college, while her older sister received an eighth-grade education. The confluence of economic, political, and material forces meant that one sister had to leave school to work and help support the family, while another, who came of age during the Great Depression, was able to continue her education. As Deborah might put it, the two sisters had different literacy sponsors.

I praised the book for calling into question a number of settled assumptions about how people learn to read and write by considering economic transformations, generational shifts in times of rapid social change, social structures that offer barriers or opportunities, and material/ideological conditions. It seemed to me at the time that this book would become important in literacy studies, and I concluded with the expectation "that we will be talking about and following the lead of her work for a long time" (2002, p. 285). Looking back from a decade later, I could take pride in my own prescience, but the truth is that I came to that review armed with a full knowledge of Deborah Brandt's previous work. I had read drafts as well as published articles, and I knew her formidable capacity to discern the significant from the less important. I also knew her fearless willingness to point out the limitations in the theories and research of others; not that she was ever unkind, but she was intellectually courageous. In 1990, when *Literacy as Involvement: The Acts of Writers, Readers, and Texts*, her first book, was published, literacy scholars like Jack Goody, David Olson, and Walter J. Ong, SJ, still dominated literacy studies, and their claims about the "great divide" between the mental capacities of literate and nonliterate peoples, the autonomous text, and the cultural discontinuities between orality and literacy were accepted by many scholars. And Deborah took them on. Drawing upon understandings developed by a process approach to writing, she examined the interactions between writers and readers, thereby calling into question the claims that still held sway in literacy studies. So when I first read *Literacy in American Lives*, I expected it to be groundbreaking, and it was.

Yet, even with the benefit of foreknowledge, I could not fully anticipate the effect that *Literacy in American Lives* would have on the field. I expected that it would be read in graduate seminars and be cited in dissertations. I imagined that Deborah Brandt's methodology of writing life histories—she once described it as "pulverizing" individual narratives—would be taken up by others. I assumed that the concept of literacy sponsor—a category I found admirably capacious but also worryingly broad enough to leave me wondering what a sponsor is *not*—would be useful. What I did not foresee was the *degree* to which this book would become indispensable in literacy studies: the numbers of graduate students who read it; the quantity of dissertations that call upon it; the ubiquity with which "sponsor" appears in scholarship, like the manuscript I read just last evening. I did not foresee the extent to which this book would become part of my own mental architecture; I thought about it even when I was not writing about literacy directly. I did not foresee a collection of articles like the ones in the current book, articles that debunk myths, complicate assumptions, extend categories, and interrogate ideologies. The scholarship collected here demonstrates the value of a capacious term like *sponsor*, putting to rest my quibble about defining its parameters, and it shows how transformative and generative Deborah's work has been—no, *is*.

While I am delighted to celebrate this moment in Deborah Brandt's career, I resist thinking of her research in the past tense. I just looked through her *Literacy and Learning*, and I'm counting on her to develop the ideas that are sketched out in "The Status of Writing." Ever since I read the National Endowment for the Arts' (2004) *Reading at Risk: A Survey of Literary Reading in America*, I have been thinking about the shifting relationship between reading and writing in American society. Amidst the report's general lament about declines in the number of readers of fiction and poetry was the finding that the number of people who reported that they are writing increased by 30 percent between 1982 and 2002. Given the expansive growth of digital technologies during the past decade, I'm sure that the percentage of increase is even greater now. If we are becoming a nation of writers, if reading is becoming a less prominent literacy practice, I want to know more about it. But it is not a survey report that I want. What I am waiting for is Brandt's carefully researched, conceptually rich, and elegantly written account of the writing done by workers in professional, administrative, and technical positions. I am waiting for her exploration of the "collision between the moral economy of reading and the commercial economy of writing" (Brandt, 2009, p. 145). I am waiting for her to address her own question: "Can mass writing claim a moral authority powerful enough to transform the social institutions that were organized to serve readers over writers?" (Brandt, 2009, p. 158). That will help me understand my world a little better, contribute to the richness of my graduate seminars, and inform my scholarship, just as *Literacy in American Lives* did.

References

Brandt, Deborah. 1990. *Literacy as Involvement: The Acts of Writers, Readers, and Texts.* Carbondale: Southern Illinois University Press.

———. 2009. *Literacy and Learning: Reflections on Writing, Reading and Society.* San Francisco: Jossey Bass, 2009.

Gere, Anne Ruggles. 2002. Review of *Literacy in American Lives*, by Deborah Brandt. *Rhetoric Review,* 21(3), 282–85.

National Endowment for the Arts. 2004. *Reading at Risk: A Survey of Literary Reading in America.* Research Report 46. Washington, DC: National Endowment for the Arts.

CONTRIBUTORS
INDEX

Contributors

Julie Nelson Christoph is an associate professor of English at the University of Puget Sound, where she directs the Center for Writing, Learning, and Teaching. Her essays have appeared in *College English, Research in the Teaching of English, Written Communication*, and other journals. She was a recipient, in 2009–10, of a Fulbright Fellowship to Zanzibar, Tanzania.

    Ellen Cushman is a professor of writing, rhetoric, and American cultures at Michigan State University. She is a Cherokee Nation citizen and has served as a Cherokee Nation Sequoyah commissioner. Her most recent book, *The Cherokee Syllabary: Writing the People's Perseverance* (2011), earned honorable mention for the 2011 MLA Mina P. Shaughnessy award and is based on six years of ethnohistorical research with her tribe. Recent essays from this research demonstrate the cultural, linguistic, and historic importance of the Cherokee syllabary and can be found in *Ethnohistory*; *Wicazo Sa Review*; *JAC: A Journal of Rhetoric, Culture, and Politics*; *College English*; and *Written Communication*. She currently serves with Mary Juzwik as coeditor of *Research in the Teaching of English*.

    Kim Donehower is an associate professor of English at the University of North Dakota, where she researches the relationship between literacy and the survival of rural communities. With Charlotte Hogg and Eileen E. Schell, Kim coauthored *Rural Literacies* and coedited *Reclaiming the Rural: Essays on Literacy, Rhetoric, and Pedagogy*.

    John Duffy is an associate professor and the Francis O'Malley director of the University Writing Program at the University of Notre Dame. His scholarly work is concerned with the relationship of rhetoric and ethics, and the historical development of literacy in cross-cultural contexts. His most recent book, *Writing from These Roots*, was awarded the 2009 Outstanding Book Award by the Conference on College Composition and Communication. He has published essays in *Written Communication, College Composition and Communication*, and other journals. Duffy is a recipient of a National Endowment for the Humanities Fellowship and the Reverend Edmund P. Joyce, CSC, Award for Excellence in Undergraduate Teaching. He teaches courses in rhetoric, writing, and literature.

    Anne Ruggles Gere is the Arthur F. Thurnau Professor and the Gertrude Buck Collegiate Professor at the University of Michigan, where she directs the

Sweetland Center for Writing and serves as cochair of the joint PhD in English and education. The study of literacy is at the center of her work, and she has published a dozen books and more than seventy-five articles.

Eli Goldblatt is a professor of English at Temple University. His composition publications focus on community literacy, writing programs, urban high school/college transitions, and memoir. He has also published poetry and books for children.

Harvey J. Graff is the Ohio Eminent Scholar in Literacy Studies and a professor of English and history at the Ohio State University, where he directs the university-wide interdisciplinary LiteracyStudies@OSU initiative. A comparative social historian, Graff is noted internationally for his research on the history of literacy (*The Literacy Myth: Literacy and Social Structure in the Nineteenth-Century City*; *The Legacies of Literacy: Continuities and Contradictions in Western Culture and Society*; *Literacy Myths, Legacies, and Lessons*), the history of children and youth (*Conflicting Paths: Growing Up in America*), and urban history (*The Dallas Myth: The Making and Unmaking of an American City*), among many other works. He is now writing a social history of interdisciplinarity. In 2013–14, he is Birkelund Fellow at the National Humanities Center.

Nelson Graff is an associate professor of English at San Francisco State University, where he coordinates the undergraduate English Education concentration within the English major. His research focuses on literacy teaching and literacy teacher education and has appeared in *Educational Research, English Journal*, the *Journal of Adolescent and Adult Literacy*, and *Teacher Education Quarterly*. He teaches courses in writing and literacy teaching at the secondary and postsecondary levels.

Gail E. Hawisher is a University Distinguished Teacher/Scholar and a professor emeritus of English at the University of Illinois, Urbana-Champaign. Her work probes the many connections between literate activity and digital media as reflected in her many books with Cynthia L. Selfe and in her book with Patrick W. Berry and Selfe, *Transnational Literate Lives in Digital Times* (2012), a multimodal, born-digital study of literacy practices across the world. She and Selfe are also founders of *Computers and Composition Digital Press*, an open-access, peer-reviewed, online book.

Bruce Horner holds the Endowed Chair in Rhetoric and Composition at the University of Louisville. His books include *Terms of Work for Composition*, winner of the 2001 Winterowd Award for the Most Outstanding Book on Composition Theory, and the coedited *Cross-Language Relations in Composition*, winner of the Conference on College Composition and Communication Outstanding Book Award.

David A. Jolliffe is a professor of English and of curriculum and instruction at the University of Arkansas, where he holds the Brown Chair in English Literacy.

Rhea Estelle Lathan is an assistant professor at Florida State University, where she teaches in the Rhetoric and Composition program. She is the author of *Freedom Writing: African American Civil Rights Literacy Activism, 1956–1962*, a manuscript which investigates how literacy is defined and the way it functions in the context of the adult literacy campaign of the civil rights movement. Her research interests include community-based literacy, African American studies, and women's studies.

Min-Zhan Lu is a professor of English and University Scholar at the University of Louisville. Her essays have received the Mina Shaughnessy and Richard Braddock Awards. Her books include *Shanghai Quartet: The Crossings of Four Women of China* and the coedited *Cross-Language Relations in Composition*, winner of the Conference on College Composition and Communication Outstanding Book Award.

Robyn Lyons-Robinson is a professor in the Department of English at Columbus State Community College in Columbus, Ohio, where she teaches composition and literature. A native of Columbus, she is also a founding member of Phenomenal Women Inc.

Carol Mattingly is a professor of English at the University of Louisville, where she teaches writing, rhetoric, and literature. Her research addresses nineteenth century women's writing, rhetoric, and literacy. Her current research examines literacy in nineteenth-century American Catholic convents and academies.

Beverly J. Moss is an associate professor of English at the Ohio State University, where she teaches in the rhetoric, composition, and literacy program. Her primary research interests include examining literacy practices in African American community settings and the teaching of writing. She is the author or editor of multiple publications, including *A Community Text Arises: A Literate Text and a Literacy Tradition in African American Churches*, *Literacy across Communities* (editor), and *Everyone's an Author* (coauthor with Andrea Lunsford, Lisa Ede, Carole Clark Papper, and Keith Walters).

Rebecca S. Nowacek is an associate professor of English at Marquette University, where she directs the Norman H. Ott Memorial Writing Center. Rebecca's research focuses on writing transfer and writing in the disciplines. Her publications include *Agents of Integration: Understanding Transfer as a Rhetorical Act* (2011) and *Citizenship across the Curriculum* (2010); her work has also appeared in *College Composition and Communication*, *College English*, *Research in the Teaching of English*, and the *Journal of General Education*. She was a Carnegie Scholar with the Carnegie Academy for the Scholarship of Teaching and

Learning and the 2012 recipient of Marquette University's Robert and Mary Gettel Faculty Award for Teaching Excellence.

Paul Prior is a professor of English and a professor and the director of the Center for Writing Studies at the University of Illinois, Urbana-Champaign. Drawing on sociohistoric theory, phenomenological approaches, and dialogic semiotics, he has explored connections among literate activity, semiotic practices, genres, and disciplinarity.

Cynthia L. Selfe is the Humanities Distinguished Professor in the Department of English at the Ohio State University. Selfe has authored or edited numerous articles and books on computers in education, including "The Movement of Air, the Breath of Meaning: Aurality and Multimodal Composing" (2009) and the coauthored *Writing New Media* (2004). With Louis Ulman, she is a founder of the DALN (Digital Archives of Literacy Narratives), housed at the Ohio State University.

Michael W. Smith is a professor in Temple University's College of Education. He has won awards for his teaching at both the high school and college levels. His research focuses both on understanding how adolescents and adults engage with texts outside school and on how teachers can use those understandings to devise more motivating and effective instruction inside schools. He has written, cowritten, or edited twelve books and monographs, including *"Reading Don't Fix No Chevys": Literacy in the Lives of Young Men*, for which he and his coauthor Jeff Wilhelm received the 2003 David H. Russell Award for Distinguished Research in the Teaching of English.

Bryan Trabold is an associate professor of English at Suffolk University, where he has also been serving as the director of the Writing Center for the past three years. His scholarly work focuses on the rhetorical and writing strategies used by South African antiapartheid activists. He received a National Endowment for the Humanities summer stipend and has published essays in *College English*, *College Composition and Communication*, and the *South African Historical Journal*. He teaches courses in writing, rhetoric, the antiapartheid movement, and the literature of war.

Morris Young is a professor of English at the University of Wisconsin, Madison. His book, *Minor Re/Visions: Asian American Literacy Narratives as a Rhetoric of Citizenship* (2004) received the 2004 W. Ross Winterowd Award and the 2006 CCCC Outstanding Book Award. *Representations: Doing Asian American Rhetoric*, coedited with LuMing Mao, received honorable mention for the 2008 Mina P. Shaughnessy Prize.

Index